Lecture Notes in Mathematics

AF063116

Edited by A. Dold and B. Eckmann

Subseries: Fondazione C.I.M.E., Firenze
Adviser: Roberto Conti

1330

A. Ambrosetti F. Gori
R. Lucchetti (Eds.)

Mathematical Economics

Lectures given at the 2nd 1986 Session of the Centro Internazionale Matematico Estivo (C.I.M.E.) held at Montecatini Terme, Italy
June 25 – July 3, 1986

Springer-Verlag
Berlin Heidelberg New York London Paris Tokyo

Editors

Antonio Ambrosetti
Scuola Normale Superiore
Piazza dei Cavalieri 7, 56100 Pisa, Italy

Franco Gori
Università di Venezia
Dipartimento di Matematica Applicata e Informatica
Dorsoduro 3825/e, 30123 Venezia, Italy

Roberto Lucchetti
Università di Milano, Dipartimento di Matematica
Via C. Saldini 50, 20133 Milano, Italy

Mathematics Subject Classification (1980): 90A, 90C, 90D

ISBN 3-540-50003-0 Springer-Verlag Berlin Heidelberg New York
ISBN 0-387-50003-0 Springer-Verlag New York Berlin Heidelberg

This work is subject to copyright. All rights are reserved, whether the whole or part of the material is concerned, specifically the rights of translation, reprinting, re-use of illustrations, recitation, broadcasting, reproduction on microfilms or in other ways, and storage in data banks. Duplication of this publication or parts thereof is only permitted under the provisions of the German Copyright Law of September 9, 1965, in its version of June 24, 1985, and a copyright fee must always be paid. Violations fall under the prosecution act of the German Copyright Law.

© Springer-Verlag Berlin Heidelberg 1988
Printed in Germany

Printing and binding: Druckhaus Beltz, Hemsbach/Bergstr.
2146/3140-543210

INTRODUCTION

In the last few years an ever increasing interest has been shown by economists and mathematicians in deepening and multiplying the many links already existing between their areas of research. Economists are looking for more advanced mathematical techniques to be applied to the analysis of formal models of greater complexity; mathematicians have found in problems from economics the stimulus to start new directions of study and to explore different trends within their theories.

The principal aim of the CIME Session on "Mathematical Economics" held at Villa La Querceta in Montecatini Terme, Italy, from June 25 to July 3 1986, has been the one of offering scholars from the two fields an opportunity of meeting and working together.

The common base of discussion was provided by four survey courses - whose texts are contained in the present volume - which were given by I. Ekeland "Some Variational Methods Arising from Mathematical Economics", A. Mas-Colell "Differentiability Techniques in the Theory of General Economic Equilibrium", J. Scheinkman "Dynamic General Equilibrium Models" and S. Zamir "Topics in Non Cooperative Game Theory".

Even if Ekeland's and Zamir's lectures were more "mathematically oriented", whereas Mas-Colell and Scheinkman put a greater emphasis on the economical contents, in every class, the focus of the discussion was placed over the connections naturally arising between problems from the two sciences.

It's our feeling that the Session was very successful in reaching its intended objectives, and we wish to express our gratitude to the four speakers, for the extremely high quality of the lectures delivered and the stimulating atmosphere they were able to create in Montecatini, and to all the participants, who supported the meeting with their interest and their lively discussions.

Our final thanks go to the CIME Scientific Committee for the invitation to organize the courses and to the CIME staff for its very effective job.

Antonio Ambrosetti
Franco Gori
Roberto Lucchetti

C.I.M.E. Session on "Mathematical Economics"

List of Participants

E. ALVONI, Istituto di Matematica Gen. e Finanz., Università, Piazza Scaravilli 2, 40126 Bologna, Italy

A. AMBROSETTI, Scuola Normale Superiore, Piazza dei Cavalieri 7, 56100 Pisa, Italy

E. BALDER, Mathematical Institute, University of Utrecht, Budapestlaan 6, 3584 CD Utrecht, The Netherlands

A. BATTINELLI, Istituto di Matematica Applicata alle Scienze Economiche e Sociali, Università, Via Montebello 7, 50123 Firenze, Italy

F. BIRARDI, Via Bertani 26, 50139 Firenze, Italy

P. CANNARSA, Via O. Tommasini 34, 00162 Roma, Italy

A. CARBONE, Dipartimento di Matematica, Università della Calabria, 87036 Arcavacata di Rende, Cosenza, Italy

E. CAVAZZUTI, Dipartimento di Matematica, Università, Via G. Campi 213/B, 41100 Modena, Italy

G. CIMATTI, Dipartimento di Matematica,Università, Via Buonarroti 2, 56100 Pisa,Italy

G. COSTA, Istituto di Economia e Finanza, Facoltà di Scienze Politiche, Via Serafini 3, 56100 Pisa, Italy

R.-A. DANA, 9 Square Port-Royal, Paris 13e, France

L. DE BIASE, Istituto Matematico, Università, Via C. Saldini 50, 20133 Milano, Italy

G. DECIMA, Dipartimento di Matematica Appl. e Inf., Università, Ca' Dolfini, 30123 Venezia, Italy

S. DELAGUICHE, 19 avenue d'Eylau, 75116 Paris, France

F. DELBONO, Linacre College, Oxford OX1 3JA, U.K.

V. DENICOLO', Dipartimento di Scienze Economiche, Piazza Scaravilli 2, 40126 Bologna, Italy

D. DI GIOACCHINO, Via Campo Ligure 30, 00168 Roma, Italy

B. D'ONOFRIO, Dipartimento di Matematica, Università dell'Aquila, Via Roma 33, 67100 L'Aquila, Italy

E. EINY, Institute of Mathematics, Hebrew University, Jerusalem 91904, Israel

I. EKELAND, CEREMADE, Université de Paris-Dauphine, Place du Maréchal De Lattre de Tassigny, 75775 Paris 16, France

P. FABBRI, Via P. Palagi 36, 40138 Bologna, Italy

L. FERRARA, Via Roccaraso 44, 00135 Roma, Italy

M. GALEOTTI, Istituto di Matematica, Facoltà di Architettura, Piazza Brunelleschi 6, 50100 Firenze, Italy

M. GILLI, Via dei Benedettini 4, 20146 Milano, Italy

F. GORI, Università di Venezia, Dipartimento di Matematica Applicata e Informatica, Dorsoduro 3825/e, 30123 Venezia, Italy

G. GOZZI, Via Carducci 5, 46100 Mantova, Italy

V. GUIDI, Dipartimento di Scienze Economiche, Università, Via Curtatone 1, 50123 Firenze, Italy

J. HERNANDEZ, Universidad Autonoma, Dep. de Matematica, 28036 Madrid, Spain

D. HOMANN, IMW, Universität Bielefeld, Postfach, 4800 Bielefeld 1, West Germany

E. LEHRER, Hebrew University, Institute of Mathematics, Givat Ram, 91904 Jerusalem, Israel

R. LEONCINI, c/o Cassola, Via del Proconsolo 5, 50122 Firenze, Italy

R. LUCCHETTI, Università di Milano, Dipartimento di Matematica, Via C. Saldini 50, 20133 Milano, Italy

L. MALAGUTI, Via G. Benassi 5, 41012 Carpi (MO), Italy

A. MAS-COLELL, Mathematical Sciences Research Institute, 1000 Centennial Drive, Berkeley, CA 94720, USA

F. MIGNANEGO, Dipartimento di Matematica, Università, Via L.B. Alberti 4, 16132 Genova, Italy

S. MODICA, Via M. Rutelli 38, 90143 Palermo, Italy

D. MONDERER, Department of Mathematics, Everyman's University, Ramat Aviv, Tel Aviv 61392, Israel

L. MONTRUCCHIO, Dipartimento di Matematica, Politecnico, Corso Duca degli Abruzzi 24, 10129 Torino, Italy

J. MORGAN, Dipartimento di Matematica e Applicazioni, Università, Via Mezzocannone 8, 80134 Napoli, Italy

A. MORI, Via S. Martino 284, 55049 Viareggio, Italy

I. NADA, Tel Aviv University, Faculty of Management, University Campus, Ramat Aviv, Tel Aviv 69978, Israel

F. NARDINI, Dipartimento Matematico, Università, Piazza di Porta S. Donato 5, 40127 Bologna, Italy

K. OLSEN, European University Institute, Badia Fiesolana, Via dei Roccettini 9, 50016 San Domenico di Fiesole, Firenze, Italy

N. PACCHIAROTTI, Dipartimento di Matematica, Università, Via G. Campi 213/B, 41100 Modena, Italy

P.-M. PACINI, Istituto Universitario Europeo, Badia Fiesolana, Via Roccettini 9, 50016 San Domenico di Fiesole, Firenze, Italy

F. PATRONE, Dipartimento di Matematica, Università, Strada Nuova 65, 27100 Pavia, Italy

E. PETAZZONI, Via Ognibene 2, 40135 Bologna, Italy

G. PIERI, Dipartimento di Matematica, Università, Via L.B. Alberti 4, 16132 Genova, Italy

C. van der PLOEG, Department of Mathematics, University of Sussex, Falmer, Brighton BN1 9QE, East Sussex, England

N. RICCIARDI, CEREMADE, Université de Paris-Dauphine, Place du Maréchal De Lattre de Tassigny, 75775 Paris 16, France

G. ROSSINI, Dipartimento di Scienze Economiche, Strada Maggiore 45, 40125 Bologna, Italy

M. SABATINI, Dipartimento di Matematica pura ed applicata, Università, Via Roma 33, 67110 L'Aquila, Italy

M. SCARSINI, Istituto di Matematica Finanziaria, Via Kennedy 6, 43100 Parma, Italy

J. SCHEINKMAN, The University of Chicago, Department of Economics, 1126 East 59th Street, Chicago, Ill. 60637, USA

A. SICONOLFI, Dipartimento di Matematica, Università della Calabria, 87036 Arcavacata di Rende, Cosenza, Italy

P. SUDHOLTER, Institut für Mathematische Wirtschartsforschung, Universitätstrasse, D-4800 Bielefeld 1, West Germany

B. TERRENI, Dipartimento di Matematica, Università, Via F. Buonarroti 2, 56100 Pisa, Italy

A. TORRE, Dipartimento di Matematica, Università, Strada Nuova 65, 27100 Pavia, Italy

A. VILLANACCI, Via Pasquini 2, 50127 Firenze, Italy

S. ZAMIR, The Hebrew University of Jerusalem, Department of Statistics, Mount Scopus, Jerusalem 91905

TABLE OF CONTENTS

SOME VARIATIONAL PROBLEMS ARISING FROM MATHEMATICAL ECONOMICS.

Ivar EKELAND, CEREMADE, Paris.

I. Ramsey problems.

Many intertemporal problems in mathematical economics can be written as infinite-horizon optimization problems :

$$(P) \qquad \begin{cases} \operatorname{Sup} \int_0^\infty e^{-\delta t} u(t,x,\dot{x})\, dt \\ (x(t),\dot{x}(t)) \in A_t \quad \text{a.e.} \\ x(0) = x_0 \quad \text{and} \quad \dot{x} \in L^1_{loc} \end{cases}$$

Here $\delta > 0$ is the discount rate and $u(t,\cdot,\cdot)$ the utility function, so that the integral to be maximized is the aggregated utility over time of the path $x : [0,\infty) \to \mathbb{R}^n$. One usually thinks of $x(t)$ as the capital stock at time t , so that $\dot{x}(t)$ is the rate of (dis-) investment. The set $A_t \subset \mathbb{R}^n \times \mathbb{R}^n$ embodies the various constraints (production technology, availability of resources) which the system has to satisfy.

This model contains seemingly more complicated ones. For instance, if one introduces the consumption $c(t)$, so that the criterion becomes

$$\int_0^\infty e^{-\delta t} u(t,c)\, dt$$

and the constraints :

$$(x(t),\dot{x}(t),c(t)) \in B_t \qquad \text{a.e.,}$$

one would simply define $A_t = \{(x,y) \mid (x,y,c) \in B_t \text{ for some } c\}$, and maximize $u(t,\cdot)$ over all c such that $(x,y,c) \in B_t$. Assuming the maximum is attained at a single point $\bar{c}(t,x,y)$, and setting

$$\bar{u}(t,\wedge,y) = u(t,\bar{c}(t,x,y))$$

brings the problem into the standard form (P) .

The first model of this kind is due to Ramsey towards the end of the last century. In the years of plenty - the sixties - very many variants of this basic model appeared, emphasizing various aspects of the theory of economic growth. We refer to the books by Intriligator [In] and by Arrow and Kurz [AK] for an introduction to this kind of literature. Unfortunately, none of the mathematical problems raised by the Ramsey problem (P) were adequately treated, or even realized at the time. A notable exception is the special issue of JET [1976] , which gives the state of the art until that time.

The main problems connected with (P) are the following :

(1) When does (P) have a solution ? In other words, what conditions on u and A_t are needed for an optimal path $\bar{x}$ to exist ?

(2) What are the necessary conditions for optimality ? In other words, does $\bar{x}$ satisfy some version of the Euler-Lagrange equation in $(0,\infty)$, and what boundary condition must $\bar{x}(t)$ satisfy when $t \to \infty$?

(3) What is the behaviour of $\bar{x}(t)$ when $t \to \infty$? Does it converge to some equilibrium state $\bar{x}(\infty)$, or can it oscillate more or less wildly ?

I don't know how to answer these questions in the full generality of problem (P). I will therefore, as the need arises, restrict myself to simpler models where I know the answer, and leave the general case to others. As a first - and considerable - simplification, let us assume that the problem is autonomous, i.e. t does not appear explicitely. It becomes :

$$(P) \qquad \begin{cases} \text{Sup} \displaystyle\int_0^\infty e^{-\delta t}\, u(x,\dot{x})\, dt \\ (x,\dot{x}) \in A \\ x(0) = x_0 \end{cases}$$

I.1 Existence.

We assume the following :

(H1) $u : \mathbb{R}^{2n} \to \mathbb{R} \cup \{-\infty\}$ is upper semi-continuous and $A \subset \mathbb{R}^{2n}$ is closed.

(H2) $\forall\, x \in \mathbb{R}^n$, $y \to u(x,y)$ is concave
$\forall\, x \in \mathbb{R}^n$, $A_x = \{y \mid (x,y) \in A\}$ is convex.

(H3) $\begin{cases} \exists\, \varphi : [0,\infty) \to \mathbb{R}, \text{ with } \varphi(t)t^{-1} \to +\infty \text{ when } t \to \infty, \\ \text{such that } u(x,y) \leqslant -\varphi(\|y\|) \text{ for all } (x,y) \in A. \end{cases}$

THM. Assume (H1),(H2),(H3). Then $(\mathcal{P})$ has at least one solution.

Proof. We refer to the books [ETu], [C] or [G] for a proof in the general case. The proof in [ETd] contains a mistake.

Let us just sketch the proof in the case where the criterion and the constraints split :

$$u(x,y) = u_1(x) + u_2(y) \quad \text{and} \quad A = A_1 \times A_2$$

Then u_2 is concave, $u_2(y) \leqslant -\varphi(\|y\|)$, and u_1 is bounded from above. Take a maximizing sequence :

$$\int_0^\infty e^{-\delta t}\,[u_1(x_n)+u_2(\dot{x}_n)]\,dt \to \text{Sup}$$

Then there is some large constant C such that :

$$C \leqslant \int_0^\infty e^{-\delta t} u_2(\dot{x}_n)\,dt \leqslant -\int_0^\infty \varphi(\|\dot{x}_n\|)e^{-\delta t}\,dt .$$

Since $[0,\infty)$ endowed with $e^{-\delta t}dt$ has finite measure, we may apply the Dunford-Pettis criterion for weak compactness in L^1, and we conclude that the sequence $\dot{x}_n$ has a weakly convergent subsequence in $L^1(0,\infty\,;\,e^{-\delta t}dt)$. Denote this subsequence by $\dot{x}_n$ again, and its limit by y :

$$\dot{x}_n \to y \qquad \text{in } L^1(0,\infty\,;\,e^{-\delta t}dt)$$

Set

$$\bar{x}(t) = x_o + \int_o^t y(s)\,ds$$

so that $y = \frac{d\bar{x}}{dt}$, and $x_n(t) \to \bar{x}(t)$ uniformly on compact subsets of $[0,\infty)$.

Using Fatou's lemma, we have :

$$\limsup_{n\to\infty} \int_o^\infty e^{-\delta t} u_1(x_n(t))\,dt \leqslant \int_o^\infty e^{-\delta t} u_1(\bar{x}(t))\,dt$$

The map $y \to \int_o^\infty e^{-\delta t} u_2(y(t))\,dt$ is concave and upper semicontinuous. By the Hahn-Banach theorem, it must also be <u>weakly</u> u.s.c. and therefore :

$$\limsup_{n\to\infty} \int_o^\infty e^{-\delta t} u_2\left(\frac{dx_n}{dt}\right) dt \leqslant \int_o^\infty e^{-\delta t} u_2\left(\frac{d\bar{x}}{dt}\right) dt$$

Adding up, we get

$$\int_o^\infty e^{-\delta t} \left(u_1(\bar{x}) + u_2\left(\frac{d\bar{x}}{dt}\right)\right) dt \geqslant \text{Sup}$$

All we have to check now is that $\bar{x}$ is admissible, that is, $\bar{x}(t) \in A_1$ and $\frac{d\bar{x}}{dt}(t) \in A_2$ for almost every t. This follows easily from the facts that :

$x_n(t) \to \bar{x}(t)$ pointwise and A_1 is closed

$\frac{dx_n}{dt} \to \frac{d\bar{x}}{dt}$ weakly in $L^1(e^{-\delta t}dt)$ and A_2 is convex closed. ∎

Note that the result holds also in the general (nonautonomous) case, as the proofs show. Note also that convexity is required with respect to the last variable $\dot{x}$ only.

I.2 Euler-Lagrange.

The derivation of necessary conditions for optimality, including some version of the Euler-Lagrange equations, requires an a priori estimates : it must first be shown that $\bar{x}$ is locally Lipschitz, that is, $\frac{d\bar{x}}{dt}$ is uniformly bounded on compact intervals of $[0,\infty)$, before anything further can be said. This delicate point is sadly missing from the literature of the sixties and seventies, although Tonelli had delved on it in his classical treatise [T] of 1921-23 . Cesari resurrected it in his recent book [C], and it was taken up again by Ball and Mizel [BM1], [BM2], and later by Clarke and Vinter [CV1], [CV2].

THM. Assume $u(x,y)$ is continuous and satisfies (H3). Let the slice $A_x = \{y \mid (x,y) \in A\}$ be closed and star-shaped with respect to the brigin, for every x . Then, if $\bar{x}$ solves (P), for any T there will be some $K > 0$ such that

$$0 \leqslant t \leqslant T \Rightarrow \left\|\frac{d\bar{x}}{dt}(t)\right\| \leqslant K \quad . \qquad \blacksquare$$

Proof. Pick $T > 0$. To simplify notations, write x instead of $\bar{x}$.

Note first that x is uniformly bounded on $[0,T]$. Indeed, setting $\inf_{t \geqslant 0} \varphi(t) = -c$, we have :

$$\begin{aligned}\int_0^T [\varphi(\|\dot{x}\|)+c\,]e^{-\delta t}dt &\leqslant \int_0^\infty [\varphi(\|\dot{x}\|)+c\,]e^{-\delta t}dt \\ &\leqslant -\int_0^\infty u(x,\dot{x})e^{-\delta t}dt + c/\delta \\ &\leqslant \frac{1}{\delta}(c-u(x_0,0))\end{aligned}$$

Since $\varphi(t)t^{-1} \to +\infty$, it follows that $\dot{x} \in L^1(0,T)$, so that $x(t)$ stays in a bounded subset, say :

$$\|x(t)\| \leqslant A \qquad \text{for} \quad 0 \leqslant t \leqslant T$$

For any $M > 0$ large enough, we can define a change of time variable $s = \sigma(t)$ by the conditions :

$$\begin{cases} \sigma(0) = 0 \\ \dfrac{d\sigma}{dt} = \|\dot{x}(t)\| & \text{if } t \in L_M \\ \dfrac{d\sigma}{dt} = 1 & \text{if } t \notin L_M \end{cases}$$

$$L_M = \{t \mid \|\dot{x}(t)\| \geqslant M \text{ and } 0 \leqslant t \leqslant T\} .$$

Define $x_M(s) = x \circ \sigma^{-1}(s)$.

Let us first check that the path x_M is admissible, that is $(x_M(s), \dot{x}_M(s)) \in A$ for almost every s . If $t \notin L_M$, we have $(x_M(s), \dot{x}_M(s)) = (x(t), \dot{x}(t)) \in A$. If $t \in L_M$, we have, with $s = \sigma(t)$:

$$(x_M(s), \dot{x}_M(s)) = (x(t) , \dot{x}(t)\|\dot{x}(t)\|^{-1})$$

which belongs to A , since $A_{x(t)}$ is star-shaped with respect to the origin.

Since x_M is admissible, we must have

$$\int_0^\infty u(x_M, \dot{x}_M) e^{-\delta s} \, ds \leqslant \int_0^\infty u(x, \dot{x}) e^{-\delta t} \, dt$$

We may assume that u is non-positive (otherwise replace $u(x,y)$ by $u(x,y)-c$). Set $s = \sigma(t)$, so that $s \geqslant t$; we have :

$$0 \leqslant \sigma(t)-t \leqslant \int_{L_M} (\|\dot{x}(t)\|-1) \, dt$$

Writing $s = \sigma(t)$ in the preceding inequality, we get :

$$\int_0^\infty u(x, \dot{x}) e^{-\delta t} \, dt \geqslant \int_0^\infty u(x_M \circ \sigma(t) , \dot{x}_M \circ \sigma(t)) \, e^{-\delta\sigma(t)} \, d\sigma(t)$$

$$\geqslant \int_0^\infty u(x_M \circ \sigma(t) , \dot{x}_M \circ \sigma(t)) \, e^{-\delta t} \frac{d\sigma}{dt} \, dt$$

Replacing $x_N \circ \sigma$ and $\dot{x}_M \circ \sigma$ by their value, we get

$$\int_{L_M} u(x,\dot{x})e^{-\delta t}\, dt \geqslant \int_{L_M} u\left(x, \frac{\dot{x}}{\|\dot{x}\|}\right) \|\dot{x}\| e^{-\delta t}\, dt$$

Hence :

$$\int_{L_M} \left[\varphi(\|\dot{x}\|) + u\left(x, \frac{\dot{x}}{\|\dot{x}\|}\right) \|\dot{x}\|\right] e^{-\delta t}\, dt \leqslant 0$$

Set $\mathrm{Max}\,\{|u(x,y)|\ \|x\| \leqslant A \text{ and } \|y\| \leqslant 1\} = B$. The preceding inequality reads :

$$\int_{L_M} [\varphi(\|\dot{x}\|) - B\|\dot{x}\|]\, e^{-\delta t}\, dt \leqslant 0$$

which is wrong as soon as $\varphi(\|\dot{x}\|)\|\dot{x}\|^{-1} \geqslant B$. This happens on L_M when M is large enough. ∎

Note that, by the preceding proof, if $u(x,y)$ does not depend on x , then $\left\|\frac{d\bar{x}}{dt}(t)\right\| \leqslant K$ on $[0,\infty)$, that is, $\bar{x}$ is Lipschitz on the whole of $\mathbb{R}_+$. More generally, if u depends on x and y , but $\|\bar{x}(t)\|$ is bounded (by A) on $[0,+\infty)$, then so is $\left\|\frac{d\bar{x}}{dt}(t)\right\|$ (by K).

If $u(x,y)$ is C^1 , this a priori bound will enable us to differentiate under the integral, and the Euler-Lagrange equations will follow.

THM. Assume $u(x,y)$ is C^1 and satisfies (H3). Assume A is convex and $A_x \neq \emptyset \Rightarrow A_x \ni 0$. Let $\bar{x}$ be an optimal path, and y an admissible path such that, for some $T > 0$, we have $y(t) = \bar{x}(t)$ if $t \geqslant T$, and $\left\|\frac{dy}{dt}\right\| \leqslant K$ for $t \leqslant T$. Then

$$\text{(E)} \qquad \int_0^T \left[\frac{\partial u}{\partial x}\left(\bar{x}, \frac{d\bar{x}}{dt}\right)(x-\bar{x}) + \frac{\partial u}{\partial y}\left(\bar{x}, \frac{d\bar{x}}{dt}\right)\left(\frac{dx}{dt} - \frac{d\bar{x}}{dt}\right)\right] e^{-\delta t}\, dt \leqslant 0$$

<u>Proof.</u> We just write :

$$0 \leqslant \int_0^\infty u\left(\bar{x}, \frac{d\bar{x}}{dt}\right)e^{-\delta t}dt - \int_0^\infty u\left(\bar{x}+h(x-\bar{x}), \frac{d\bar{x}}{dt} + h\left(\frac{dx}{dt} - \frac{d\bar{x}}{dt}\right)\right)e^{-\delta t}\, dt$$

divide by h and let $h \to 0$. ∎

We shall discuss the interpretation of (E) in the particular case when there are only state constraints : $A = A_1 \times \mathbb{R}^n$, with A convex and $\text{Int } A \neq \emptyset$.

If $\bar{x}(t_o)$ belongs to the interior of A_1 , then so does $\bar{x}(t)$ for $|t-t_o| \leqslant \eta$, and (E) gives the familiar Euler-Lagrange equations

$$\frac{d}{dt}\left(\frac{\partial u}{\partial y}\left(\bar{x}, \frac{d\bar{x}}{dt}\right) e^{-\delta t}\right) = \frac{\partial u}{\partial x}\left(\bar{x}, \frac{d\bar{x}}{dt}\right) e^{-\delta t}$$

In the general case, the allowable variations $y = x - \bar{x}$ must satisfy $y(t) \in T(\bar{x}(t),A)$ (tangent cone to A at $\bar{x}(t)$) for every t . We then have :

$$\int_0^T \left|\frac{\partial u}{\partial x}\left(\bar{x}, \frac{d\bar{x}}{dt}\right) y + \frac{\partial u}{\partial y}\left(\bar{x}, \frac{d\bar{x}}{dt}\right) \frac{dy}{dt}\right| e^{-\delta t} \, dt \leqslant 0$$

for every Lipschitz function y such that $u(t) \in T(\bar{x}(t),A)$, $y(0) = 0$ and $y(t) = 0$ for $t \geqslant T$. Since $\frac{d\bar{x}}{dt} \in L^\infty$, so do $\frac{\partial u}{\partial x}\left(\bar{x}, \frac{d\bar{x}}{dt}\right)$ and $\frac{\partial u}{\partial y}\left(\bar{x}, \frac{d\bar{x}}{dt}\right)$, and the inequality holds in fact for all y such that $\frac{dy}{dt} \in L^1$, $y(t) \in T(\bar{x},t),A)$, $y(0) = 0$ and $y(t) = 0$ for $t \geqslant T$. Integrate by parts :

$$\int_0^T \left|-\int_0^t \frac{\partial u}{\partial x}\left(\bar{x}, \frac{d\bar{x}}{dt}\right) e^{-\delta s} \, ds + \frac{\partial u}{\partial y}\left(\bar{x}, \frac{d\bar{x}}{dt}\right) e^{-\delta t}\right| \frac{dy}{dt} \, dt \leqslant 0$$

Set :

$$f(t) = -\int_0^t \frac{\partial u}{\partial u}\left(\bar{x}, \frac{d\bar{x}}{dt}\right) e^{-\delta s} \, ds + \frac{\partial u}{\partial y}\left(\bar{x}, \frac{d\bar{x}}{dt}\right) e^{-\delta t} \in L^\infty$$

$$Au(t) = \int_0^t u(s)ds \in C^o , \text{ with } u \in L^1(0,T) \text{ and } \int_0^T u(s)ds = 0$$

$$C = \{v \in C^o([0,T]) \mid v(t) \in T(\bar{x}(t),A) \ \forall t\}$$

Then C is a cone with non-empty interior in C^o . Letting $C^\perp$ be its polar cone, which is a subset of $\mathcal{U}$, the set of all Radon measures on $[t_o-\eta, t_o+\eta]$:

$$C^\perp = \left\{\mu \in \mathcal{U} \mid \int v \, d\mu \leqslant 0 \quad \forall v \in C\right\}$$

we have the standard formula from convex analysis :

$$[A^{-1}C]^{\perp} = A^{\star}C^{\perp}$$

So $f \in A^{\star}C^{\perp}$. This means that there is some $\bar{\mu} \in C^{\perp}$ and some constant $\xi \in \mathbb{R}^{2n}$ such that :

$$f(t) - \xi = \bar{\mu}([0,t]) - \operatorname{Supp} \bar{\mu}$$

This relation is equivalent to the following (use the theory of desintegration of measures) : there is a measurable vector-valued function $\nu : [0,\infty) \to \mathbb{R}^n$, with $\nu(t) \in N(\bar{x}(t),A)$ (the normal cone to A at $\bar{x}(t)$), and a scalar-valued non-negative Radon measure ρ on $[0,\infty)$, such that :

$$f(t) - \xi = \int_0^t \nu(s)\, e^{-\delta\tau}\, d\rho(s)$$

In other words :

$$e^{\delta t}\frac{df}{dt} = \frac{d}{dt}\left(\frac{\partial u}{\partial y}\left(\bar{x},\frac{d\bar{x}}{dt}\right)\right) - \delta\frac{\partial u}{\partial y}\left(\bar{x},\frac{d\bar{x}}{dt}\right) - \frac{\partial u}{\partial x}\left(\bar{x},\frac{d\bar{x}}{dt}\right)$$

$$= \nu(t)\, d\rho$$

where the right-hand side is to be understood as a measure.

I.3 Transversality condition at infinity.

A very original approach to this problem is due to Ph. Michel [M]. Here, I will favour the Ekeland-Scheinkman approach [ES], which has a broader scope.

THM. Assume that

(1) $u(x,y)$ is C^1 , concave in y , and satisfies (H3).

(2) A is convex and $A_x \neq \emptyset \Rightarrow 0 \in A_x$.

Let $\bar{x}$ be a solution of problem (P), and let x be another admissible path such that :

(3) $\frac{d\bar{x}}{dt}$ is uniformly bounded on finite intervals.

(4) for some constants α and some $f \in L^1(e^{-\delta t}dt)$, we have

$$\frac{\partial u}{\partial x}(\xi,\eta)(x(t)-\xi) + \frac{\partial u}{\partial y}(\xi,\eta)\left(\frac{dx}{dt}(t)-\eta\right) \geqslant \alpha u(\xi,\eta) + f(t)$$

for all $(\xi,\eta) \in A$ and $t \geqslant 0$.

Set :

$$f(t) = \left[\frac{\partial u}{\partial x}\left(\bar{x}, \frac{d\bar{x}}{dt}\right)(x-\bar{x}) + \frac{\partial u}{\partial y}\left(\bar{x}, \frac{d\bar{x}}{dt}\right)\left(\frac{dx}{dt} - \frac{d\bar{x}}{dt}\right)\right] e^{-\delta t}$$

Then f is Lebesgue-integrable and $\int_0^\infty f(t)\, dt \leqslant 0$. ■

For the proof, we refer to [ES]. The problem is that we do not assume that $\int_0^\infty u\left(x, \frac{dx}{dt}\right) e^{-\delta t}\, dt$ is finite. We therefore approximate the infinite-horizon problem by finite-horizon ones.

Condition (4) is automatically satisfied in the case when u is concave in both variables, and $\int_0^\infty u\left(x, \frac{dx}{dt}\right) e^{-\delta t}\, dt$ is finite. Indeed, by concavity :

$$\frac{\partial u}{\partial x}(\xi,\eta)(x(t)-\xi) + \frac{\partial u}{\partial y}(\xi,\eta)\left(\frac{dx}{dt}(t)-\eta\right) \geqslant u\left(x(t), \frac{dx}{dt}(t)\right) - u(\xi,\eta)$$

It is also satisfied if, for instance, $n = 1$ and

$$A = \{(x,y) \mid x \geqslant 0 , y \leqslant \varphi(x)\}$$

(φ is the production function), with $u(x,y) = \bar{u}(\varphi(x)-y)$ where $\bar{u}(c) = c^\beta$ (with $0 < \beta < 1$) or $\bar{u}(c) = -c^\beta$ (with $\beta < 0$). Indeed, the left-hand side of inequality (4) becomes

$$|\beta|(\varphi(\xi)-\eta)^{\beta-1}\left[(x(t)-\xi)\,\varphi'(\xi) + \left(\frac{dx}{dt}(t)-\eta\right)\right] \geqslant$$

$$\geqslant -|\beta|(\varphi(\xi)-\eta)^\beta + \frac{dx}{dt}|\beta|\,(\varphi(\xi)-\eta)^{\beta-1}$$

provided $\xi\varphi'(\xi) \leqslant \varphi(\xi)$ (the production function does not grow exponentially). If $\int_0^\infty \left|\frac{dx}{dt}\right| e^{-\delta t} dt < \infty$, then x satisfies assumption (4).

Let us illustrate the theorem on an example.

Corollary. Assume (1) and (2). Assume that $(0,0) \in A$ and that, for some constants α and γ :

$$\forall (x,y) \in A , \qquad x \frac{\partial u}{\partial x}(x,y) + y \frac{\partial u}{\partial y}(x,y) \leqslant \alpha u(x,y) + \gamma$$

Then (after correcting on a set of measure zero) for any solution $\bar{x}$ of (P) we have :

$$\liminf_{t \to \infty} \left[\frac{\partial u}{\partial y}\left(\bar{x}, \frac{d\bar{x}}{dt}\right) \bar{x}(t)\, e^{-\delta t}\right] \geqslant 0$$

Proof. Comparing $\bar{x}$ with the path x defined by

$$x(t) = (1-t)x_o \qquad \text{for } 0 \leqslant t \leqslant 1$$

$$x(t) = 0 \qquad \text{for } t \geqslant 1$$

we find that

$$0 \leqslant \int_1^\infty \left[\frac{\partial u}{\partial x}\left(\bar{x}, \frac{d\bar{x}}{dt}\right) \bar{x} + \frac{\partial u}{\partial y}\left(\bar{x}, \frac{d\bar{x}}{dt}\right) \frac{d\bar{x}}{dt}\right] e^{-\delta t} dt \leqslant \infty$$

so that $\int_T^\infty \left|\frac{\partial u}{\partial x} \bar{x} + \frac{\partial u}{\partial y} \frac{d\bar{x}}{dt}\right| e^{-\delta t} dt \to 0$ when $T \to \infty$.

We want to prove that, for every $\varepsilon > 0$, there is some T_o such that the measure of the set

$$\left\{t \geqslant T_o \mid \frac{\partial u}{\partial y}\left(\bar{x}, \frac{d\bar{x}}{dt}\right) \frac{d\bar{x}}{dt} e^{-\delta t} \geqslant \varepsilon\right\} = A(T_o)$$

is zero.

Choose first T_1 so large that, for all $T \geqslant T_o$:

$$\int_T^\infty \left|\frac{\partial u}{\partial x}\left(\bar{x}, \frac{d\bar{x}}{dt}\right) \bar{x} + \frac{\partial u}{\partial y}\left(\bar{x}, \frac{d\bar{x}}{dt}\right) \frac{d\bar{x}}{dt}\right| e^{-\delta t} dt \leqslant \frac{\varepsilon}{7}$$

If $A(T_o)$ has positive measure, there must be some point $t_o \in A(T_o)$ such that (here we use the fact that $\frac{d\bar{x}}{dt}$ is locally bounded, so $\frac{\partial u}{\partial y}\left(\bar{x}, \frac{d\bar{x}}{dt}\right) \frac{d\bar{x}}{dt}$ is locally integrable) :

$$\lim_{\alpha \to 0} \frac{1}{\alpha} \int_{t_o}^{t_o+\alpha} \frac{\partial u}{\partial y}\left(\bar{x}, \frac{d\bar{x}}{dt}\right) \bar{x}(t_o) e^{-\delta t}\, dt \leqslant -\varepsilon$$

Define the path x_α as follows :

$$x_\alpha(t) = \bar{x}(t) \qquad \text{for } 0 \leqslant t \leqslant t_o$$

$$x_\alpha(t) = \left(1 - \frac{t-t_o}{\alpha}\right) \bar{x}(t_o) \qquad \text{for } t_o \leqslant t \leqslant t_o+\alpha$$

$$x_\alpha(t) = 0 \qquad \text{for } t \geqslant t_o+\alpha$$

The theorem then gives

$$0 \geqslant \int_{t_o}^{t_o+\alpha} \left[\frac{\partial u}{\partial x}\left(1 - \frac{t-t_o}{\alpha}\right) \bar{x}(t_o) - \frac{\partial u}{\partial y} \frac{1}{\alpha} \bar{x}(t_o)\right] e^{-\delta t}\, dt$$

$$- \int_{t_o}^{\infty} \left[\frac{\partial u}{\partial x} \bar{x}(t) + \frac{\partial u}{\partial y} \frac{d\bar{x}}{dt}(t)\right] e^{-\delta t}\, dt$$

Letting $\alpha \to 0$, we get : $0 \geqslant \varepsilon - \frac{\varepsilon}{7} = \frac{6\varepsilon}{7}$, which contradicts the fact that $\varepsilon > 0$. Hence the result. ∎

II . Hamiltonian formalism.

From the preceding section, we extract the following information.

THM. Assume $u(x,y)$ is C^1, concave in y, and there is some $\varphi : [0,\infty) \to \mathbb{R}$ with $\varphi(t)t^{-1} \to +\infty$ when $t \to \infty$ such that $u(x,y) \leqslant -\varphi(\|y\|)$ for all $(x,y) \in A$. Assume A is convex, closed, and there is some $\bar{x} \in \mathbb{R}^n$ and $\varepsilon > 0$ such that, whenever $\|\bar{x}-\xi\| \leqslant \varepsilon$, we have :

$$(\xi,0) \in \operatorname{Int} A$$

$$\frac{\partial u}{\partial x}(x,y)(\xi-x) - \frac{\partial u}{\partial y}(x,y)y \geqslant \alpha u(x,y) + \gamma \qquad \forall (x,y) \in A$$

Then (P) has an optimal solution at least, and every optimal solution $x(t)$ satisfies

$$(1) \qquad \frac{d}{dt}\left[\frac{\partial u}{\partial y}\left(\bar{x}, \frac{d\bar{x}}{dt}\right) e^{-\delta t}\right] = \frac{\partial u}{\partial x}\left(\bar{x}, \frac{d\bar{x}}{dt}\right) e^{-\delta t}$$

$$(2) \qquad \lim_{t \to \infty} \frac{\partial u}{\partial y}\left(\bar{x}, \frac{d\bar{x}}{dt}\right) e^{-\delta t} = 0 \qquad \blacksquare$$

If we assume that $u(x,y)$ is strictly concave in y for all x, we can write these equations in Hamiltonian form. Define

$$H(x,p) = \operatorname{Min} \{(p,y) - u(x,y) \mid (x,y) \in A\}$$

The equations then become

$$(H) \qquad \begin{cases} \dot{p} - \delta p = -\dfrac{\partial H}{\partial x} \\ \dot{x} = \dfrac{\partial H}{\partial p} \end{cases}$$

$$(T) \qquad \lim_{t \to \infty} p(t)\, e^{-\delta t} = 0$$

Among all trajectories of the flow (H), the optimal ones are singled out by (T), the transversality condition at infinity. Note for instance that any trajectory of (H) such that $p(t)$ remains bounded as $t \to \infty$ automatically satisfies (H), and is therefore a candidate for optimality. The question whether such solutions exist is a question about the global behaviour of the flow, and we shall answer it in some particular cases, using Lyapounov stability theory. The basic facts about Lyapounov functions and ω-limit sets can be found in [HS] or in [NS].

Before we begin, we should note that, if u is globally convex, then the Hamiltonian H is convex in p and concave in x. This is in stark contrast with Hamiltonians arising from physics, which tend to be convex in both variables. The corresponding flows have completely different behaviours.

THM1. (Separable case). Assume $H(x,p) = H_1(x) + H_2(p)$ where H_1 and H_2 are C^2 functions on $\mathbb{R}^n$, and H_2 is strictly convex and attains its minimum at $\bar{p}$

$$H_2(p) > H_2(\bar{p}) \qquad \forall\, p \neq \bar{p}$$

Assume in addition that the equation $\frac{\partial H_1}{\partial x}(x) = \delta\bar{p}$ has finitely many solutions $\bar{x}_1,\ldots,\bar{x}_K$, with $K \geqslant 1$. Then the flow (H) has at least one bounded trajectory $\left[\sup_{t \geqslant 0} \{\|p(t)\|, \|x(t)\|\} < \infty\right]$, and every such trajectory must converge to one of the $(\bar{x}_k, \bar{p})$, $1 \leqslant k \leqslant K$. ∎

Proof. Set $V(x,p) = H_1(x) + H_2(p) - \delta(\bar{p},x)$. I claim it is a Lyapounov function for (H).

Indeed, the calculation gives

$$\frac{d}{dt} V(x(t),p(t)) = \left(\frac{\partial H_1}{\partial x}, \frac{\partial H_2}{\partial p}\right) + \left(\frac{\partial H_2}{\partial p}, -\frac{\partial H_1}{\partial x} + \delta p\right) - \delta(\bar{p},x)$$

$$= \delta\left(p-\bar{p}, \frac{\partial H_2}{\partial p}(p)\right) \geqslant 0 .$$

So $V(x(t),p(t))$ increases along every trajectory. If $(x(t),p(t))$

remains bounded as $t \to \infty$, it is known that the ω-limit set is a compact, connected, non-empty, invariant set contained in

$$\Omega = \left\{(x,p) \mid \delta\left(p-\bar{p}, \frac{\partial H_2}{\partial p}(p)\right) = 0\right\}$$

So $\Omega = \mathbb{R}^n \times \{\bar{p}\}$. If $(x,\bar{p}) \in \Omega$, we have

$$(\dot{x},\dot{p}) = \left(0, -\frac{\partial H}{\partial x}(x) + \delta\bar{p}\right),$$

which leaves Ω unless $-\frac{\partial H}{\partial x}(x) + \delta\bar{p} = 0$, hence $x = x_k$ for some $k \in \{1,\dots,K\}$. The connectedness requirement then allows us to conclude that the ω-limit set is one of the $(x_k,\bar{p})$, and hence that the whole trajectory converges to that point.

If the flow (H) had no bounded trajectory, since it is always transversal to the level sets $V(x,p) \geq h$, it could be used to build a diffeomorphism of two level sets $V(x,p) \geq h_1$ and $V(x,p) \geq h_2$, with

$$h_1 < H_2(\bar{p}) + \operatorname*{Max}_x \{H_1(x) - \delta(\bar{p},x)\} < h_2$$

assuming there are no other critical value of V between h_1 and h_2. This leads to a contradiction, since $V \geq h_2$ is $V \geq h_1$ with finitely many n-cells attached.

Alternatively, note that the condition $(V'(z),f(z)) \geq 0$ with $z = (x,p)$ and $f(z) = \left(\frac{\partial H_2}{\partial p}, -\frac{\partial H_1}{\partial p} + \delta p\right)$, near $\bar{z} = (\bar{x}_k,\bar{p})$ leads to :

$$(V''(\bar{z})f'(\bar{z})z, z) \geq 0 \qquad \forall z$$

It follows that, if $V''(\bar{x})$ has a negative eigenvalue, then $f'(\bar{z})$ must have an eigenvalue with non-positive real part, and a corresponding real invariant subspace. ∎

THM2. (Concave-convex case). Assume that

$$H(x,p) = \operatorname*{Min}_y \{(p,y) - u(x,y)\}$$

where $u : \mathbb{R}^n \times \mathbb{R}^n \to \mathbb{R}$ is concave and attains its maximum at $(\bar{x},0)$, with u'' negative definite. Let B be any ball around $(\bar{x},0)$. Then there is some δ_o such that, for any $\delta < \delta_o$, any half-trajectory $(x(t),p(t))$ which is contained in B must converge to $(\bar{x},0)$.

Proof : Consider the function :

$$W(x,p) = (p,x-\bar{x})$$

We have :

$$\frac{dW}{dt}(x,p) = \delta(p,x-\bar{x}) + \left(p , \frac{\partial H}{\partial p}\right) - \left(\frac{\partial H}{\partial x} , x-\bar{x}\right)$$

$$= \delta\left(\frac{\partial u}{\partial y}, x-\bar{x}\right) + \left(\frac{\partial u}{\partial y}, y\right) + \left(\frac{\partial u}{\partial x}, x-\bar{x}\right)$$

Hence $\frac{d}{dt}(e^{-\delta t}(p,x)) \leqslant 0$. If $(x(t),p(t))$ is a half-trajectory contained in Ω_δ , its ω -limit set must be compact, invariant, non-empty and satisfy $\frac{dW}{dt} = 0$. For $\delta > 0$ small enough, the only solution is $(\bar{x},0)$. ■

This example is interesting for two reasons :

(a) if u is such that

$$\left(\frac{\partial u}{\partial y}, y\right) + \left(\frac{\partial u}{\partial x}, x-\bar{x}\right) + \delta\left(\frac{\partial u}{\partial y}, x-\bar{x}\right) \leqslant 0 \qquad \forall\ (x,y)$$

for $0 < \delta < \delta_o$, then every bounded solution must converge to $(\bar{x},\bar{p})$.

(b) the linearized equations near $(\bar{x},0)$ are

$$\dot{x} = \frac{\partial^2 H}{\partial p\, \partial x} x + \frac{\partial^2 H}{\partial p^2} p \quad , \quad \dot{p} = -\frac{\partial^2 H}{\partial x^2} x - \frac{\partial^2 H}{\partial p\, \partial x} p + \delta p$$

If $n = 1$, for instance, both eigenvalues have positive real part if $\frac{\partial^2 H}{\partial p\, \partial x}(\bar{x},0) > 0$ and δ is large enough. The point $(\bar{x},0)$ then becomes unstable, and no bounded solution can converge to $(\bar{x},0)$.

Combining both situations, we can construct an example where, for small δ , the optimal path converges to $(\bar{x},0)$, whereas, for larger δ , the behaviour is more complicated.

BIBLIOGRAPHY

[AK] K. Arrow and M. Kurz, "Optimal taxation policy", Saunders, 1968

[BM1] J. Ball and V. Mizel, "Singular minimizers for regular one-dimensional problems in the calculus of variations", Bull. AMS 11, 1984, p. 143-6

[BM2] J. Ball and V. Mizel, "One-dimensional variational problems whose minimizers do not satisfy the Euler-Lagrange equation", Archive for Rational Mechanics, 1986

[C] L. Cesari, "Optimization: Theory and applications", Springer, New York, 1983

[CV1] F. Clarke and R.Vinter, "On the conditions under which the Euler equation or the maximum principle hold", Appl. Math. and Opt. 12, 1984, p 73-79

[CV2] F. Clarke and R.Vinter, "Regularity properties of solutions to the basic problem in the calculus of variations". Trans. AMS, 1987 , p.133-179

[ETe] I. Ekeland and R. Temam, "Convex analysis and variational problems" , North-Holland, 1976

[ETu] I. Ekeland and T.Turnbull, "Infinite-dimensional optimization and convexity", Chicago University Press, 1978

[ES] I. Ekeland and J. Scheinkman, "Transversality conditions for some infinite horizon discrete time optimization problems", Math. of Operations Research, 11, 1986, p.216-229

[G] M. Giaquinta, "Multiple integrals in the calculus of variations and nonlinear elliptic systems", Annals of Mathematics studies 105, Princeton University Press, 1985

[HS] M. Hirsch and S. Smale, "Dynamical systems", Ac. Press, 1978

[I] M. Intriligator, "Optimal growth theory", Wiley, 1969

[IT] A. Ioffe and V. Tikhomirov, "Theory of extremal problems", North Holland Elsevier

[L] M. Lavrentiev,"Sur quelques problèmes du calcul des variations", Ann. Mat. Pura Appl. 4,1926,p.7-28

[M] PH. Michel, "La condition de transversalité à l'infini", Econometrica, 1983

[NS] A. Nemitskii and P. Stepanov, " Qualitative theory of differential equations", Princeton University Press.

[T] L. Tonelli, "Fondamenti di Calcolo delle Variazioni", 2 vol, Zanichelli, 1921-23 (also as vol. 13 of "Opere scelte", Edizioni Cremonese, Roma, 1961)

Four Lectures on the Differentiable Approach to General Equilibrium Theory

Andreu Mas-Colell
Harvard University

With few exception the material from the first three lectures is taken from A. Mas-Colell: *The Theory of General Economic Equilibrium: A Differentiable Approach*, Cambridge University Press, 1985. We refer to this text for many extensions and the basic references. The names of the developers of the differentiable approach (at least for the parts covered in these lectures) should, however, be mentioned at the outset: G. Debreu, S. Smale, E. Dierker, and Y. Balasko.

The fourth lecture gives an account of a recent and fascinating development. A major and deep application of the differentiable approach to an area, incomplete market theory, not covered by the above reference.

Lecture I: Single Consumer Theory

I.1 Preference and Utility

The consumers making an appearance in these lectures have preferences defined over nonnegative vectors of R^ℓ, ℓ being the number of commodities. The *consumption set* is thus R^ℓ_+.

A preference relation $\succsim$ is a relation $\succsim \subset R^\ell_+ \times R^\ell_+$ with the properties:

(i) $x \succsim x$ for all $x \in R^\ell_+$ (*reflexivity*).

(ii) "$x \succsim y$ and $y \succsim z$" $\Rightarrow$ "$x \succsim z$" (*transitivity*)

(iii) for every x, y we have that either $x \succsim y$ on $y \succsim x$ (*completeness*).

In addition we always assume that $\succsim$ satisfies a topological property (which does not belong to the essence of the concept of preferences).

(iv) $\succsim$ is a closed set (*continuity*).

By a classic theorem (due to Eilenberg and Debreu) every relation $\succsim$ satisfying (i)–(iv) is representable by a utility function, i.e., there is a $u : R^\ell_+ \to R$ such that "$x \succsim y$" $\Leftrightarrow$ "$u(x) \geq u(y)$". Moreover u can be taken to be continuous. Of course, u is not unique What is intrinsic to $\succsim$ are the family of level curves of u (called *indifference sets*), not the particular indexing (see Figure I.1):

We read $x \succsim y$ as "at least as good", if $x \succsim y$ does hold but $y \succsim x$ does not (resp. does) then we say that x is preferred to y (resp., is indifferent to x), denoted $x \succ y$ (resp., $x \sim y$).

I.2 Properties of Preferences

(i) *Monotonicity:* $A \succsim$ is *monotone* (resp., strictly monotone) if "$x \geq y$" $\Rightarrow$ "$x \succsim y$" (resp., $x \geq y$, $x \neq y \Rightarrow$ "$x \succ y$"). That is, commodities are not noxious (resp., they are desirable). See Figure I.2.

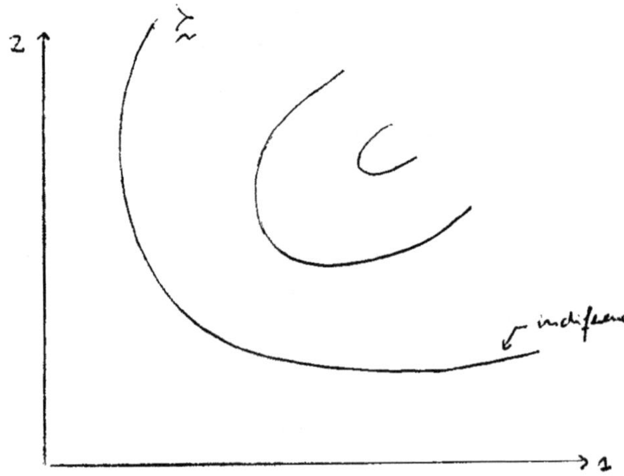

Figure I.1

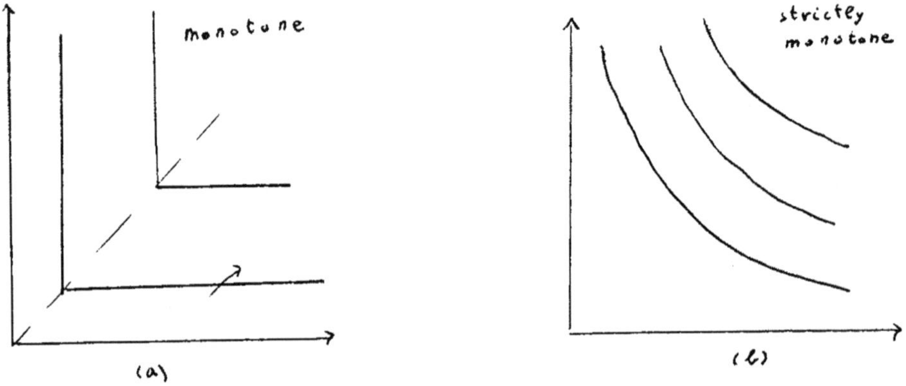

Figure I.2

(ii) *Boundary Condition:* Given $\succsim$, for every $x >> 0$ the at least as good set $\{y: y \succsim x\}$ is closed relative to R^ℓ, i.e., every commodity is indispensable. See Figure I.3.

N.B.: *Unless otherwise stated we assume from now on that preferences satisfy the strict monotonicity and the boundary conditions.*

It is to be emphasized that these restrictions are not essential to the theory. They simply allow for ease of presentation. In particular, the boundary condition allows us to regard $R^\ell_{++} = \{x \in R^\ell: x >> 0\}$ as the consumption set.

(iii) *Convexity:* A $\succsim$ is *convex* (resp., strictly convex) if $\{y: y \succsim x\}$ is a convex set for every y (resp., $\alpha y + (1-\alpha)x \succsim x$ whenever $y \succsim x$ and $0 \le \alpha < 1$). See Figure I.4.

If $\succsim$ is generated from a concave (resp., strictly concave) utility then $\succsim$ is convex (resp., strictly convex). The converse need not hold (i.e., there are convex preferences not generated by concave utilities).

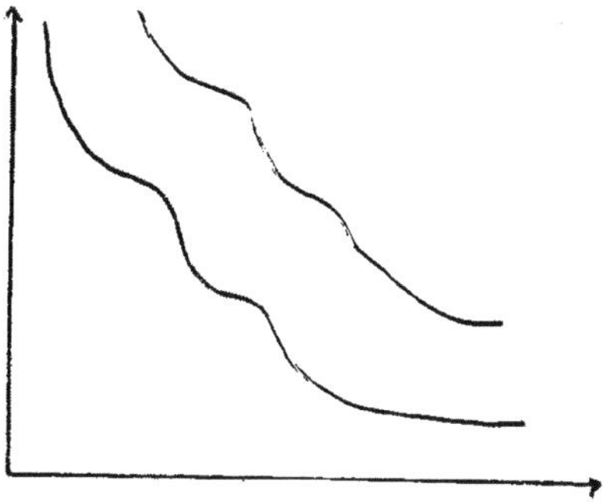

Figure I.3

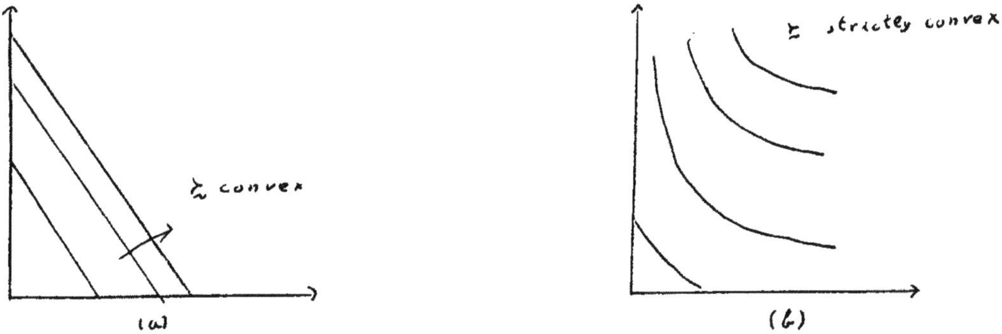

Figure I.4

I.3 Smooth Preferences

Definition. *A $\succsim$ is of class C^r, $r \geq 1$, if the indifference set $I = \{(x,y): x \sim y\} \subset R^\ell \times R^\ell$ (= B dry $\succsim$) is a C^r manifold (i.e., for every $\bar{z} \in I$ there is a C^r function $g : V \to R$ defined on a neighborhood $V \subset R^\ell \times R^\ell$ of $\bar{z}$ s.t. $\partial g(z) \neq 0$ for all $z \in V$ and $g^{-1}(0) = V \cap I$).*

We state without proof.

PROPOSITION. *$\succsim$ is C^r, $r \leq 2$, if and only if $\succsim$ is representable by a C^r utility function $u: R^\ell_{++} \to R$ with no critical point, i.e., $\partial u(x) \neq 0$ for all x.* (The validity of the Proposition does not depend on the maintained monotonicity and boundary conditions.)

Example. $\succsim \subset [-1,1] \times [-1,1]$ is defined by $x \succsim y \Leftrightarrow |x| \leq |y|$. Then $\succsim$ does not have a smooth boundary (Fig. I.5). There is a C^∞ utility for $\succsim$ (i.e., $u(x) = -x^2$) but no C^2 utility with *no vertical point.*

I.4 Curvature

N.B.: *Unless otherwise stated we assume that our preferences are of class C^2 and that utility functions are C^2 have no critical points.*

If a C^2 function $u : R^\ell \to R$ is concave then $\partial^2 u(x)$ is negative semidefinite. If $\partial^2 u(x)$ is in fact negative definite then we say that u is differentiably strictly concave.

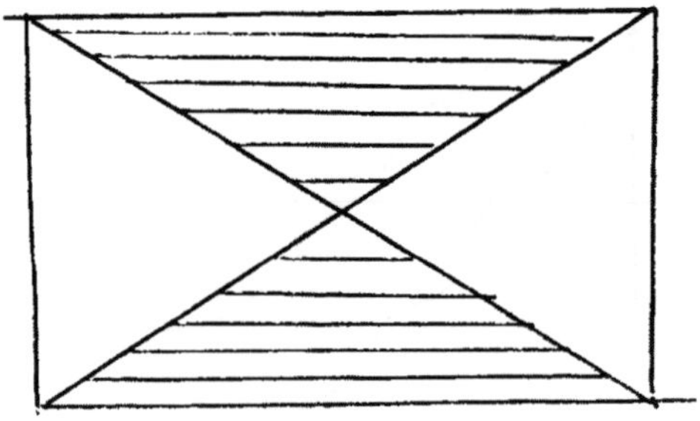

Figure I.5

Given a convex preference relation $\succsim$ we shall now search for a concept of "differentiably strictly convex." Consider $\succsim$ at the point x represented in Fig. I.6. The indifference set at x can be viewed as the boundary of the preferred set. Looking at the curvature of this boundary at x suggests itself.

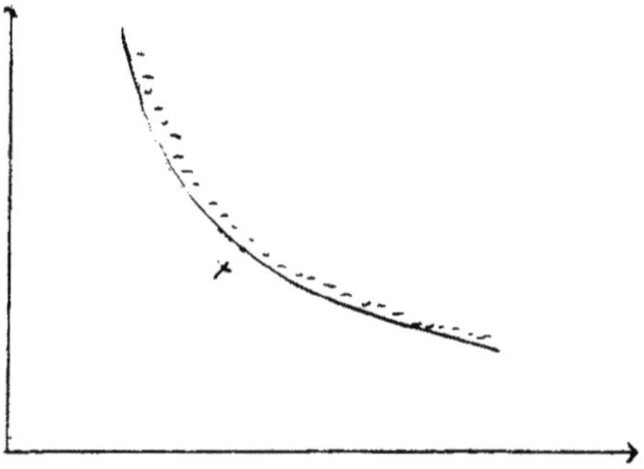

Figure I.6

Definition. *The preference relation* $\succsim$ *is differentiably strictly convex if it is convex (because of the Boundary Condition this is in fact redundant) and for every* $x \in R^\ell_{++}$ *the Gaussian curvature of* $I_x = \{y : y \sim x\}$, *viewed as the boundary of* $\{y : y \succsim x\}$, *is nonzero.*

The Gaussian curvature is defined as follows: let $g : R^\ell_{++} \to S^{\ell-1}$ be given by $g(y) = (1/\|\partial u(y)\|)\partial u(y)$, where u is an arbitrary utility function for $\succsim$ (the definition is independent of the particular u). See Figure I.7. Let $T_y = \{v \in R^\ell : \partial u(y)v = 0\}$. Then at any x, $\partial g(x)$ maps T_x into T_x. The determinant of this linear map is the Gaussian curvature (up to a sign).

There is a simple characterization in terms of utility functions.

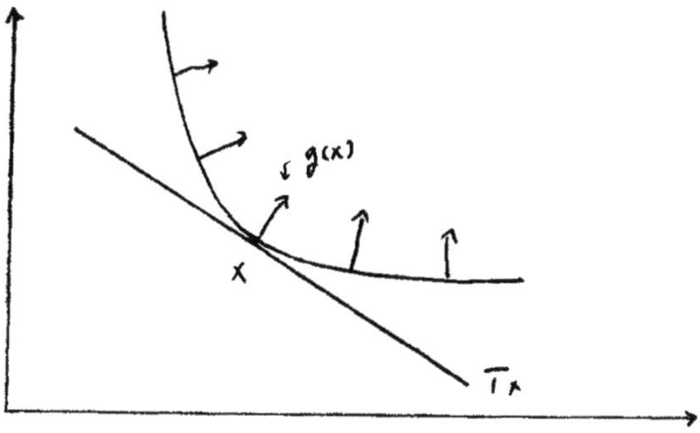

Figure I.7

PROPOSITION: $\succsim$ *is differentiably strictly convex if*

$$\begin{vmatrix} \partial^2 u(x) & \partial u(x) \\ [\partial u(x)]^T & O \end{vmatrix} \neq 0$$

for all x *and some* u *representing* $\succsim$.

The Proposition should be plausible enough if: (i) we remember the definition of Gaussian curvature, and (ii) take into account that for matrices $\underset{n\times n}{A}$ and $\underset{m\times n}{B}$ ($m < n$, B nonsingular) the determinant of $\begin{bmatrix} A & B \\ -B^T & O \end{bmatrix}$ has the sign of the determinant of the linear map obtained by restricting A to Kernel B and projecting then back into Kernel B, and (iii) we carry out the simple computation allowing one to verify

$$\begin{vmatrix} \partial^2 g(x) & \partial g(x) \\ [\partial g(x)]^T & O \end{vmatrix} \neq 0 \quad \Leftrightarrow \quad \begin{vmatrix} \partial^2 u(x) & \partial u(x) \\ [\partial u(x)]^T & O \end{vmatrix} \neq 0 \ .$$

Yet another interesting characterization is:

PROPOSITION. $\succsim$ *is differentiably strictly convex if, for any smooth utility for* $\succsim$ *and any* x, $\partial^2 u(x)$ *is negative definite on* T_x, *i.e.,* $v \cdot \partial^2 u(x) v < 0$ *for* $v \neq 0$, $\partial u(x) v = 0$.

Therefore if u has no critical point and it is differentiably strictly concave then $\succsim$ is differentiably strictly convex. There is an (easy) partial converse to this:

PROPOSITION. *If* $\succsim$ *is differentiably strictly convex then for every convex compact* $K \subset R^{\ell}_{++}$ *there is a smooth utility function for* $\succsim$ *which is concave on* K.

Note. We cannot take $K = R^{\ell}_{++}$ in the above. Another necessary condition for concavifiability is that all the at least as good sets $\{y : y \succsim x\}$ have the same asymptotic cone.

I.5 The Demand Function

In this section the strictly convex preference relation $\succsim$ remains fixed.

We shall at last introduce prices. Given a vector of strictly positive prices $p \in R^{\ell}_{++}$ and a level of income (or wealth) w the demand function $\varphi(p, w)$ is defined as the unique maximizer of $\succsim$ on the budget set $\beta(p, w) = \{x \in R^{\ell}_{++} : p \cdot x \leq w\}$. Such a maximum exists by the continuity and boundary hypotheses on $\succsim$. See Figure I.8.

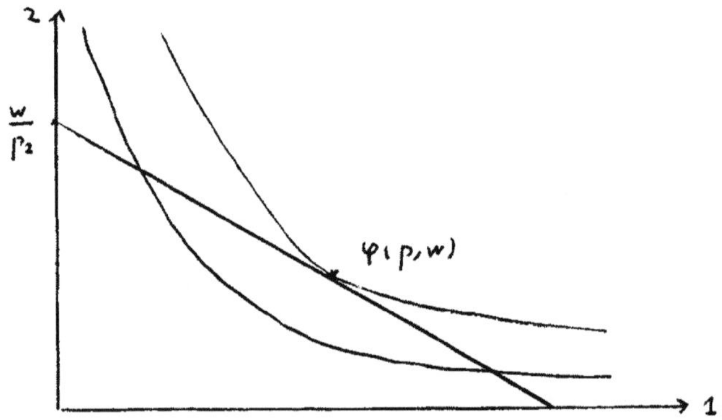

Figure I.8

Some of the obvious, or relatively straightforward properties of the demand function are:

(i) $\varphi(\alpha p, \alpha w) = \varphi(p, w)$ for all p, w and $\alpha > 0$ (*Homogeneity of degree zero*)

(ii) $p \cdot \varphi(p, w) = w$ for all p, w (*Walras law*)

(iii) $\varphi(p, w)$ is singlevalued

(iv) φ is a continuous function on $R^{\ell}_{++} \times R_{+}$.

So far we did not use the smoothness of utility. It is logical to expect that this will be the crucial property in order to get the differentiability of demand.

Suppose that u is a C^2 utility function for $\succsim$ with no critical point. Then, given $(\bar{p}, \bar{w})$, x is the demand vector, i.e., $\bar{x} = \varphi(\bar{p}, \bar{w})$, if and only if (iff) there is $\bar{\lambda}$ such that $(\bar{x}, \bar{\lambda})$ solves the system of equations:

$$(*) \quad \begin{cases} \partial u(x) - \bar{p} = 0 \\ \bar{p} \cdot x = -\bar{w} = 0 \end{cases}$$

Thus, by the Implicit Function Theorem (IFT), $\varphi(p, w)$ will be a differentiable function iff the Jacobian determinant of (*) is nonsingular. But the Jacobian determinant of (*) is

$$\begin{vmatrix} \partial^2 u(x) & \partial u(x) \\ [\partial u(x)^T & O \end{vmatrix}$$

which, as we saw in the previous section, is nonzero iff the nonzero Gaussian curvature condition is satisfied at x. Summarizing: *if there is a smooth utility with no critical point the necessary and sufficient condition for differentiability of demand is that preferences be differentiably strictly convex.*

I.6 The Expenditure Function

Let $\succsim$ be representable by $u(\cdot)$ and fix a $\bar{u} \in u(R^{\ell}_{++})$.

Definition. *The expenditure function* $e_{\bar{u}}: R^{\ell}_{++} \to R$ *is defined as* $e_{\bar{u}}(p) = \min\{p \cdot v : u(v) \geq \bar{u}\}$. *The corresponding (unique) minimizer is denoted* $h_{\bar{u}}(p) \in R^{\ell}_{++}$. *See Figure I.9.*

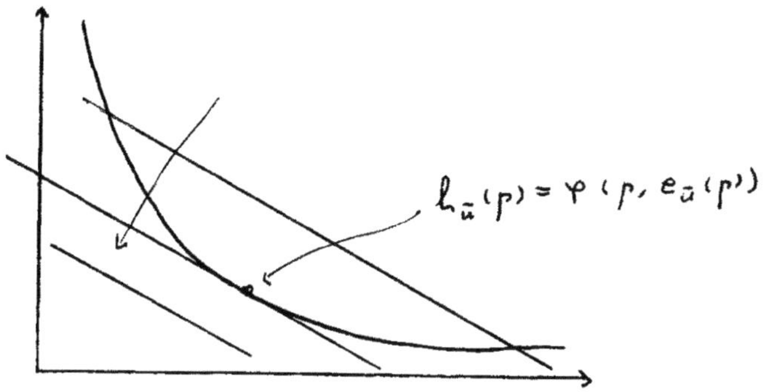

Figure I.9

The function $h_{\bar{u}}(p)$ is called the "compensated demand function." It relates to the demand function of the previous section by $h_{\bar{u}}(p) = \varphi(p, e_{\bar{u}}(p))$.

Mathematically, $e_{\bar{u}}$ is nothing but the support function of a (convex) set. From this some important properties follow:

(i) $e_{\bar{u}}$ is homogeneous of degree one.

(ii) $e_{\bar{u}}$ is concave.

(iii) $e_{\bar{u}}$ is C^1 and $\partial e_{\bar{u}}(p) = h_{\bar{u}}(p)$.

Property (i) is obvious; (ii) is easy to verify directly; for (iii) note that the linear function $p \cdot h_{\bar{u}}(\bar{p})$ majorizes $h_{\bar{u}}(p)$. Hence, if $e_{\bar{u}}$ is differentiable we must have $\partial e_{\bar{u}}(\bar{p}) = h_{\bar{u}}(\bar{p})$.

As we see the compensated demand function $h_{\bar{u}}(\cdot)$ satisfies nice properties but, in contrast with $\varphi(p, w)$, it is not directly observable in the marketplace (the utility function u enters its definition). It turns out however that we can use the properties of $h_{\bar{u}}(\cdot)$ to generate restrictions on the observable market demand function $\varphi(p, w)$. Indeed we have $\partial e_{\bar{u}}(p) = h_{\bar{u}}(p) = \varphi(p, e_{\bar{u}}(p))$ for all p. Hence, letting $u(\varphi(\bar{p}, \bar{w})) = \bar{u}$, $e_{\bar{u}}(\bar{p}) = \bar{w}$, we always have:

$$\partial^2 e_{\bar{u}}(p) = \partial_p \varphi(p, e_{\bar{u}}(p)) + \partial_w \varphi(p, e_{\bar{u}}(p)) \underbrace{(\partial e_{\bar{u}}(p))^T}_{\varphi(p, e_{\bar{u}}(p))} .$$

Evaluating at $(\bar{p}, \bar{w}, \bar{u})$:

$$\partial^2 e_{\bar{u}}(p) = \partial_p \varphi(\bar{p}, \bar{w}) + \partial_w \varphi(\bar{p}, \bar{w})(\varphi(\bar{p}, \bar{w}))^T \quad .$$

The right-hand side only involves the derivatives of φ and it is called the Substitution or Slutzky matrix. The left-hand side is the Hessian matrix of a concave function; therefore, it is negative semidefinite. Note that we always have $p \cdot \partial^2 e_{\bar{u}}(p) = 0$ and $\partial^2 e_{\bar{u}}(p)p = 0$. So, $\partial^2 e_{\bar{u}}(p)$ cannot be negative definite. However, it is always negative definitive on $T_p = \{v: p \cdot v = 0\}$. Summarizing:

PROPOSITION. *For all* (p, w), *the substitution matrix*

$$\partial_p \varphi(p, w) + \partial_w \varphi(p, w)(\varphi(p, w))^T$$

is negative definite on $T_p = \{v: p \cdot v = 0\}$.

The above is the fundamental economic property of demand.

I.7 The Indirect Utility Function

As before we let $\succsim$ be a C^2, differentially strictly convex preference relation and u a corresponding smooth utility function.

Definition. *The indirect utility function is defined (for* $p >> 0$, $w > 0$*) by* $v(p, w) = u(\varphi(p, w))$.

The theory of the direct (u) and the indirect utility function (v) is rich in duality relations. We shall not get into them now. We merely mention:

PROPOSITION. *The sets* $\{(p, w): v(p, w) \leq \bar{v}\}$ *are convex for all* $\bar{v}$. *If* v *is* C^1 *at* $(\bar{p}, \bar{w})$ *then:*

(i) $\partial_w v(\bar{p}, \bar{w}) = -\frac{1}{\bar{w}} \bar{p} \cdot \partial_p v(\bar{p}, \bar{w})$

(ii) $\varphi(\bar{p}, \bar{w}) = -\frac{1}{\partial_w v(\bar{p}, \bar{w})} \partial_p v(\bar{p}, \bar{w})$.

The fundamental property is (ii) (also called Roy's identity). It is again a consequence of the properties of the support functions of convex sets; in particular, of the fundamental duality fact $\partial e_{\bar{u}}(\bar{p}) = h_{\bar{u}}(\bar{p})$. Indeed, we have the identity $v(p, e_{\bar{v}}(p)) = \bar{v}$. Differentiate and recall that $\partial \varphi_{\bar{u}}(\bar{p}) = \varphi(\bar{p}, \bar{w})$. For (i) differentiate $v(\lambda \bar{p}, \lambda \bar{w}) - v(\bar{p}, \bar{w}) = 0$ with respect to λ and evaluate at $\lambda = 1$.

It is also (ii) which accounts for the usefulness of indirect utility functions. Indeed, (ii) tells us that it is very easy to derive demand from indirect utility (this is in contrast to deriving demand from the direct u). It is "almost" like taking a derivative. The "almost" is for the $1/\partial_w \varphi(\bar{p}, \bar{w})$ factor. In applications it is often possible to go around this factor and get a fully linear dependence of $\varphi(\cdot)$ on $v(\cdot)$. We discuss two illustrative examples.

Example 1. Fix $w = 1$ and denote $v(p) = v(p, w)$. This is just a normalization. We say that the indirect utility function $v(\cdot)$ is logarithmically homogeneous if $v(\alpha p) = v(p) - \ell n\ \alpha$ for $\alpha > 0$ (i.e., it is the ℓn transformation of an homogeneous of degree one function). Then it is easy to verify that $\varphi(p, 1) = -\partial v(p)$ (because $p \cdot \partial v(p) = -1$). So $v \mapsto \varphi$ acts linearly on the convex set of logarithmically homogeneous indirect utility functions.

Example 2. Let v be an indirect utility function. Define quadratic perturbations of $v(p,w)$ by $v_Q(p,w) = v(p,w) + \frac{1}{w^2}\, p \cdot Qp$ where Q is an symmetric matrix. Denote the corresponding demand by φ_Q. With $\mathcal{Q}$ the set of symmetric $\ell \times \ell$ matrices let

$$\mathcal{Q}_p = \{Q \in \mathcal{Q}: p \cdot Q = 0\} \quad .$$

It is then easy to verify that at any fixed $(\bar{p},\bar{w})$ $\varphi_Q(\bar{p},\bar{w})$ and $\partial_w \varphi_Q(\bar{p},\bar{w})$ are invariant to Q and $Q \mapsto \partial_p \varphi_Q(\bar{p},\bar{w})$ acts linearly.

Lecture II: Pareto Optimality

II.1. Definitions and Preliminaries

We shall now proceed to put n consumers together.

Each consumer $i = 1, ..., n$ has a preference relation $\succsim_i$ on R^ℓ_+. We let $\succsim_i$ be represented by a utility function $u_i : R^\ell_+ \to R$. We always assume that $\succsim_i$ satisfies the defining properties of a preference relation plus strict monotonicity. Also, $u_i(0) = 0$, all i.

There is a total endowment of commodities, i.e., a vector $\omega \in R^\ell_+$.

A vector $x = (x_1, ..., x_n) \in R^{\ell n}_+$ is an *allocation* if $\sum_i x_i \leq \omega$. In these lectures there shall be no production of commodities by means of commodities. Thus the only economic problem is the allocation of the total vector of goods ω. We shall also not bring to bear during these lectures considerations of fairness. Thus from the welfare point of view we shall not aim at singling out very definite outcomes but just at delimitating the class of nonwasteful ones.

Definition. *The allocation x is a Pareto Optimum* (P.O.) *if there is no other x' such that $x'_i \succ_i x_i$ for every i.*

Because of strict monotonicity this definition is equivalent to the more correct: "there is no other x' such that $x'_i \succsim_i x_i$ for all i with at least one strict preference."

Denote by $P \subset R^{\ell n}_+$ the set of P.O. allocations.

For two consumers and two goods the set of allocations can be represented in the so-called Edgeworth's box, i.e., $\{z : 0 \leq z \leq \omega\}$, where z stands for the allocation $(z, \omega - z)$. The following figures provide some examples of Pareto sets P.

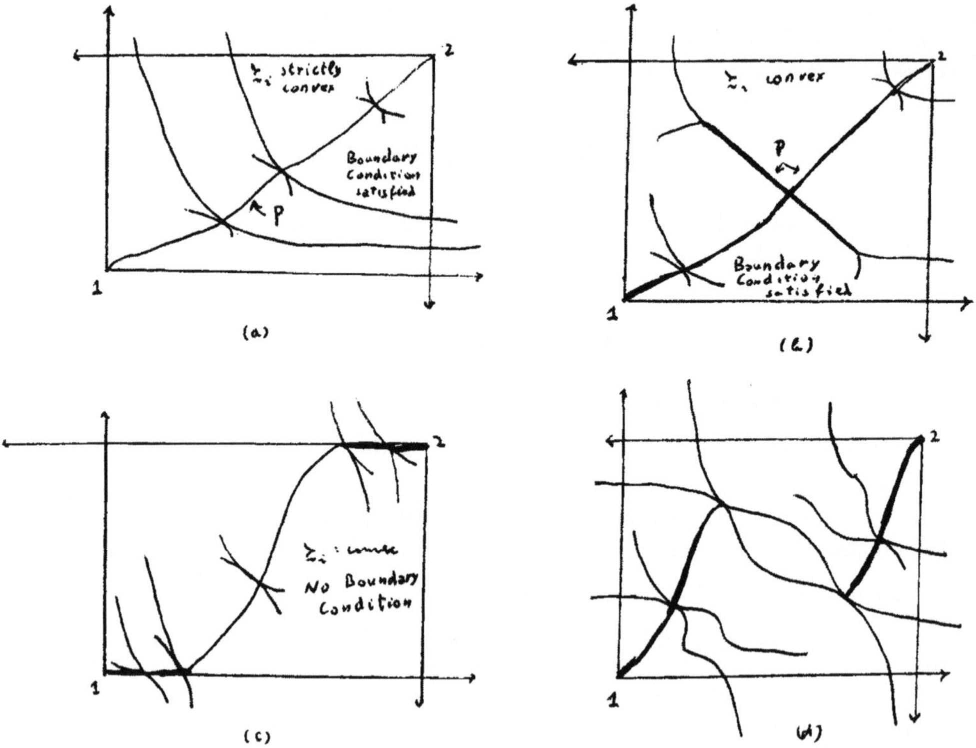

Figure II.1

Another set of interest is:

$$U = \{u = (u_1, ..., u_n) \in R^n : u \leq u(x) = (u_1(x_1), ..., u_n(x_n)),$$
$$\text{for } x = (x_1, ..., x_n) \text{ an allocation}\}$$

Graphically:

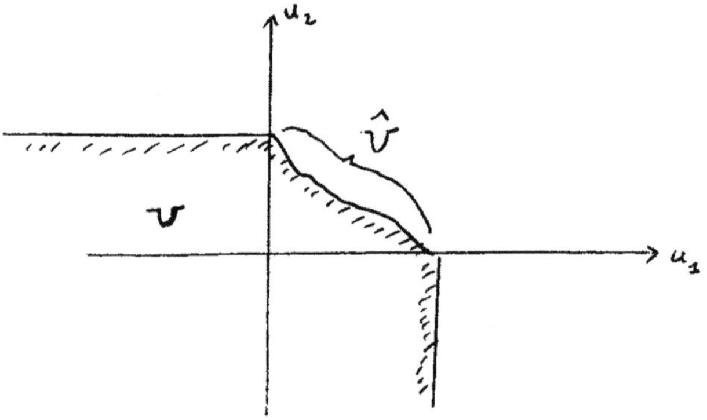

Figure II.2

By monotonicity $U - R^n_+ \subset U$. Hence U is what is called a comprehensive set. The upper frontier of U, $\hat{U} = Bdry U \cap R^n_+$ is, by definition and strict monotonicity (which implies that if $u' \leq u$, $u', u \in \hat{U}$ then $u' = u$) the utility image of the Pareto set P. Note that

$$u\left(\left\{x \in R^{\ell n}_+ : \sum_i x_i \leq \omega\right\}\right) = U \cap R^n_+.$$

It can be shown that $\hat{U}$ is topologically a simplex. We call $\hat{U}$ the utility Pareto set.

II.2. The First Fundamental Theorem

We now proceed to introduce prices.

Definition. *The vector* $x = (x_1, \ldots, x_n)$ *is a* price equilibrium *if there is* $p \in R^\ell$, $p \neq 0$, *such that* $v \succ_i x_i$ *implies* $p \cdot v > p \cdot x_i$ *for every* i.

PROPOSITION. *If* x *is a price equilibrium then it is a Pareto optimum allocation for* $\omega = \sum_i x_i$.

Proof. Note first that because of monotonicity we must have $p \geq 0$. Let now $x' = (x'_1, \ldots, x'_n)$ be such that $x'_i \succ_i x_i$, all i. Then $p \cdot x'_i > p \cdot x_i$ for all i. Hence $p \cdot (\sum_i x'_i) > p \cdot \sum_i x_i = \omega$. So $\sum_i x'_i \leq \omega$ cannot occur. ∎

Simple as this result is it is of fundamental economic importance.

The converse to the proposition need not be true (see Fig. II.3 for a one consumer counterexample), although as we shall see it is almost true if convexity hypotheses are added.

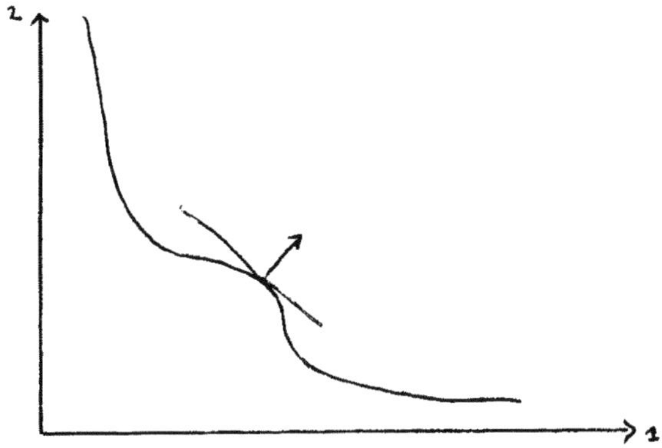

Figure II.3

A "dual" of the Proposition in utility space goes as follows. Let $\lambda \in R^n_+$, $\sum_i \lambda_i = 1$ and consider (for given ω):

$$\operatorname{Max} \sum_i \lambda_i u_i$$
$$\text{s.t. } u \in U.$$

Then if $\bar{u}$ solves this problem it follows that $\bar{u}$ is a P.O. utility allocation. The proof is of course obvious.

II.3. First Order Necessary Conditions

We take for granted the following Kuhn-Tucker like mathematical fact.

Let $f : R^s \to R^t$ be a vector of C^1 objective functions and $h : R^s \to R^m$ a vector of C^1 constraints. The constraint set is $E = \{x \in R^s \;:\; h(x) \geq 0\}$. We say that $x \in E$ is a *local weak optimum* of f subject to h if for some neighborhoods V of x there is no $x' \in E \cap V$ such that $f(x') >> f(x)$.

First Order Necessary Conditions (FONC): If x is a local weak optimum of f subject to h then there are $(\lambda, \mu) \in R^t_+ \times R^m_+$ s.t.:

(i) $(\lambda, \mu) \neq 0$

(ii) If $h_j(x) > 0$ then $\mu_j = 0$

(iii) $\sum_{i=1}^t \lambda_i \partial f_i(x) + \sum_{j=1}^m \mu_j \partial h_j(x) = 0$

Suppose, to get back to the economics, that the utility functions are C^1 and strictly increasing. The next proposition is an easy consequence of the FONC.

PROPOSITION. *Let x be a* P.O. *allocation. Then there are $p \in R^\ell_{++}$ and $\lambda \in R^n_{++}$ such that: $\lambda_i \partial u_i(x_i) \leq p$ for all i and $x_i \cdot [p - \lambda_i \partial u_i(x_i)] = 0$ for all i.*

(Hint for the application of the FONC: forgetting about the nonnegativity constraints we have here: $s = \ell n$, $t = n$, $m = \ell$.)

In particular, if $x >> 0$ then $\lambda_i \partial u_i(x_i) = p$ for all i.

We will see later that under convexity hypotheses the multipliers λ, p are rich in economic interpretations.

The FONC interact nicely with the price equilibrium concept.

PROPOSITION. (i) *If $\bar{x}$ is a price equilibrium with respect to $\bar{p}$ then for some $\bar{\lambda}$, $(\bar{p}, \bar{\lambda})$ solve the* FONC.

(ii) *If $\bar{u}$ solves* Max $\sum_i \bar{\lambda}_i u_i$, $u \in U$, $\bar{\lambda} \geq 0$, and $u(\bar{x}) = \bar{u}$, then for some $\bar{p}$, $(\bar{p}, \bar{\lambda})$ solve the FONC at $\bar{x}$.

The proof is easy and will not be given. Figure II.4 illustrates the proposition.

One could ask: when are the FONC sufficient to determine (p, λ) uniquely (up to a positive factor)? An answer is: when x is *linked*, i.e., when it is not possible to split consumers and commodities into two groups in such a way that no consumer of one of the groups consumes any commodity consumed by any consumer of the second group.

II.4 The Second Fundamental Theorem

We assume now that preferences are convex. To obtain the cleanest theory we assume a bit more, that every u_i is concave. Under this hypothesis the set U is convex.

The implications of the last two sections will now also be valid in the reverse direction: if x satisfies the FONC then it is an optimun and if x satisfies the FONC then it can be supported as a price equilibrium or be supported by utility weights. Formally, we begin by this second fact:

PROPOSITION. *Let x satisfy the* FONC *with respect to (p, λ). Then:*

(i) *x is a price equilibrium with respect to p.*

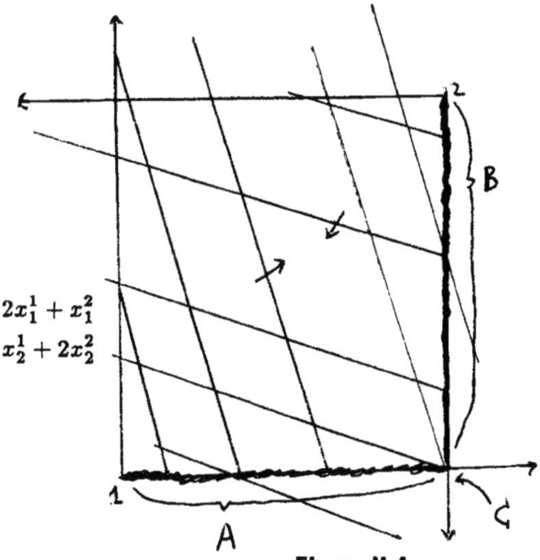

$u_1(x_1) = 2x_1^1 + x_1^2$

$u_2(x_2) = x_2^1 + 2x_2^2$

Region A $\begin{cases} \bar{p} &= (1,2) \\ \bar{\lambda} &= (\frac{1}{2},1) \end{cases}$

Region B $\begin{cases} \bar{\bar{p}} &= (2,1) \\ \bar{\bar{\lambda}} &= (1,\frac{1}{2}) \end{cases}$

At C any convex combination of $(\bar{p},\bar{\lambda})$ and $(\bar{\bar{p}},\bar{\bar{\lambda}})$ will do.

Figure II.4

(ii) $u(x)$ *solves* Max $\sum_i \lambda_i u_i$, $u \in U$.

Proof. (i) To be simple we look at the case $x >> 0$. Then the FONC yield $\partial u_i(x_i) = (1/\lambda_i)p$ which, recalling the definition of the demand function at p, yields $x_i = \varphi_i(p,\ p \cdot x_i)$ for all i. Hence x is a price equilibrium with respect to p.

(ii) For all i, if $\sum_i x_i' \leq \sum_i x_i = \omega$ we have

$$p \cdot (x_i' - x_i) \underset{\text{FONC}}{\geq} \lambda_i \partial u_i(x_i)(x_i' - x_i) \underset{\text{Concavity}}{\geq} \lambda_i(u_i(x_i') - u_i(x_i)).$$

Hence

$$\sum_i \lambda_i u_i(x_i) \geq \sum_i \lambda_i u_i(x_i') - \sum_i p \cdot (x_i' - x_i) \geq \sum_i \lambda_i u_i(x_i') \qquad \blacksquare$$

As a graphical illustration:

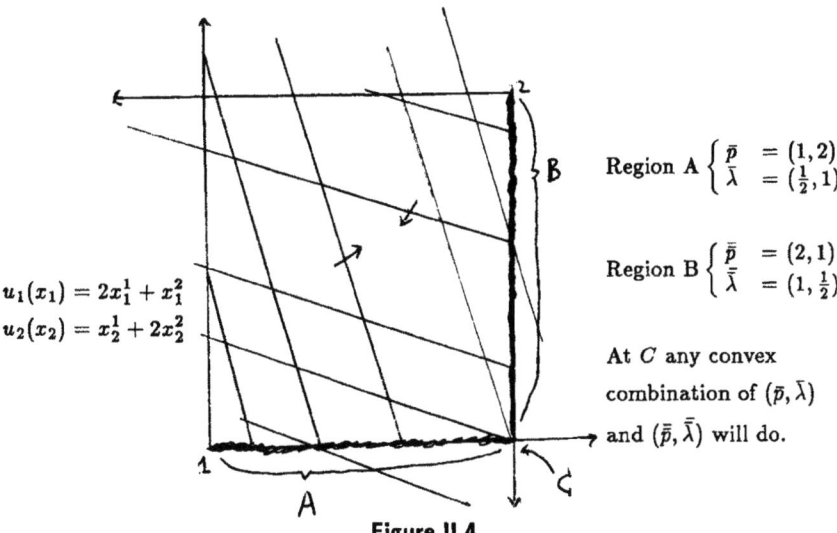

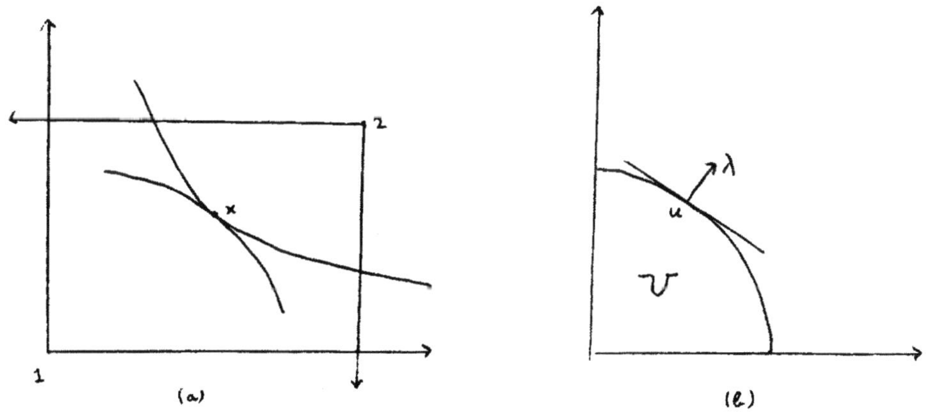

Figure II.5

Of course, an implication of the above proposition is:

PROPOSITION. *If x is a P.O. allocation then there are p, λ such that* (i) *and* (ii) *of the previous proposition are satisfied.*

For yet another, more geometric proof of (i), (ii):

(i) For x a P.O. allocation defines $V = \sum_i \{v_i : v_i \succsim_i x_i\} - \omega$. Then V is convex and $0 \in BdryV$. If we let p support V at 0 then we are done (see Figure II.6.(a)).

(ii) Let $\bar{u}$ be a P.O. utility allocation. Then $\bar{u} \in B(dry)U$. If we let λ support U at $\bar{u}$ we are done (see Fig. II.6.(b)).

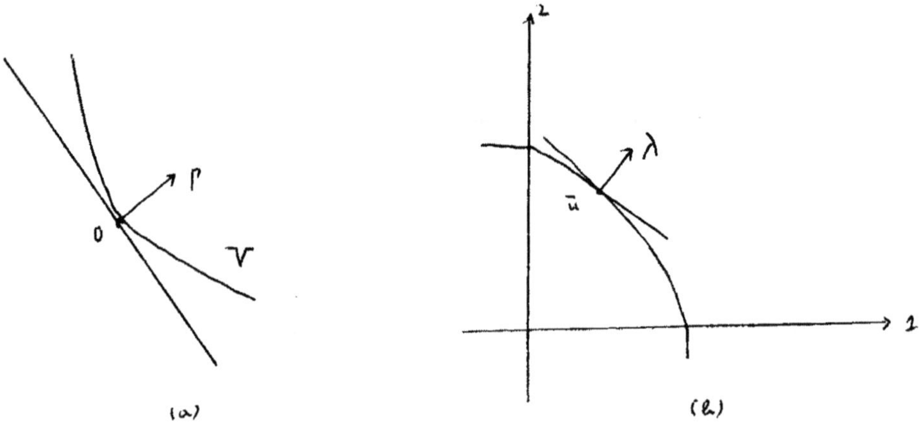

Figure II.6

We can at this point interpret economically the multipliers $(\bar{p}, \bar{\lambda})$ associated to a P.O. allocation $\bar{x}$:

(i) p is the vector shadow prices of the commodities for the social evaluation function $\sum_i \lambda_i u_i(x_i)$. That is, consider:

$$\text{Max} \sum_i \bar{\lambda}_i u_i(x_i)$$
$$\text{such that} \sum_i x_i - \omega \leq 0 \ .$$

Then the $\bar{p}_j$ are the multipliers for this problem and so p_j is the social value of increasing the endowment of the j good by a small infinitesimal amount.

(ii) $\bar{\lambda}_i$ is the reciprocal of the marginal utility of income of consumer i at the price-income combination $(\bar{p}, \bar{p}\cdot\bar{x}_i)$. Indeed, recall that (neglecting inequalities) $\partial u_i(x_i) - (1/\bar{\lambda}_i)\bar{p} = 0$. So $1/\bar{\lambda}_i$ is a multiplier for the problem:

$$\text{Max } u_i(x_i)$$
$$\text{s.t. } \bar{p}\cdot x_i - \bar{p}\cdot\bar{x}_i = 0 \ .$$

Assuming the strict convexity of $\succsim_i$ we can say something of interest about the global topology of P.

PROPOSITION. *P is homeomorphic to the $(n-1)$ simplex.*

Proof. Clearly this is the case for $\hat{U}$. Note then that the natural map $u \mapsto \{x : u(x) = u\}$ from $\hat{U}$ to $R_+^{\ell n}$ is singlevalued (obvious) and continuous (easy). ∎

If preferences are C^2, differentially strictly concave and satisfy the boundary condition then $\hat{U} \cap R_{++}^n$ and $P \cap R_{++}^{\ell n}$ are in fact diffeomorphic under this natural map and both are also diffeomorphic to the open unit simplex under, for example, $\lambda \mapsto \bar{u}$: solution to Max $\sum_i \lambda_i u_i$, $u \in U$.

II.5 Second Order Conditions

In this section preferences are C^2 but not necessarily convex.

The analysis of second order conditions can be quite subtle. Here I will be very rough. I will only look at sufficient conditions and stay away from boundaries.

Let $x >> 0$ satisfy the FONC with respect to (p, λ).

PROPOSITION. *A sufficient condition for x to be a local* P.O. [*the definition of local* P.O. *is the obvious one*] *is that the bilinear form*

$$B(v, v') = \sum_i \lambda_i \partial^2 u_i(x_i)(v_i, v_i')$$

(defined on $R^{\ell n} \times R^{\ell n}$) be negative definite on $K = \{v \in \prod_{i=1}^n T_p : \sum_{i=1}^n v_i = 0\} \subset R^{\ell n}$.

Illustrations:

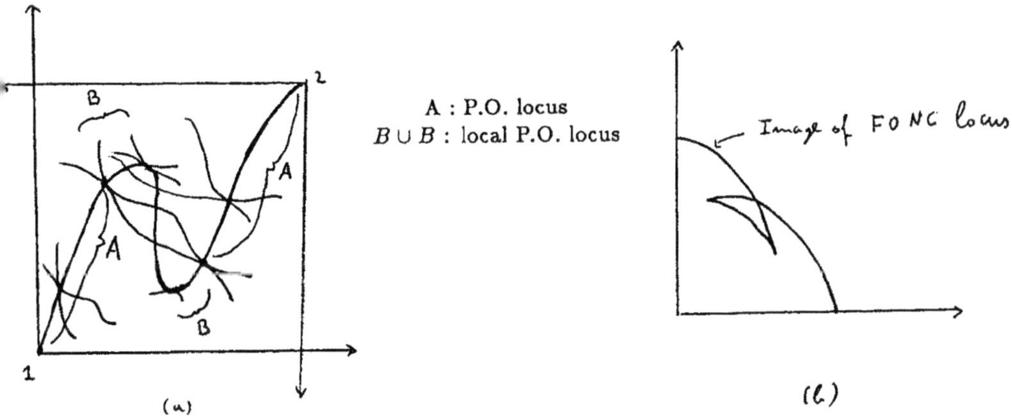

Figure II.7

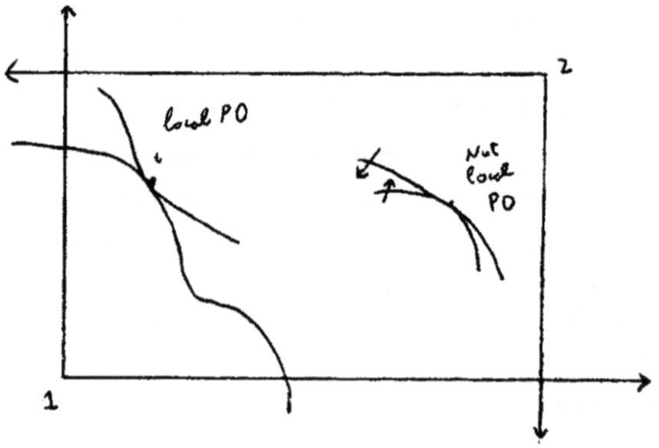

Figure II.8

For an interesting application:

PROPOSITION. *Let* $x >> 0$ *satisfy the second order sufficient conditions. Then, except for at most* $\ell - 1$ *agents,* $\partial^2 u_i(x_i)$ *is negative definite on* T_p.

That is, if n is much larger than ℓ then only exceptionally consumers will not be in local price equilibrium.

Proof. Define $J_i = \{v_i \in T_p : \partial^2 u_i(x_i)(v_i, v_i) \geq 0\}$. Note that $-J_i = J_i$. Suppose that $J_i \neq \{0\}$ for ℓ consumers. Since T_p is $(\ell - 1)$ – dimensional we can find $v_i \in J_i$, not all zero, such that $0 = \sum_i v_i$. But this contradicts the negative definiteness of $\sum_i \lambda_i \partial^2 u_i(x_i)$ on K. ■

Lecture III: Walrasian Equilibrium

III.1 Basic Definitions

To the exchange set-up of the previous lecture we now add a further consideration: individual consumers have entitlements (i.e., own) to a part of the social endowments. In consequence we impose as an equilibrium condition that the value of individual consumptions be the same as the value of individual endownments.

As before we have N consumers endowed with preferences $\succsim_i$ on R^ℓ_+. Every $\succsim_i$ is strictly monotone and representable by a concave utility function u_i. Every consumer i is also endowed with an initial endowment vector $\omega_i >> 0$. We put $\omega = (\omega_1, ..., \omega_N)$.

Definition. *The allocation* x *is a Walrasian equilibrium if there is a price vector* $p \neq 0$ *such that* x *is a price equilibrium with respect to* p *and* $p \cdot x_i = p \cdot \omega_i$ *for all* i. *In other words, for every* i, x_i *maximizes* u_i *on the budget set* $\{z : p \cdot z \leq p \cdot \omega_i\}$.

Because of the First Fundamental Theorem a Walrasian equilibrium is a Pareto Optimum. It also follows from strict monotonicity that at an equilibrium we must have $p >> 0$.

The following figure illustrates the concept of equilibrium.

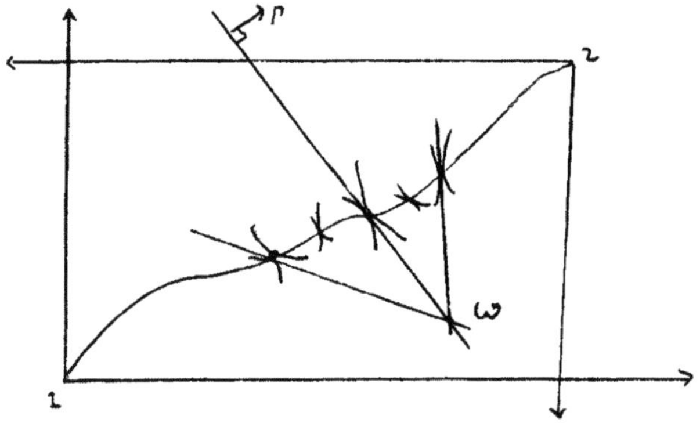

Figure III.1

III.2 Equilibrium Equations

In order to study the properties of equilibria it is convenient to express them as the zeroes of a system of equations. This can be done in several different ways.

Let every u_i be C^1 and assume for simplicity that at equilibrium every consumer consumes strictly positive amounts of every good (i.e., goods are indispensable). Then $x = (x_1, \ldots, x_N)$ is a Walrasian equilibrium if and only if for some $p >> 0$ and $\lambda = (\lambda_1, \ldots, \lambda_N) \in R^N$ the following system of equations is satisfied:

[I] $$\partial u_i(x_i) - \lambda_i p = 0\,, \qquad \text{all } i$$

[II] $$p \cdot (x_i - \omega_i) = 0\,, \qquad \text{all } i$$

[III] $$\sum_i x_i - \sum_i \omega_i = 0\,.$$

This would be called the universal system of equations. In applications it may be convenient to look at more consolidated systems. For example, [I] and [III] can be used to solve p and x_i as a function of λ, i.e., $p(\lambda)$, $x_i(\lambda)$. Replacing this in [II] we end up with an equation system $p(\lambda) \cdot (x_i(\lambda) - \omega_i) = 0$, $1 \leq i \leq N$, that involves only λ. The search for equilibrium is viewed as the search for the social weights having the property that if a Pareto Optimum is chosen by maximizing the weighted sum of utilities then the value of individual consumptions (evaluated at the imputed shadow prices) is equal to the value of individual endowments. If we are dealing with few consumers and many commodities this is a particularly convenient way to formalize equilibria.

Nonetheless we shall focus on a more traditional reduction of the universal system. It is in a sense dual to the one just described. Assume that every u_i is strictly concave. Using [I] and [II] we can express λ and x_i as a function of p, i.e., $\lambda(p)$, $x_i(p)$. Replacing in [III] we have $\sum_i (x_i(p) - \omega_i) = 0$. The function $f(p) = \sum_i (x_i(p) - \omega_i)$ is called the (aggregate) *excess demand function.*

The function $f(p)$ is related to the demand function $\varphi_i(p, w_i)$ of the first lecture as follows: $x_i(p) = \varphi_i(p, p \cdot \omega_i)$. There we can immediately conclude on some of the basic properties of $f : R^{\ell}_{++} \to R$:

(i) f is homogeneous of degree zero, i.e., $f(\alpha p) = f(p)$, all p and $\alpha > 0$.

(ii) f is continuous (and differentiable if every $\succsim_i$ is differentiably strictly concave).

(iii) f is bounded below. Indeed, $f(p) \geq -\sum_i \omega_i$ for all p.

(iv) f satisfies the so-called Walras' law: $p \cdot f(p) = 0$ for all p.

(v) f is a proper map on any domain $\{p : p \cdot v = 1\}$ (where $v \geq 0$, $v \neq 0$). That is to say, if $p_n \to p$, $p_n \cdot v \geq 1$ and $p^j = 0$ for some j then $\|f(p^j_n)\| \to \infty$.

Property (v) follows from (iii) and the strict monotonicity of every $\succsim_i$.

III.3 Existence of Equilibrium

The existence of a Walrasian equilibrium is not difficult to prove. The traditional tool for establishing the existence of a zero of the excess demand function has been Brouwer's fixed point theorem or any of its variants. For later reference we will avoid an explicit fixed point route.

Denote by $S = \{p \in R^{\ell}_{++} : \|p\| = 1\}$ the strictly positive part of the unit sphere. Because of the homogeneity of degree one of f if p is an equilibrium price vector then so is $(1/\|p\|)p$. Hence without loss of generality we can confine our search of equilibrium to S. Walras' law tells us that $p \cdot f(p) = 0$ for all p, or $f(p) \in T_p = \{v \in R^{\ell} : p \cdot v = 0\}$, i.e., $f(p)$ is nothing but a tangent vector fields on S. Properties (iii) — boundedness below — and (v) — properness — of f imply that f point inwards at the boundary. See Figure III.2. This inward pointing property will be preserved if we replace S by a slightly trimmed closed subset $\bar{S}$ having a smooth boundary. (More precisely, what is preserved is the property of being homotopic to an inward pointing vector field.) As it is well-known: (i) the mod 2 Euler number of an inward pointing vector field on a (connected) manifold with boundary is nonzero if the Euler characteristic of the manifold is nonzero, and (ii) if the mod 2 Euler number of the vector field is different from zero then the vector field has at least one zero. Because $\bar{S}$ is homotopic to the $\ell - 1$ ball it has a nonzero Euler characteristic. Hence f has at least one zero.

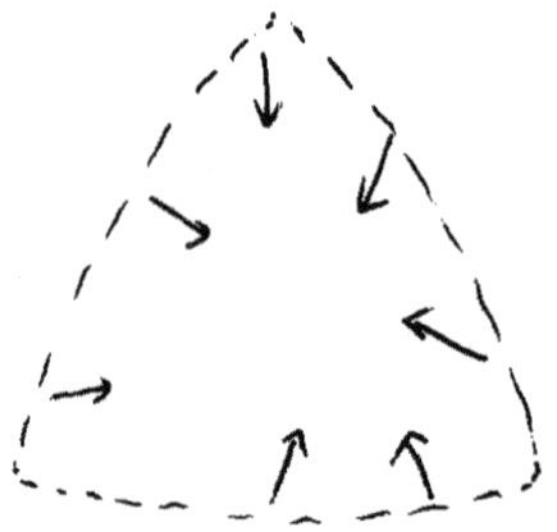

Figure III.2

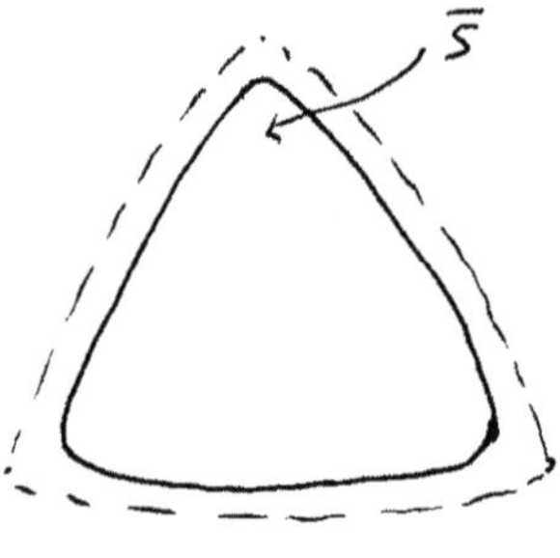

Figure III.3

For later reference it is convenient to rephrase the above argument in a more general manner. Admittedly at this point it will appear as uncalled for generality.

A tangent vector field f or, more precisely, its graph, can be viewed as a section of the tangent bundle $\tau_{\bar{S}}$ of $\bar{S}$. The total space of $\tau_{\bar{S}}$ is $T\bar{S} = \{(p, v) \in \bar{S} \times R^{\ell} : p \cdot v = 0\}$.

Denote by $\sigma_0 : \bar{S} \to T\bar{S}$ the zero section of $\tau_{\bar{S}}$, i.e., $\sigma_0(p) = (p, 0)$, all $p \in \bar{S}$. Then p is an equilibrium if and only if $\sigma_0(p) = (p, 0)$. Therefore the existence of a zero for f is equivalent to σ_0 and Graph f having a nonempty intersection. Because the fibers of $\tau_{\bar{S}}$ are convex, any two sections are homotopic. Furthermore, inward pointing sections will not only be homotopic but will have the same Euler intersection number with the zero section. If this number is different from zero then the intersection must be nonempty. Summarizing: in order to prove the existence of equilibrium it is enough to exhibit a section having a nonzero intersection number with σ_0. But this is easy. Pick an arbitrary $\bar{p}$ and let $g(p)$ equal the perpendicular projection of $p - \bar{p}$ on T_p. Clearly, $g(p) = 0$ only for $p = \bar{p}$. Strictly speaking in order to prove that the intersection number with σ_0 is nonzero we should argue that $\bar{p}$ is not a coincidental zero. This should be obvious enough (it is geometrically trivial — and easy to verify: see the next three sections — that g and σ_0 intersect transversally).

III.4 Local Uniqueness

Is the equilibrium, which existence has already been established, unique? Figure III.1 tells us immediately that not necessarily. We are dealing with highly nonlinear problem (e.g., the excess demand function can never be linear) and there is no general hope of uniqueness (of course, uniqueness is possible in particular and well studied cases).

On the other hand a count of equations and unknowns tells us that there are $\ell - 1$ effective unknowns (the dimension of S) and $\ell - 1$ possibly independent equations (because of Walras' law one component of excess demand is dependent on the others). So one may hope that the equilibrium be locally determinate. As Figure III.4 shows, this need not be the case. In the figure we have a continuum of equilibria. Nonetheless, the situation seems quite pathological (i.e., coincidental) and prompts the following question: is the local uniqueness of equilibrium a generic property of economies?

By using a differentiable approach we shall see in the next two sections that the answer is affirmative. Although we shall not go into it here, it is worth pointing out that this is no longer true in more general contexts, e.g., it may fail in economies with infinitely many commodities and agents. This is one of the active areas of current research.

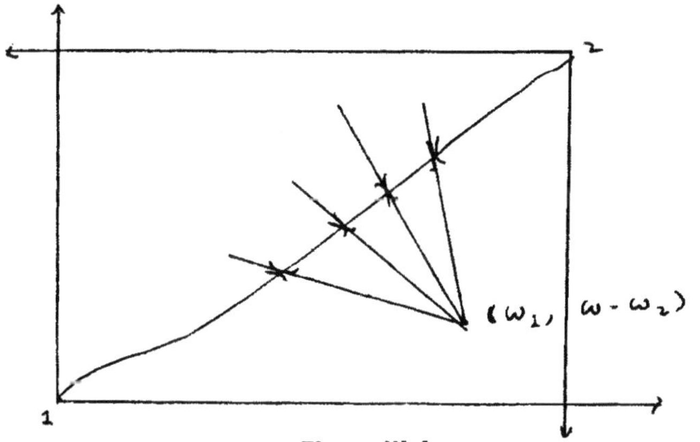

Figure III.4

III.5. Regular Economies

From now on we assume that the excess demand function $f : S \to R^\ell$ is C^1. Go back to Lecture I for the conditions on preferences that imply this. In particular, we are assuming that consumption always takes place in the interior of the positive orthant.

Viewed as a matrix $\partial f(p)$ is $(\ell-1)\times\ell$ and therefore always singular. However, because of Walras' law, $\partial f(p)$ maps T_p into T_p whenever $f(p) = 0$, i.e., at equilibrium (**proof:** differentiate $p \cdot f(p) = 0$ to get $p \cdot \partial f(p) + f(p) = 0$). This motivates the next definition.

Definition. *The equilibrium price vector* p *is regular if* $\partial f(p)$ *maps* T_p *into* T_p.

There are many equivalent forms of the regularity definition. Thus, p is regular if and only if the $(\ell-1)\times(\ell-1)$ matrix obtained by deleting any row and corresponding column from $\partial f(p)$ is nonzero, or if and only if Graph f and σ_0 are transversal at $(p, 0)$ when viewed as submanifolds of TM, etc.

We say that the economy is *regular* if every equilibrium price is regular. The following fact is easy to prove:

PROPOSITION. *A regular economy has a finite number of equilibrium.*

From now on we implicitly let preferences be fixed but want to consider variations on initial endowments $\omega \in R^{\ell N}_{++}$. Thus, we identify the economy with ω and denote the corresponding excess demands by $f_\omega(\cdot)$ or $f(\cdot, \omega)$.

By the implicit function theorem, if $\bar{p}$ is a regular equilibrium for the economy $\bar{\omega}$ then locally p can be solved as a function of ω. This immediately implies that the set of regular economies is an open subset of $R^{\ell N}_{++}$.

We shall see in the next section that the set of nonregular (or critical) economies has Lebesgue measure zero (which constitutes quite a demanding test of negligibility). In particular, the set of regular economies is dense in $R^{\ell N}_{++}$. To prove this will require the use of a comparatively powerful mathematical tool: Sard's theorem. Thus it may be worthwhile to show that a weaker result can be proved by elementary means:

PROPOSITION. *The set of economies for which some equilibrium is regular is dense in* $R^{\ell N}_{++}$.

Proof. Let ω be an arbitrary economy and $f_\omega(p) = 0$. Put $w_i = p \cdot \omega_i$, $x_i = \varphi(p, w_i)$, $u_i = u(x_i)$. For $0 \le t \le 1$ define $\omega(t) = (tx_1 + (1-t)\omega_1, \ldots, tx_N + (1-t)\omega_N)$. Of course, $\sum_i \omega_i(t) = \sum_i \omega_i$ and $p \cdot \omega_i(t) = w_i$. Therefore, $f_{\omega(t)}(p) = 0$ for all t. Let $\alpha(t)$ be the determinant of the linear map $\partial f_{\omega(t)}(p)$ from T_p to T_p.

Denote by $S_i = \partial^2 e_{u_i}(p)$ the substitution matrix for i at (p, w_i); see Section I.6. Simple computations give:

$$\partial f_{\omega(t)}(p) = \sum_i (S_i - (1-t)\partial_w \varphi_i(p_i, w_i)(x_i - \omega_i)^T) \ .$$

Hence $\alpha(t)$ is a polynomial of t. Also $\alpha(1) \neq 0$ because $\sum_i S_i$ is negative definite on T_p. Therefore $\alpha(t)$ is a nondegenerate polynomial which implies $\alpha(t) \neq 0$ for a t arbitrarily close to 0. Since then p is a regular equilibrium for $\omega(t)$ we have what we wanted. □

III.6 Genericity of Regular Economies

Now we shall prove:

PROPOSITION. *The set of regular economies has measure zero in* $R^{\ell N}_{++}$.

Proof. Let $E = \{(p,\omega) : f_\omega(p) = 0\}$ be the equilibrium set. The proof proceeds in three steps: (i) E is a C^1 manifold of dimension ℓN, (ii) ω is a regular economy if and only if it is a regular value of the projection $\pi : E \to R^{\ell N}$, (iii) the set of critical values of π has measure zero. See Figure II.5.

Step (i) follows from the implicit function theorem once one notices that rank $\partial_\omega f(p,\omega) \geq \ell - 1$ for all p,ω (in fact $\partial_\omega f(p,\omega)(v) = -\sum_i v_i$ whenever $p \cdot v_i = 0$ for all i).

Step (ii) is a simple exercise.

Step (iii) is precisely the easy part of Sard's theorem: the set of critical values of a C^1 function between C^1 manifolds of the same (finite) dimension is null in its range. □

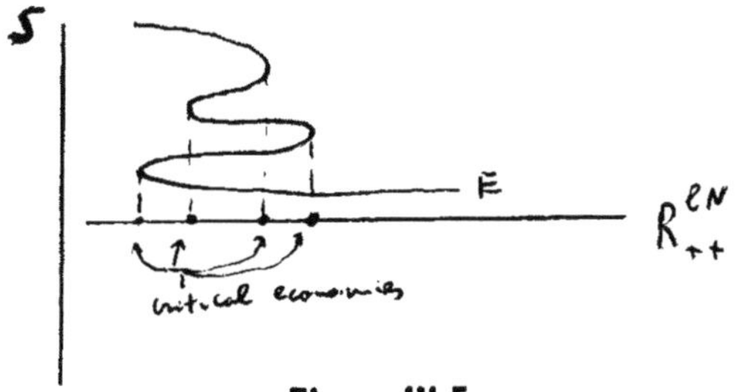

Figure III.5.

Lecture IV: Equilibrium with Incomplete Markets

IV.1 Basic Definitions

We now consider sequential trade under uncertainty. A basic reference is R. Radner, "Existence of Plans, Prices and Price Expectations in a Sequence of Markets," *Econometrica*, 1972. To be simple we consider only two dates: 0 and 1. At date 1, one of S states occurs and spot trade in ℓ commodities takes place according to prices $p_s \in R^\ell_{++}$. Given a system of contingent prices $p = (p_1, \ldots, p_S)$, at date 0 there is trade in $K \leq S$ assets. A unit of asset k delivers a (return) vector $a_{ks} \in R^\ell_+$ of goods if state s occurs. Thus the result of asset trade at date 0 determines the initial endowment at every of the possible states in date 1. At date 0 economic agents have correct anticipation on date 1 prices (conditional, of course, on the state).

Denote by $y_i \in R^K$, $x_i \in R^{\ell S}_+$ the trade and consumption plans of agent i. Put $y = (y_1, \ldots, y_N)$, $x = (x_1, \ldots, x_N)$.

Definition. *The plans* $(\bar{y}, \bar{x})$ *and prices* $q \in R^K$, $p \in R^{\ell S}_{++}$ *constitute an equilibrium if:*

(i) *Every* $\bar{y}_i$, $\bar{x}_i$ *maximizes* $u_i(x_i)$ *subject to* $q \cdot y_i \leq 0$ *and* $p_s \cdot x_{is} \leq p_s \cdot \omega_{is} + \sum_k y_{ik}(a_{ks} \cdot p_s)$ *for every* s.

(ii) $\sum_i y_i = 0$, $\sum_i (x_i - \omega_i) \leq 0$.

Note: During this lecture we are assuming that the $u_i(\cdot)$ satisfy all the appropriate technical conditions. We also let $\omega_i >> 0$.

Given a vector $p \in R^{\ell S}_{++}$ the return vector (in value terms) for asset k is $g_k(p) = (p_1 \cdot a_{k1}, \ldots, p_S \cdot a_{kS}) \in R^S$.

It is not difficult to see that in the definition of equilibrium the trades $\bar{y}$ and prices q of assets can be, so to speak, swept under the rug. In fact, the previous definition is equivalent (in the sense of yielding the same real allocations) to the following (we leave the proof of this as an exercise).

Definition. *The pair* $(\bar{p}, \bar{x}) \in R^{\ell S}_{++} \times R^{\ell S N}_{+}$ *constitutes an equilibrium if:*

(i) *Every* $\bar{x}_i$ *maximizes* $u_i(x_i)$ *subject to* $p \cdot x_i \leq p \cdot \omega_i$ *and* $(p_1 \cdot (x_{i1} - \omega_{i1}), \ldots, p_S \cdot (x_{iS} - \omega_{iS})) \in L(p)$ *where* $L(p) \subset R^S$ *is the subspace spanned by* $g_1(p), \ldots, g_S(p))$.

(ii) $\sum_i (x_i - \omega_i) \leq 0$.

A further, and trivial, redefinition will prove helpful.

Denote by $G^{S,K} = \{L \subset R^S : L$ is a K-dimensional subspace$\}$. This is the so-called Grassman manifold of K planes in R^S. Denote $\tilde{G}^{S,K} = \bigcup_{K' \leq K} G^{S,K}$.

For every p and $L \in \tilde{G}^{S,K}$ let $f(p, L) \in R^{\ell S}$ be the aggregate excess demand vector for commodities obtained in the usual way except that the consumption set of every consumer is not $R^{\ell S}_{+}$ but $\{x_i \in R^{\ell S}_{+} : (p_1 \cdot (x_{i1} - \omega_{i1}), \ldots, p_S \cdot (x_{iS} - \omega_{iS})) \in L\}$.

We can then rephrase the definition of equilibrium as:

Definition. *The pair* $(p, L) \in R^{\ell S}_{++} \times \tilde{G}^{S,K}$ *constitutes an equilibrium if:*

(i) $f(p, L) = 0$, *and*

(ii) $L =$ span$\{g_1(p), \ldots, g_K(p)\}$.

In this lecture, we investigate the existence problem for this equilibrium concept. Note that if rank$\{g_1(p), \ldots, g_K(p)\} = S$ for all p then putting $L = R^S$ we have a problem identical to the one in Lecture III. This is called the complete market case. Beyond the budget constraint there is no restriction on transfers of purchasing power across states. We will be interested in the case where there may be such restrictions (typically because $K < S$). This is the incomplete market case.

IV.2. Equilibrium May Not Exist

It was shown by O. Hart ("On the Optimality of Equilibrium when Markets are Incomplete," *Journal of Economic Theory*, 1975) that under the standard conditions an equilibrium may not exist in this model. The idea of the example can be briefly explained.

Let $\ell = 2$ and $S = 2$. There are two assets. Each asset is a future contract delivering one of two commodities independently of the state of the world, i.e., $a_{11} = (1,0)$, $a_{12} = (1,0)$, $a_{21} = (0,1)$, $a_{22} = (0,1)$. Note that then $L(p) = R^2$, i.e., markets are complete, if and only if p_1 and p_2 are not collinear (i.e., relative prices are not the same in the two states). If p_1 and p_2 are collinear, then $L(p)$ is one-dimensional and contains some positive nonzero vector. Because of the budget constraint this means that whatever the preferences $f(p, L(p)) = f(p, \{0\})$, i.e., it is as if no transfer were possible across the two states.

Hence, if p is an equilibrium price vector, then either (i) $f(p, L) = 0$ and p_1, p_2 are not collinear, or (ii) $f(p, \{0\}) = 0$ and p_1, p_2 are collinear. It should be reasonably clear that an f can be found so that neither (i) or (ii) holds (i.e., every equilibrium, if markets are complete, should have the same relative prices in the two states while every equilibrium of the incomplete markets situation should have distinct relative prices in the two states). For this f no equilibrium can exist.

There is something that appears coincidental in this example, namely, the equality of relative prices in the two states under the complete market structure. It prompts the following question: if not always, can we at least assert that equilibrium exists generally? As we shall try to suggest in the rest of this lecture the answer is positive. The basic paper is by Duffie and Shafer ("Equilibrium in Incomplete Markets: I. Basic Model of Generic Existence," *Journal of Mathematical Economics* **14**, 1985). We follow M.D. Hirsch–Magill–Mas-Colell ("A Geometric Approach to a Class of Equilibrium Existence Theorem," forthcoming in *Journal of Mathematical Economics*). These papers contain further references.

IV.3. Pseudoequilibrium

We shall focus on a concept more general than equilibrium.

Definition. *The pair* $(p, L) \in R^{\ell S}_{++} \times G^{S,K}$ *constitutes a pseudoequilibrium if:*

(i) $f(p, L) = 0$, *and*

(ii) $g_k(p) \in L$ *for all* $k = 1, \ldots, K$.

Note that a pseudoequilibrium (p, L) is an equilibrium if $\{g_1(p), \ldots, g_K(p)\}$ are linearly independent. Thus, this allows us to divide the proof of generic existence into two parts: (i) show that generically a pseudoequilibrium is an equilibrium, and (ii) show that a pseudoequilibrium exists under standard conditions.

IV.4. The Genericity Argument

The pseudoequilibrium conditions are:

[I] $f(p, L) = 0$

[II] $g_k(p) \in L$, all $k \leq K$.

How many equations and unknowns do these represent? As for unknowns p gives ℓS minus normalizations. There is one normalization for the budget constraint and $S - K$ for the fact that we always have $f(p, L) \in L$. Thus, p gives $\ell S - (1 + S - K)$. It is immediate that [I] yields the same number of possibly independent constraints. As for L the grassmanian $G^{S,K}$ is a C^∞ manifold of dimension $K(S - K)$. This is precisely the same number of equations needed to represent [II].

Summarizing: the system [I]–[II] has the same number of equations as of unknowns. This means that if we throw in any other constraint, say the linear dependency of $\{g_1(p), \ldots, g_K(p)\}$, then the system is overdetermined and an application of Sard's theorem similar to the one of Lecture III should yield the result that for almost every parameter of the model, the solutions of [I]–[II] will have $\{g_1(p), \ldots, g_K(p)\}$ linearly independent, i.e., will be true equilibrium

Which parameters should be used as perturbation variables? As in Lecture III, the initial endowment vectors ω_i are a clear possibility. They will certainly provide enough variation directions for [I]. Unfortunately, they are of no help with [II] since ω_i does not enter into this part of the equation system. There seems no alternative (using p itself does not quite do it) to using the return vectors a_{ks}. This is the state of the art. It is a bit unsatisfactory because from many points of view it would be preferable to have a generic result for arbitrarily given return vectors.

IV.5. Existence of Pseudoequilibrium

It is a remarkable fact that in order to prove the existence of a pseudoequilibrium tools stronger than Brouwer's fixed-point theorem or any of its variants (such as the ones used in Lecture III) appear to be required. This is remarkable because it is a novelty in economics.

To focus on essentials let us make the strong simplification that for fixed $L \in G^{S,K}$ there is a single $p(L)$ of unit norm such that $f(p(L), L) = 0$. Defining $g_i(L) = g_i(p(L))$ the existence of pseudoequilibrium reduces then to the question: *Given* K *functions* $g_i : G^{S,K} \to R^S$ *is there an* L *such that* $g_i(L) \in L$ *for every* i? We assume that each of the functions is continuous (in the obvious topology of $G^{S,K}$).

The answer is positive and a proof can be given following the same section of vector bundles approach of Lecture III. The difference is that we should now work with a vector bundle different to the tangent vector bundle having as base space the positive portion of the sphere. Clearly, our base space will now be $G^{S,K}$. The fiber associated with L will be $\{L\} \times \overbrace{L^{\perp} \times \ldots \times L^{\perp}}^{K \text{ times}}$. Note that the dimension of the fibers is the same as the dimension of the base space. For every L let $\pi_{L^{\perp}}$ denote the projection map of R^S on $L^{\perp}$. Define a section σ of the vector bundle by $\sigma(L) = (L, \pi_{L^{\perp}} g_K(L), \ldots, \pi_{L^{\perp}} g_K(L))$. Then L yields a pseudoequilibrium if and only if $\sigma(L) = (L, 0)$, or, in other words, if and only if $\sigma(L) = \sigma_0(L)$ where σ_0 is the zero section.

The existence of a pseudoequilibrium follows then from the fact that any section of the above vector bundle must intersect the zero section. To see this note: (i) any two sections are homotopic (the base space is compact and boundaryless), hence all sections have the same mod 2 intersection number with σ_0, (ii) the mod 2 intersection number must be nonzero since there is a smooth section σ' which intersects σ_0 transversally at a single point. Indeed, let $a_1, \ldots, a_K \in R^S$ be linearly independent. Put $\sigma'(L) = (L, \pi_{L^{\perp}} a_1, \ldots, \pi_{L^{\perp}} a_K)$. Obviously $\sigma'(L) = (L, 0)$ if and only if $L = \text{span}\{a_1, \ldots, a_\kappa\}$. To see that σ' is transversal to σ_0 is straightforward but tedious — we would need among other things to specify the differentiable structure on $G^{S,K}$. Finally, (iii) if the mod 2 intersection number of σ and σ_0 is nonzero then the intersection is actually nonempty.

The above is of course no more than a sketch of proof. There is an interesting point of comparison with the arguments of Lecture III. There phrasing or not our proof as a fixed point, argument was simply a matter of taste. This is not the case here. The base space $G^{S,K}$ may not have the fixed point property (consider $S = 2$, $K = 1$). Thus a rigid adherence to the fixed point proves in this case not to be helpful.

IV.6. An Open Problem

We have seen that proving the existence of pseudoequilibrium necessitates tools stronger than Brouwer's fixed point theorem. (Incidentally, it is a useful exercise to verify that the fixed-point like result on $G^{S,K}$ claimed in the last section implies Brouwer's and also the Borsuk-Ulam theorem, a result more advanced than Brouwer's.) Strictly speaking, however, to establish this one must, roughly speaking, show that the underlying economics places no restrictions on the functions g_i beyond continuity. A careful analysis of this problem leads to the following question.

Open Problem. *Let* $J < M$ *and consider* $G_+^{M,J} = \{L \in G^{M,J}\} : L \cap R_+^M = \{0\}\}$. *Suppose that* $F : G_+^{M,J} \to R^M$ *is a continuous function such that* $F(L) \in L$ *for all* $L \in G_+^{M,J}$.

Let $E \subset G_+^{M,J}$ *be closed. Is there an economy such that for every* $L \in E$, $F(L)$ *represents the aggregate excess demand vector when every consumer maximizes utility subject to its net trade* $x_i - \omega_i$ *to lie in* $L - R_+^M$*?*

For $J = M - 1$ the function F is nothing but the classical excess demand function of Lecture III. The positive answer to the problem is the well known Sonnenschein-Mantel-Debreu theorem (see A. Mas-Colell, "The Theory of ..." for more on this theorem). Thus we are asking for a generalization of this theorem (the comparatively simpler additional case seems to be $J = 1$).

Dynamic General Equilibrium Models - Two Examples

by

José A. Scheinkman
Department of Economics
University of Chicago

Introduction

In these lectures I exhibit two examples of dynamic general equilibrium models. These are two of a series of models developed over the last few years by economists with the goal of clarifying questions relating to assets valuation, the role of money, fiscal policy, and many aspects of economic fluctuations.[1/] In this literature, in contrast to earlier efforts, one starts by a formal description of agents and how they interact. The treatment is explicitly dynamic and the equilibrium notion encompasses not only actions but also beliefs. It should be emphasized that "equilibrium" as used here may accommodate oligopolistic elements, impossibility of completing certain trades, etc. and certainly does not preclude motion over time.

The increased interest in this type of formulation on the part of the economics profession stems partly from curiosity as to how aggregate economic phenomena are created, and also from the realization that an equilibrium account is essential in order to evaluate hypothetical policy interventions.

The model in the first part is a natural development in the Arrow-Debreu-McKenzie tradition. Variants of it have been used to study asset prices (Lucas [1978], Brock [1982]), and aggregate fluctuations (Kydland and Prescott [1982], Lucas [1987]). My approach here is inspired by Arrow [1964] and was first used to study asset pricing (Scheinkman [1977]). The presence of enough trading opportunities and agents' characteristics can be used to demonstrate that the equilibrium stochastic process solves a single agent optimization problem that is essentially like the Brock and Mirman [1972] optimal growth model. This result is then used to derive properties of equilibrium asset prices, consumption, etc.

The second part discusses a model of Scheinkman and Weiss [1986]. Here markets are incomplete: individuals face risky labor income streams and are not allowed to borrow except what they could pay back with probability one. There is a single durable asset that agents may accumulate in order to consume in periods of low labor income. The existence of an equilibrium is proved and properties of the equilibrium allocations are discussed and contrasted with the ones of the first model.

I have opted here for a careful presentation of two examples rather than for an attempt at surveying the literature. Perhaps the most crucial omission concerns the literature on overlapping generations models including the important points raised, at least initially, in that literature, i.e., indeterminancy of equilibrium, existence of stationary rational expectations equilibria in which intrinsic uncertainty matter, deterministic "chaotic" time paths, etc. The reader interested in these issues should consult the excellent survey by Woodford [1984].

Though an effort was made to make these lectures self-contained, familiarity with the Walrasian model as in Debreu [1959] is essential. I have also assumed elementary concepts in convex analysis, dynamic programming and probability theory.

My thanks to Blake LeBaron for able research assistance and to the NSF through grant SES-8420930 and grant NSF INT-8413966 (USA-France, Binational). These lectures were prepared during my stay at CEREMADE, University of Paris, IX in the Spring of 1986.

1. The Brock-Mirman Model

A. The Equilibrium Model

Optimal growth models suitably interpreted are the simplest examples of dynamic general equilibrium models. We will describe here an example whose study can be reduced to the one of the Brock and Mirman [1972] model of optimal growth under uncertainty.

There are an infinite number of time periods $t=1,2,\ldots$ and at each t a random variable $\theta_t \in S$, S a finite set, is chosen. We write $\theta^t=(\theta_1,\ldots,\theta_t)$ for the histories up to t. Let $\nu_t(\theta^t)$ denote the probability that $\theta^t \in S^t$ obtains. For simplicity we assume $\nu_t(\theta^t)>0$ and let $\pi(\theta^t,\theta_{t+1}) = \nu_{t+1}(\theta^t,\theta_{t+1})/\nu_t(\theta^t)$. In order to preserve a symmetric notation we will treat S^0 as a singleton and write $\pi(\theta^0,\theta_1)$ for $\nu_1(\theta^1)$.

There is, at each time t, a single consumption good which is also the capital good -- and labor. There are J firms. Each firm $j=1,\ldots,J$ is described by a family of production functions

$$f^j(\cdot,\cdot,\theta^t):\ R_+^2 \to R_+$$
$$(k,\ell) \to f^j(k,\ell,\theta^t)$$

that indicates the amount produced at t, if history θ^t obtains, given that the firm used the quantity of capital (labor) $k(\ell)$ at time $t-1$. There are also I consumers and each consumer $i=1,\ldots,I$ has a utility function given by

$$E_0 \sum_{t=0}^{\infty} \delta^t u^i(c_t(\theta^t),\ell_t(\theta^t),\theta^t)$$

where $c_t(\theta^t)$ denotes the consumption of the single consumption good at t if history θ^t obtains, $\ell_t(\theta^t)$ analogously for labor and E_0 denotes the expectation at time zero, and for each θ^t, $u^i(\cdot,\cdot,\theta^t)$: $R_+ x[0,1] \to R$ satisfies

A-1: u^i is strictly concave, continuous, differentiable in the interior of its domain, increasing in c, decreasing in ℓ and

$$\sup_{(c,\ell,\theta^t)} \{|u(c,\ell,\theta^t)|<\infty / c\in R_+, \ell\in[0,1]\}.$$

Further,

$$\text{if } \ell>0 \ \lim_{c\to 0} \frac{\partial u(c,\ell,\theta^t)}{\partial c} = +\infty, \text{ if } c>0 \ \lim_{\ell\to 1} \frac{\partial u(c,\ell,\theta^t)}{\partial \ell} = -\infty,$$

$$\text{and } \lim_{\ell\to 0} \partial u(c,\ell,\theta^t)/\partial \ell = 0.$$

We will also use

A-2: $f^j(\cdot,\cdot,\theta^t)$ is strictly concave, continuous and $f^j(0,0,\theta^t)=0$. Further,

$$\sup_{(k,\ell,\theta^t)} f^j(k,\ell,\theta^t)<\infty.$$

As we mentioned above, we wish to exhibit a model whose solution can be shown to be equivalent to the optimization problem studied by Brock and Mirman [1972]. One way to proceed would be to postulate the existence of a complete set of contingent claims markets, i.e., firms and consumers could buy and sell claims to the consumption good and labor contingent on the realization of a history θ^t at time zero.[2/] Debreu's theorem [1954] on the Pareto optimality of complete markets competitive equilibrium would guarantee that under concavity the equilibrium must solve the problem of maximizing a weighted sum of utilities subject to the aggregate production possibility, i.e., a problem such as (G) in section (b) below. In order to do this formally in a set up such as ours where there are an infinite number of contingent commodities, one must, however, assume <u>a priori</u> certain restrictions on the price system. In particular, one must assume certain "boundedness" property of prices in order to be able to assign finite value to an adequate set of contingent claims.[3/]

We will proceed here in a different manner following the approach initiated by Kenneth Arrow in the context of a finite number of dates and states. Arrow [1964] noticed that we can price "by arbitrage" all contingent claims if we are willing to assume that at each t history θ^t there exist complete spot markets and contingent markets for at least one commodity for every $t+1$ history θ^{t+1} that may follow θ^t and further that consumers have <u>perfect foresight about the spot and contingent prices that would prevail in all future date-event pairs</u>. In our case of an infinite time horizon, it is clear that one needs to impose some restrictions on allowable trades to rule out the strategy of consuming at each t arbitrary amounts, financing the consumption by the sale of goods for delivery at time $t+1$ and repeating this operation <u>ad infinitum</u> (Ponzi schemes). Without such a restriction no equilibrium would exist. This is usually accomplished by placing some lower bound on net debt at each t. We will thus proceed with Arrow's approach except that we will also introduce a set of extra "long-lived" assets, i.e., claims to future profits of the firms. These assets will turn out to be superfluous but this will allow us to discuss their valuations.

We will consider two types of markets. At each time t, given history θ^t, contingent markets will exist for the delivery of the consumption good at time $t+1$ if θ_{t+1} occurs for each $\theta_{t+1} \in S$. We will denote by $p_t(\theta^t, \theta_{t+1})$ the price quoted in such markets. This will express the number of time t consumption goods that must be delivered at t in order to assure a unit of the consumption good at $t+1$ if θ_{t+1} occurs. In a "spot" market labor at t will be exchanged for the consumption good. The wage rate $w_t(\theta^t)$ will express the number of consumption goods that must be paid for each unit of labor. In another set of spot markets, shares entitling the owner to the profits of each firm will be traded. We will write $q^j_t(\theta^t)$ for the price (again in terms of the consumption good at t) of the total number of shares of firm j at time t given that θ^t has obtained.

All agents take prices as given. Each firm j then solves at each θ^t,

$$\max_{(k,\ell)} \sum_{\theta_{t+1}\in S} f^j(k,\ell,\theta^t,\theta_{t+1})p(\theta^t,\theta_{t+1})-k-w_t(\theta^t)\ell.$$

Since f is stricly concave a solution to this problem, if it exists, is unique and we denote it $k^j_t(\theta^t)$ and $\ell^j_t(\theta^t)$. Further, the maximized value, that we write $\gamma^j_t(\theta^t)$, is non-negative. Clearly, all such quantities depend on prices and wages but we omit this dependence where unnecessary.

Notice that each firm's maximum problem is truly static. At time t if history θ^t has occurred, price per unit of output on all possible subsequent histories (θ^t,θ_{t+1}) are quoted (as well as the price of labor) and the maximization problem is independent of future (or past) prices. The situation is quite different in the case of consumers.

Each consumer $i=1,\ldots,I$ at each period t given that history θ^t obtained takes as given prices $p(\theta^t,\theta_{t+1})$, the wage rate $w_t(\theta^t)$, the price of shares $q^j_t(\theta^t)$ as well as the profits $\gamma^j_t(\theta^t)$ of each of the firms. He also expects that for each $\tau>t$ if θ^τ obtains prices $p(\theta^\tau,\theta_{\tau+1})$, $w_\tau(\theta^\tau)$, $q^j_\tau(\theta^\tau)$ $j=1,\ldots,J$ and profits $\gamma^j_\tau(\theta^\tau)$ occur. Based on the observed prices and profits and his expectations about future prices and profits, at each t, given that θ^t has occured he chooses his consumption $c^i_t(\theta^t)$, his labor supply $\ell^i_t(\theta^t)$, the fraction of the shares of firm j, $s^{ij}_t(\theta^t)$ that he wishes to hold between period t and period t+1, and the amount $x(\theta^t,\theta_{t+1})$ of units of the consumption good that he wants to buy in the contingent markets to be delivered to him if θ_{t+1} occurs.

In general, of course, the prices (or profits) that he expects at time t to prevail at time t' will vary with t and, in particular, may be distinct from the ones which actually occur at t'. These, in turn, will be determined by consumers' demand behavior which, of course, is a function of expected future prices. We close this system by imposing equilibrium expectations, i.e., that the prices expected at time $t<t'$ to prevail at time t' actually clear the market at t', and that the expected future profits are the ones that actually occur. In particular, all expectations of future values are commonly held and do not change over time.

Formally, we search for non-negative sequences $p_t(\theta^t,\theta_{t+1})$, $w_t(\theta^t)$, $q_t^j(\theta^t)$ such that:

if we define $\gamma_t^j(\theta^t) = \max_{(k,\ell)} \sum_{\theta_{t+1}\in S} f^j(k,\ell,\theta^t,\theta_{t+1})p(\theta^t,\theta_{t+1})-k-w_t(\theta^t)\ell$

and if agents solve (P^i):

$$\text{Max } E_0 \sum_{t=0}^{\infty} \delta^t u^i(c_t^i(\theta^t),\ell_t^i(\theta^t),\theta^t)$$

s.t.

$$\text{(C.1)} \qquad c_t^i(\theta^t) + \sum_{j=1}^{J} ([s_t^{ij}(\theta^t)-s_{t-1}^{ij}(\theta^{t-1})]q_t^j(\theta^t))$$

$$+ \sum_{\theta_{t+1}\in S} x_t^i(\theta^t,\theta_{t+1})p_t(\theta^t,\theta_{t+1})$$

$$= x_{t-1}^i(\theta^t)+\sum_{j=1}^{J} s_{t-1}^{ij}(\theta^{t-1})\gamma_t^j(\theta^t)+\ell_t^i(\theta^t)w_t(\theta^t)$$

and

(C.2) for all infinite histories $(\theta_1,\theta_2,\ldots)$

$$\liminf_{t\to\infty} (\sum_{\theta_{t+1}\in S} [x_t^i(\theta^t,\theta_{t+1})p_t(\theta^t,\theta_{t+1})]) > -\infty,$$

$s_t^{ij}\geq 0$ $\ell^i(\theta^t)\leq 1$, with $x_{-1}^i(\theta^0)>0$, and $s_0^{ij}\geq 0$ given and $\sum_{i=1}^{I} s_0^{ij}=1$ for all $j=1,\ldots,J$

then

(i) $$\sum_{j=1}^{J} f^j(k_t^j(\theta^t), \ell_t^j(\theta^t), \theta^t, \theta_{t+1}) - \sum_{i=1}^{I} x_t^i(\theta^t, \theta_{t+1})$$

(ii) $$\sum_{j=1}^{J} \ell_t^j(\theta^t) = \sum_{i=1}^{I} \ell_t^i(\theta^t)$$

(iii) $$\sum_{i=1}^{I} s_t^{ij}(\theta^t) = 1 \quad \text{for each } j=1,\ldots,J.$$

(iv) $$\sum_{j=1}^{J} k_t^j(\theta^t) + \sum_{i=1}^{I} c_t^i(\theta^t) = \sum_{j=1}^{J} f^j(k_{t-1}^j(\theta^{t-1}), \ell_{t-1}^j(\theta^{t-1}), \theta^{t-1}, \theta_t)$$

Equation (i) express the clearing of the contingent markets. Equations (ii), (iii) says the labor (stock) market(s) is(are) in equilibrium. The last one requires the equalities between demand for the consumption good at t in event θ^t and its supply and it's right hand side should be interpreted for $t=0$ as $\sum_{i=1}^{I} x_{-1}^i(\theta^0)$.

The first constraint in (P^i) has a straightforward interpretation. Consumption $(c_t^i(\theta^t))$, the amount spent on the acquisition of shares $\sum_{j=1}^{J}[s_t^{ij}(\theta^t)-s_t^{ij}(\theta^{t-1})]q_t^j(\theta^t)$ and the purchases in the contingent markets must be financed with the amounts delivered from purchases in the past period $x_{t-1}^i(\theta^t)$, dividends received $\sum_{j=1}^{J} s_{t-1}^{ij}(\theta^{t-1})\gamma_t^j(\theta^t)$ and the payments received for his work $\ell_t^i(\theta^t)w_t(\theta^t)$.

The second constraint is necessary since, if not present, a consumer could set $\ell_t^i(\theta^t)=0$ and finance any desired consumption $c_t^i(\theta^t)$ through sales of contingent claims. Constraint (C.2) says that along any possible infinite history $\bar{\theta}=(\theta_1,\theta_2,\theta_3,\ldots)$ the <u>debt</u> the individual at t remains bounded below.

Even after imposing constraint (C.2), problem (P^i) may very well fail to have a solution. If say $p_t(\theta^t,\theta_{t+1})=0$ and $\pi_t(\theta^t,\theta_{t+1})\neq 0$ clearly no solution exists. We will not try here to state explicitly conditions under which (P^i) has a solution. Henceforth, such sequences $p_t(\theta^t,\theta_{t+1}),w_t(\theta^t)$ and $q_t^j(\theta^t)$ will be called an equilibrium of the sequential model. The corresponding allocations, $\ell_t^i(\theta^t)$, $c_t^i(\theta^t)$, $\ell_t^j(\theta^t)$, $k_t^j(\theta^t)$, $s_t^{ij}(\theta^t)$ will be called equilibrium allocations.

B. **An Equivalent Growth Model**

At this point, the task of characterizing the equilibrium allocations even in this rudimentary model seems quite complicated. One must guess a sequence of functions and solve the implied optimization problems and see whether an infinite number of equations are simultaneously solved. As we mentioned in the introduction, we wish to show that the study of the equilibria of this economy can be reduced to the one of an "optimal growth model" under uncertainty. We start by a proposition whose proof is immediate.

Proposition 1.1: Let $\{p_t(\theta^t,\theta_{t+1}),\ w_t(\theta^t),\ q_t^j(\theta^t)\}$, $t=0,1,\ldots$, $j=1,\ldots,J$ be an equilibrium for the sequential model with corresponding allocations of labor and consumption $\{\ell_t^i(\theta^t),\ c_t^i(\theta^t)\}$ $t=0,1,\ldots$ $i=1,\ldots,I$. Then for each $\theta^t \in S$ with $\nu_t(\theta^t)>0$,

(a)
$$p_t(\theta^t,\theta_{t+1})\frac{\partial u^i}{\partial c}(c_t^i(\theta^t),\ell_t^i(\theta^t),\theta^t)$$
$$= \delta\pi_t(\theta^t,\theta_{t+1})\frac{\partial u^i}{\partial c}(c_{t+1}^i(\theta^t,\theta_{t+1}),\ell_{t+1}^i(\theta^t,\theta_{t+1}),\theta^t,\theta_{t+1})$$
for each $\theta_{t+1}\in S$, for each $i=1,\ldots,I$.

(b)
$$-\left[\frac{\partial u^i}{\partial c}(c_t^i(\theta^t),\ell_t^i(\theta^t),\theta^t)\right]^{-1}\left[\frac{\partial u^i}{\partial \ell}(c_t^i(\theta^t),\ell_t^i(\theta^t),\theta^t)\right] = w_t(\theta^t).$$

From now on, we fix an equilibrium and for each x and s^{ij} let,

$$V^i(x,s^{ij},\theta^t) = \text{Max } E\{\sum_{\tau=t}^{\infty} \delta^\tau u^i(c^i_t,\ell^i_t,\theta^\tau)|\theta^t\}$$

s.t. (C.1) and (C.2) of (P^i)

and $x^i_{t-1}(\theta^t)=x,\ s^{ij}_{t-1}(\theta^{t-1})=s^{ij}\quad j=1,\ldots,J$

i.e., the value of the problem for consumer i when he starts at t with (x,s^{ij}) $j=1,\ldots,J$.

Clearly, for fixed θ^t, V is concave and by A.1 there exists M such that $|V^i(x,s^{ij},\theta^t)|\le\delta^t M$. For each f concave we write $p\in\partial f(x)$ iff $\langle p,y-x\rangle \ge f(y)-f(x)$ for each y. Even though in equilibrium $s^{ij}_{t-1}(\theta^{t-1})\ge 0$, we may since $c^i_t(\theta^t)>0$ extend V^i to an open neighborhood of $(x^i_{t-1}(\theta^t),s^{ij}_{t-1}(\theta^t))$ and this extension is still bounded. Hence there exists $h^i(\theta^t)\in\partial V^i(x^i_{t-1}(\theta^t),s^{ij}_{t-1}(\theta^{t-1}),\theta^t)$ and further,

$$\text{(1.1)}\qquad \langle h^i(\theta^t),(x^i_{t-1}(\theta^t),s^{ij}_{t-1}(\theta^{t-1}))\rangle \le V^i(x^i_{t-1}(\theta^t),s^{ij}_t(\theta^{t-1}),\theta^t)$$

$$- V^i((1/2)\,x^i_{t-1}(\theta^t),(1/2)s^{ij}_{t-1}\,(\theta^{t-1}),\theta^t) \le 2\delta^t M.$$ Q.E.D.

<u>Proposition 1.2</u>: $$h^i(\theta^t) = \frac{\partial u^i}{\partial c}(c^i_t(\theta^t),\ell^i_t(\theta^t),\theta^t)$$
$$(1,q^1_t(\theta^t)+\gamma^1_t(\theta^t),\ldots,q^J_t(\theta^t)+\gamma^J_t(\theta^t))$$

<u>Proof</u>:

Let: $$\bar V(x,s^{ij})=\delta^t[u^i(c^i_t(\theta^t)+x-x^i_{t-1}(\theta^t)$$
$$+\sum_{j=1}^{J}(q^j_t(\theta^t)+\gamma^j_t(\theta^t))(s^{ij}-s^{ij}_{t-1}(\theta^{t-1})),\ell(\theta^t),\theta^t)$$
$$+ E\{V^i(x^i_t(\theta^{t+1}),s^{ij}_t\,(\theta^t),\theta^{t+1})|\theta^t\}]$$

Since $c(\theta^t)>0$, $\bar V$ is well defined in a neighborhood of $x^i_t(\theta^t),s^{ij}_t(\theta^t)$. Also, $V^i\ge\bar V$ and $V^i(x^i_{t-1}(\theta^t),s^{ij}_{t-1}(\theta^{t-1}),\theta^t)=\bar V^i(x^i_{t-1}(\theta^t)s^{ij}_{t-1}(\theta^{t-1}))$. Thus,

$$(\langle h^i(\theta^t),(x,s^{ij})-(x^i_{t-1}(\theta^t),s^{ij}_t(\theta^{t-1})\rangle) \geq \hat{V}(x,s^{ij})-\hat{V}(x^i_{t-1}(\theta^t),s^{ij}_t(\theta^{t-1}))$$

i.e., $h^i(\theta^t)\in\partial\hat{V}(x^i_{t-1}(\theta^t),s^{ij}_{t-1}(\theta^{t-1}))$. The result follows from the fact that $\hat{V}$ is C^1 at $(x^i_{t-1}(\theta^t),s^{ij}_{t-1}(\theta^{t-1}))$ and from the computation of its derivative.

Q.E.D.

Remark 1: Proposition (1.2) together with equation (1.6) above tells us that

$$\frac{\partial u^i}{\partial c}(c^i_t(\theta^t),\ell^i_t(\theta^t),\theta^t).$$

$$[x^i_{t-1}(\theta^t)+\sum_{j=1}^{J}(q^j_t(\theta^t)+\gamma^j_t(\theta^t))s^{ij}_{t-1}(\theta^{t-1})]$$

$\leq 2\delta^t M$ and, in particular

$$(1.2)\quad \lim_{t\to\infty}\{\frac{\partial u^i}{\partial c^i}(c^i_t(\theta^t),\ell^i_t,\theta^t)[x^i_{t-1}(\theta^t)+\sum_{j=1}^{J}(q^j_t(\theta^t))s^{ij}_{t-1}(\theta^{t-1})]\}=0$$

This last condition is frequently called the "transversality condition at infinity." From now on we let,

$$(1.3)\qquad f(k,\ell,\theta^t) = \text{Max}\{\sum_{j=1}^{J} f^j(k^j,\ell^j,\theta^t)\,|\sum_{j=1}^{J} k^j=k,\sum_{j=1}^{j}\ell^j=\ell\}$$

and

$$(1.4)\qquad \nu(c,\ell,\theta^t) = \text{Max}\{\sum_{i=1}^{I}\lambda^i u^i(c^i,\ell^i,\theta^t)\,|\sum_{i=1}^{I} c^i=c,\sum_{i=1}^{I}\ell^i=\ell\}.$$

Thus, ν is well defined over $R^n_+ x[0,1]$ and it represents the maximum attainable aggregate utility when individual i's utility has weight λ^i. The function f describes the economy-wide production possibilities. For each set of weights $\lambda^1,\ldots,\lambda^I$ $\lambda^i>0$, let us consider

(G) $$\operatorname{Max} E_0 \sum_{t=0}^{\infty} \delta^t \nu(c_t(\theta^t), \ell_t(\theta^t), \theta^t)$$

subject to

$$c_t(\theta^t)+k_t(\theta^t) = f(k_{t-1}(\theta^{t-1}), \ell_{t-1}(\theta^{t-1}), \theta^t)$$

$$f(k_{-1}, \ell_{-1}, \theta_0) \text{ given.}$$

Except for the presence of labor this is exactly the model of Brock and Mirman [1972].

We are now ready to prove:

Theorem 1.1: If $\{p_t(\theta^t,\theta_{t+1}), w_t(\theta^t), q_t^j(\theta^t)\}$ $t=0,1,\dots,$ $j=1,\dots,J$ is a competitive equilibrium and if $c_t(\theta^t)=\sum_{i=1}^I c_t^i(\theta^t)$, $\ell_t(\theta^t)=\sum_{i=1}^I \ell_t^i(\theta^t)$, $k_t(\theta^t)=\sum_{j=1}^J k^j(\theta^t)$ then (c,ℓ,k) solves (G) for some $(\lambda^1,\dots,\lambda^I)$ with $\lambda^i>0$.

Proof: Write $y_t(\theta^t)=k_t(\theta^t)+c_t(\theta^t)$. Let $(\tilde{c}_t,\tilde{\ell}_t,\tilde{k}_t)$ be another feasible path for G and $\tilde{y}_t(\theta^t)=\tilde{k}_t(\theta^t)+\tilde{c}_t(\theta^t)$. By lemma 1.1 and the maximum problem for the firms we have

(1.5) $$E\{\delta(y_{t+1}(\theta^t,\theta_{t+1})-\tilde{y}_{t+1}(\theta^t,\theta_{t+1}))\frac{\partial u^1}{\partial c}(\theta^t,\theta_{t+1})|\theta^t\}$$

$$-\frac{\partial u^1}{\partial c}(\theta^t)[y_t(\theta^t)-c_t(\theta^t)-\tilde{y}_t(\theta^t)+\tilde{c}_t(\theta^t)]$$

$$+\frac{\partial u^1}{\partial \ell}(\theta^t)[\ell_t(\theta^t)-\tilde{\ell}_t(\theta^t)] \geq 0.$$

where $$\frac{\partial u^1}{\partial c}(\theta^t) = \frac{\partial u^1}{\partial c}(c_t^1(\theta^t),\ell_t^1(\theta^t),\theta^t)$$

and $$\frac{\partial u^1}{\partial \ell}(\theta^t) = \frac{\partial u^1}{\partial \ell}(c_t^1(\theta^t),\ell_t^1(\theta^t),\theta^t)\dots.$$

Now since by A.1 $c_t^1(\theta^t)>0$, and $\ell_t^1(\theta^t)=0$ if and only if $\ell_t^i(\theta^t)=0$, $i=1,\dots,I$. We have that

$$\lambda^1\left(\frac{\partial u^1}{\partial c}(\theta^t), \frac{\partial u^1}{\partial \ell}(\theta^t)\right)\in\partial\nu(c_t(\theta^t),\ell_t(\theta^t),\theta^t)$$

if ν is given by (1.4). Hence,

$$D_T = E_0 \sum_{t=0}^{T} \delta^t[\nu(\tilde{c}_t(\theta^t),\tilde{\ell}_t(\theta^t),\theta^t)-\nu(c_t(\theta^t),\ell_t(\theta^t),\theta^t)]$$

$$\leq E_0 \sum_{t=0}^{T} \lambda^1\delta^t\left\{\frac{\partial u^1}{\partial c}(\theta^t)[\tilde{c}_t(\theta^t)-c_t(\theta^t)]+\frac{\partial u^1}{\partial \ell}(\theta^t)[\tilde{\ell}_t(\theta^t)-\ell_t(\theta^t)]\right\}.$$

Using (1.5) and the law of iterated expectations, we have,

$$D_T\leq\lambda^1E_0\left\{\sum_{t=0}^{T}\delta^t\left[\delta\frac{\partial u^1}{\partial c}(\theta^t,\theta_{t+1})(y_{t+1}(\theta^t,\theta_{t+1})-\tilde{y}_{t+1}(\theta^t,\theta_{t+1}))\right.\right.$$

$$\left.\left.-\frac{\partial u^1}{\partial c}(\theta^t)[\tilde{y}_t(\theta^t)-y_t(\theta^t)]\right]\right\}$$

$$= \lambda^1E_0\left\{\delta^{T+1}\frac{\partial u^1}{\partial c}(\theta^T,\theta_{T+1})[y_{T+1}(\theta^T,\theta_{T+1})-\tilde{y}_{T+1}(\theta^T,\theta_{T+1})]\right\}$$

$$\leq \lambda^1E_0\,\delta^{T+1}\frac{\partial u^1}{\partial c}(\theta^T,\theta_{T+1})y_{T+1}(\theta^T,\theta_{T+1}),$$

since u is increasing in c and $\tilde{y}_{T+1}\geq 0$. Now $y_{T+1}(\theta^T,\theta_{T+1})=\sum_{i=1}^{I}x_T^i(\theta^T,\theta_{T+1})$ and

$$\lambda^i\frac{\partial u^i}{\partial c}(\theta^T,\theta_{T+1}) = \lambda^1\frac{\partial u^1}{\partial c}(\theta^T,\theta_{T+1}).$$

Further, by Remark 1 and the fact that $s_t^{ij}(\theta^t)\geq 0$, $q_t^j(\theta^t)\geq 0$, $\gamma_t^j(\theta^t)\geq 0$, we have that $D_T\leq\delta^T D$ for some constant $D>0$.

Q.E.D.

C. **Asset Price, etc.**

As we mentioned in the introduction, trading in shares of firms was introduced explicitly to allow us to discuss asset valuation. We start by noting that $s_t^{i,j}(\theta^t)>0$ for at least one i, we must have

$$(1.6) \qquad q_t^j(\theta^t)\frac{\partial u^i}{\partial c}(c_t^i(\theta^t),\ell_t^i(\theta^t),\theta^t)$$
$$=\delta E\{[q_{t+1}^j(\theta^t,\theta_{t+1})+\gamma_{t+1}^j(\theta^t,\theta_{t+1})]\frac{\partial u^i}{\partial c}(c_t^i(\theta^t,\theta_{t+1}),\ell_t^i(\theta^t,\theta_{t+1}),\theta^t,\theta_{t+1})|\theta^t\}$$

and since $\frac{\partial u^i}{\partial c}=\frac{\lambda^i\partial\nu}{\partial c}$

$$(1.7) \qquad q_t^j(\theta^t)=\delta\left[\frac{\partial\nu}{\partial c}(\theta^t)\right]^{-1}E\left\{[q_{t+1}^j(\theta^t,\theta_{t+1})+\gamma_{t+1}^j(\theta^t,\theta_{t+1})]\frac{\partial\nu}{\partial c}(\theta^t,\theta_{t+1})|\theta^t\right\}$$

where here as in the proof of theorem 1.1

$$\frac{\partial\nu}{\partial c}(\theta^t)=\frac{\partial\nu}{\partial c}(c_t(\theta^t),\ell_t(\theta^t),\theta^t) \text{ etc.}$$

again using the law of iterated expectations we get,

$$(1.8) \qquad q_t^j(\theta^t)=\sum_{s=t+1}^{T}E\left\{\delta^{s-j}\gamma_s^j(\theta^s)\frac{\partial\nu}{\partial c}(\theta^s)\cdot\left[\frac{\partial\nu}{\partial c}(\theta^t)\right]^{-1}|\theta^t\right\}$$
$$+E\left\{\delta^{T-t}q^j(\theta^T)\frac{\partial\nu}{\partial c}(\theta^T)|\theta^t\right\}.$$

From (1.2) we know that

$$\lim_{t\to\infty}\lambda^i\frac{\partial u^i}{\partial c^i}(c_t^i(\theta^t),\ell_t^i(\theta^t),\theta^t)[q^j(\theta^t)s_{t-1}^{ij}(\theta^{t-1})+x_{t-1}^i(\theta^t)]=0$$

or summing over i and using $\sum_{i=1}^{I}s_{t-1}^{ij}(\theta^{t-1})=1$ and $\sum_{i=1}^{I}x_{t-1}^i(\theta^t)\geq 0$

$$\lim_{T\to\infty} \delta^{T-t} q_T^j(\theta^T) \frac{\partial \nu}{\partial c} (\theta^T)=0$$

thus

$$q_t^j(\theta^t) = \sum_{s=t+1}^{\infty} \delta^{s-t} E\left[\gamma_s^j(\theta^s)\frac{\partial \nu}{\partial c}(\theta^s) \left[\frac{\partial \nu}{\partial c}(\theta^t)\right]^{-1} \middle| \theta^t\right] \tag{1.9}$$

Equation (1.9) says that the value of an asset is given by the discounted value of its dividends. Dividends in event θ^s are priced according to the marginal utility of consumption at θ^s relative to the m.u.c. at θ^t. The right hand side of (1.9) is sometimes referred to by economists as the asset's "market fundamental." The price of an asset cannot simply reflect expected future prices as seems possible from (1.6). This is a consequence of the transversality condition at infinity expressed in (1.2) above and this in turn is a consequence of the existence of sufficient trading opportunities. The model presented in part 2 has exactly the opposite property, namely an asset which yields always zero dividends and exhibits nonetheless a positive price.[4/]

The model discussed in this section, though it seems very particular, is in reality "too" general. In fact, if we dispense with the strict concavity and boundedness of u and f we can readily see that all the other assumptions place no testable implications on either prices or consumption except no-arbitrage relationships such as (1.9).[5/] More restricted models have, of course, stronger implications. In particular, if one is willing to assume that histories do not effect individual's utility functions one has

Proposition 1.1: Suppose $u^i(c,\ell,\theta^t)=\bar{u}^i(c,\ell)$ for each $\theta^t \in S^t$ $i=1,\ldots,I$. Then $c^i(\theta^t)=c^i(c(\theta^t),\ell(\theta^t))$ and $\ell^i(\theta^t)=\ell^i(c(\theta^t),\ell(\theta^t))$ $i=1,\ldots,I$.

Proof: Clearly ν defined by (1.4) also satisfies $\nu(c,\ell,\theta^t)=\bar{\nu}(c,\ell)$ for each $\theta^t \in S^t$. Also since $c^i(\theta^t)>0$ and $\ell^i(\theta^t)=0$ if and only if $w(\theta^t)=0$ we have from (1.4) that

$$\frac{\partial \bar{\nu}}{\partial c}(c(\theta^t),\ell(\theta^t)) = \lambda^i \frac{\partial \bar{u}^i}{\partial c}(c^i(\theta^t),\ell^i(\theta^t))$$

$$\ell^i(\theta^t)\frac{\partial \bar{\nu}}{\partial \ell}(c(\theta^t),\ell(\theta^t)) = \ell^i(\theta^t)\lambda^i \frac{\partial \bar{u}^i}{\partial \ell}(c^i(\theta^t),\ell^i(\theta^t))$$

for some $\lambda^i > 0$ $i=1,\ldots,I$.

The result follows from the fact that each $\bar{u}^i$ (and hence, using (1.4), $\bar{\nu}$) is strictly concave. Q.E.D.

The above proposition shows that if utility functions are not dependent on histories then each individual's consumption and labor supply depends only on aggregate consumption and labor supply. In equilibrium agents insure each other and all individual uncertainty is eliminated.

Suppose further that

$$f^j(k,\ell,\theta^t) = f^j(k,\ell,\theta_t) \tag{1.10}$$

and that when we write $S=\{s_k\}_{k=1}^N$, there exists matrix $\alpha_{kk'}$ such that $\pi_t(\theta^t,\theta_{t+1})=\alpha_{kk'}$ if and only if $\theta_t=s_k$, $\theta_{t+1}=s_{k'}$. In this case, recalling that $y_t(\theta^t)=k_t(\theta^t)+c_t(\theta^t)$ is aggregate output at time t, we know that by Bellman's principle applied to problem (G) that $k_t(\theta^t)=k(y_t,\theta_t)$ and $c_t(\theta^t)=c(y_t,\theta_t)$, $\ell_t(\theta^t)=\ell(y_t,\theta_t)$. Hence using the last proposition we have that $c_t^i(\theta^t)=\xi^i(y_t,\theta_t)$ and $\ell_t^i(\theta^t)=\mu^i(y_t,\theta_t)$.

A parametric version of a model much like ours with $I=1$ and incorporating the assumptions of proposition 1.1 and equation (1.10) has been used to study economic fluctuations (Kydland and Prescott [1982] and Lucas [1987]). The model variables e.g., y_t, c_t, ℓ_t etc. are identified with output, consumption and employment etc. in the U.S. economy. Some parameter values were provided by microeconomic evidence whereas a few others were chosen so that the output of the model match the data. Though it seems to "fit" some of the data characteristics well, e.g., relative variability of consumption and investment, the comovements of output and hours worked, it did much worse in dealing with other aspects of the cycle, e.g., it predicts a much too high variability of average product of labor than is found on the data. Further, the emphasis on market clearing precludes the model from being used to study the important question of the variation of unemployment throughout the cycle.

2. Borrowing Contraints

A. Description of Model and Existence of an Equilibrium

I consider a model with two types of infinitely long-lived individuals, indexed by $i=1,2$. Each agent will at each moment of time choose how much to consume and how much to work.

The productivity of labor is state dependent. In state i, $i=1,2$ labor of type i can produce one unit of consumption per unit of labor input, both measured as flows per unit time. Labor of type $j\neq i$ in state i is not productive at all. The duration of time between state changes is random and has an exponential probability distribution with mean duration $1/\lambda$. In order to fix notation let $N_t(\omega)$ be a Poisson counting process with rate λ on a probability space (Ω,F,P). Define $s_t(\omega)=1$ if $N_t(\omega)$ is odd and $s_t(\omega)=2$ if $N_t(\omega)$ is even. In particular, $P\{s_{t+h}(\omega)=i|s_t(\omega)=j\}=\lambda h+o(h)$ if $i\neq j$.

Consumers are assumed to be able to observe the "histories" of the process $s_t(\omega)$. In order to make this precise I write $\mathbf{F}_t$ for the smallest sub σ-algebra of $\mathbf{F}$ which makes all random variables $s_\tau(\omega), \tau\leq t$ measurable. $\{\mathbf{F}_t\}_{t=0}^{\infty}$ is a nondecreasing family of σ-algebras and each $\mathbf{F}_t$ summarizes the information given by the histories. Consumer choices at time t should be $\mathbf{F}_t$ measurable, i.e., independent of future $s_\tau(\omega)$. <u>Every real valued function indexed by t that appears in the sequel is assumed to be $\mathbf{F}_t$ measurable</u>. (I.e., the inverse image of a Borel subset of reals is assumed to belong to

F_t.) Similarly, all equations are to be interpreted as holding almost surely (e.g., $c(t,\omega)=0$ means that for almost all (t,ω), $c(t,\omega)=0$).

I assume the existence of a good called "money" which can be neither augmented or depleted and choose units in such a way that where one type holds a unit per capita, the other type holds zero. Agents forecast that at each time t and at each event ω, one unit of money would trade for $q(t,\omega)$ units of the consumption good and that this "price" is not affected by his actions. Agents of type $i=1,2$ take $q(t,\omega)$ as given and choose $c^i(t,\omega)$ and $\ell^i(t,\omega)$ to solve

$$
\begin{aligned}
(P^i)\quad & \text{Max } E[\{\textstyle\int_0^\infty e^{-\beta t}[\log(c^i(t,\omega))-\ell^i(t,\omega)dt\}|F_0] \\
& \text{s.t. } y^i(0,\omega)=y_o^i \\
& \dot{y}^i(t,\omega)=(\ell^i(t,\omega)-c^i(t,\omega))/q(t,\omega) \quad \text{if } s_t(\omega)=i \\
& \dot{y}^i(t,\omega) = -c^i(t,\omega)/q(t,\omega) \\
& \ell^i(t,\omega) = 0 \quad \text{if } s_t(\omega)=j\neq i \\
& y^i(t,\omega)\geq 0,\ \ell^i(t,\omega)\geq 0,\ c^i(t,\omega)\geq 0.
\end{aligned}
$$

In (P^i), notice that in state i individual of type i chooses both consumption and labor supply, while in state $j\neq i$ it sets its labor supply at zero and chooses consumption. The constraint $y^i(t,\omega)\geq 0$ means that <u>no borrowing is allowed</u>.

Now for an arbitrary $q(t,\omega)$, $y^1(t,\omega)+y^2(t,\omega)\neq 1$ i.e., demand and supply of money will not balance. An <u>equilibrium</u> is a stochastic process $q(t,\omega)$ such that the solution to (P^i) $y^i(t,\omega)$ satisfy

$$(2.1)\qquad y^1(t,\omega)+y^2(t,\omega)=1.$$

One should note that we assume that agents will use the equilibrium stochastic process $q(t,\omega)$ in solving their maximization problem. This is the hypothesis of equilibrium or rational expectations.

Finding an equilibrium thus involves, in general, a fixed point problem coupled with (two) control problems. Economic considerations suggest, however, another route to compute at least one equilibrium.

Let $z(t,\omega)$ denote the average amount of money held by type 1 at time t in event ω. I will look for an equilibrium in which $q(t,\omega)=q(z(t,\omega),s_t(\omega))$ where for $s_t(\omega)$ fixed, q is a C^1 function of $z(t,\omega)$. In order to treat the two types symmetrically, assume that $q(z,1)=q(1-z,2)$ for each $0\leq z\leq 1$. Thus one may think that consumers take $z(t,\omega)$ and the function $q:[0,1]\times\{1,2\}\to R$ as given and solve P^i. Assume further that consumers forecast that z will be an absolutely continuous function such that, where the derivative exists,

$$\dot{z}(t,\omega) = h(z,s_t(\omega)), \quad \text{with} \quad h(z,1)+h(1-z,2)=0, \tag{2.2}$$

where $h(\cdot,i)$ is a C^1 function for each $i=1,2$. In particular, it only depends on z and the state.

With this structure, redefine an equilibrium as a function $q:[0,1]\times\{1,2\}\to R$ with $q(z,1)=q(1-z,2)$, and a stochastic process $z(t,\omega)$ with values in $[0,1]$, such that if consumer i solves (P^i) with $q(t,\omega)=q(z(t,\omega),s_t(\omega))$ and $y_0^1=z(0,\omega)$, $y_0^2=1-z(0,\omega)$ then $\dot{y}^1(t,\omega)=\dot{z}(t,\omega)$ and $\dot{y}^2(t,\omega)= -\dot{z}(t,\omega)$, i.e., type i holds the predicted amounts of money.

Let $L(y,\dot{y},z,1)=\sup\{\log c-\ell \ / \ \ell\cdot c=q(z,1)\dot{y}\}$ and $L(y,\dot{y},z,2)=\log(-q(z,2)\dot{y})$. If $y>0$ then $(0,-q(z,1))=\nabla L(y,\dot{y},z,1)$ and if $y>0$ and $\dot{y}<0$ then $(0,1/\dot{y})=\nabla L(y,\dot{y},z,2)$. Let

(2.3) $p(t,\omega) = q(z(t,\omega),1)$ if $s_t(\omega)=1$

and

(2.4) $p(t,\omega) = -1/h(z(t,\omega),2)$ if $s_t(\omega)=2$.

Suppose $q(z,i)$ and $z(t,\omega)$ form an equilibrium. Then $e^{-\lambda t}p(t,\omega)$ is exactly the marginal utility of a unit of money at time t for type 1, in equilibrium. If there were no uncertainty, since money yields no dividends, in order for agents of type 1 to hold the asset in every period, such marginal utility would have to be a constant. Hence it seems natural to conjecture that in an equilibrium $(e^{-\beta t}p(t,\omega),F_t)$ form a <u>Martingale</u>, i.e., $E\{e^{-\beta(t+\tau)}p(t+\tau)|F_t\} = e^{-\beta t}p(t,\omega)$. In fact, the concavity of $L(\cdot,\cdot,z,s)$ for fixed (z,s) can be used to establish the following theorem.

<u>Theorem 2.1</u>: Suppose $0<z(t,\omega)<1$ for all (t,ω) and,

(i) $(e^{-\beta t}p,F_t)$ form a Martingale

(ii) For each $T>0$, $\operatorname{ess\,sup}_{(t,\omega)} |p(t,\omega)|$ $t\leq T$ is finite

(iii) $\lim_{t\to\infty} |e^{-\beta t}p(t,\omega)z(t,\omega)|=0$

(iv) $|\operatorname{ess\,sup}_{(t,\omega)} \dot{z}(t,\omega)|<\infty$

Then $y^1(t,\omega)=z(t,\omega)$ solves P^1 with $y^1(0,\omega)=z(0,\omega)$ and symmetrically $y^2(t,\omega)=1-z(t,\omega)$ solves P^2 with $y^2(0,\omega)=1-z(0,\omega)$ among all $y^1(t,\omega)$, $(y^2(t,\omega))$, with

$$\operatorname{ess\,sup}_{(t,\omega)} |\dot{y}^1(t,\omega)|<\infty , \quad (\text{resp } \operatorname{ess\,sup}_{(t,\omega)} |\dot{y}^2(t,\omega)|<\infty)$$

<u>Proof</u>: By concavity,

$$E_0 \int_0^T e^{\beta t}(L(\dot{y},y,z,s))-L(z,\dot{z},z,s))\leq E_0 \int_0^T e^{-\beta t}p(t,\omega)(\dot{z}(t,\omega)-\dot{y}(t,\omega))dt$$

For each ω since $p(t,\omega)$ is of bounded variation (a.s.),

$$\int_0^T e^{-\beta t} p(t,\omega)[\dot{z}(t,\omega)-\dot{y}(t,\omega)]dt$$

$$= e^{-\beta T} p(T,\omega)[z(T,\omega)-y(T,\omega)]$$

$$+ \int_0^T (y(t,\omega)-z(t,\omega)]d(e^{-\beta t} p(t,\omega)).$$

Now in each $[0,T]$, both y and z are essentially bounded. Thus the last integral is the limit of integrals of non-anticipative bounded step functions whose $E(\cdot|F_0)$ is zero by (i) and the law of iterated expectations. Also,

$$\left| \int_0^T \psi(t,\omega)\ d(e^{-\beta t} p(t,\omega)) \right|$$

$$< 4T \operatorname*{ess\ sup}_{(t,\omega),t\leq T} |\psi(t,\omega)| \operatorname*{ess\ sup}_{(t,\omega),t\leq T} |p(t,\omega)| N_T(\omega),$$

where $N_T(\omega)$ is the value of the Poisson Process at T in event ω. The right hand side of this last expression has clearly an expected value and thus by the dominated convergence theorem the last integral has zero expected value. Hence by Fatou's Lemma, and (iii),

$$\limsup_{T\to\infty} E_0 \int_0^T e^{-\beta t}(L(y,\dot{y},z,s)-L(z,\dot{z},z,s))dt \leq 0.$$

Q.E.D.

Theorem 2.1 tells us sufficient conditions for an equilibrium. Further insights can be gained if we make explicit the Martingale condition (i). First note that since $(z(t,\cdot), s_t(\cdot))$ forms a Markov process, and z is F_t measurable this is equivalent to conditioning on $z(t,\omega)$ and $s_t(\omega)$. From now on we write $A(z)=(-h(z,2))^{-1}$ and $B(z) = q(z,1)$.

Then the Martingale condition reads since $s_t(\omega)$ is defined by a Poisson process with parameter λ, for $0<z<1$.

(2.5) $\quad e^{-\beta t}p(z,\omega) = E(e^{-\beta(t+dt)}p(z(t+dt,\omega),s_{t+dt}(\omega)|z_t(t,\omega)=z,\ s_t(\omega)=1)$ or,

$$e^{-\beta t}p(z,\omega) = e^{-\beta t}B(z)+e^{-\beta t}\{B'(z)h(z,1)-(\beta+\lambda)B(z)+\lambda A(z)\}+o(dt)$$

Hence we must have

(2.6) $\quad B'(z)h(z,1)=(\beta+\lambda)B(z)-\lambda A(z)$

and similarly conditioning on $s_t(\omega)=2$ we get,

(2.7) $\quad A'(z)=A(z)(\lambda B(z)-(\beta+\lambda)A(z))$

Since $h(z,1)+h(1-z,2)=0$ we may rewrite (2.6) as

(2.8) $\quad B'(z) = A(1-z)((\beta+\lambda)B(z)-\lambda A(z))$

Further since in equilibrium $h(0,2)=0$, we must have

(2.9) $\quad (\beta+\lambda)B(1) = \lambda A(1).$

If A and B are solutions to (2.7), (2.8), and (2.9) and if we define $p(t,\omega)$ using (2.3) and (2.4), in order for $p(t,\omega)$ to be well defined for $t\in[0,\infty]$ we must have

(2.10) $\quad \lim_{z\to 0} A(z) = \infty.$

System (2.7)-(2.10) is somewhat nonstandard due to the appearance of $A(1-z)$ in equation (2.8). However, the usual approach utilizing the contraction mapping theorem may be used to show that a solution to (2.7) and (2.8) exists for given values of $A(1/2)$ and $B(1/2)$ and one can then show that at least one positive solution satisfying (2.9) and (2.10) exists. The following theorem can be obtained from the results in appendix A and B in Scheinkman and Weiss [1986].

<u>Theorem 2.2</u>: There exists a positive solution $A(z)$, $B(z)$ to equations (2.7)-

(2.10). Further, $B'(z)<0$, $A'(z)<0$, $A(z)\geq B(z)$ and $(\beta z)^{-1}\geq A(z)\geq((\beta+\lambda)^{z)-1}$.

The solution described in theorem (2.2) satisfies all assumptions of theorem (2.1). To see this note that $p(t,\omega)\leq A(z(t,\omega))$ and hence $p(t,\omega)z(t,\omega)\leq\beta^{-1}$ i.e., (iii) is satisfied. Further

$$|\dot{z}(t,\omega)|\leq\sup_{z}(A(z))^{-1}=(A(1))^{-1}\leq\beta+\lambda$$

i.e., (iv). Assumption (ii) follows if one shows that for any T, there exists $\delta>0$ such that $\delta < \operatorname{ess\,inf}_{(t,\omega)} z(t,\omega) \quad t\leq T$.

Clearly, we may assume $s_t(\omega)=2$, for $t\in[0,T]$, for if $s_t(\omega)=1$, $\dot{z}(t,\omega)>0$. Hence, $\dot{z}(t,\omega) = -A^{-1}(z)<0$ and the map $T(z)$ defined by $z(T(z),\omega)=z$ is well defined with $T'(z) = -A(z)$. Hence

$$T(\delta) = \int_{\delta}^{z_0} A(z)dz \geq \int_{\delta}^{z_0} (\lambda+\beta)^{-1}z^{-1}dz.$$

Hence

$$\lim_{\delta\to 0} T(\delta)=\infty.$$

It remains to be shown that (p,F_t) is a Martingale.

As observed above, $E(e^{-\beta(t+\tau)}p(t+\tau,\omega)|F_t) = E(e^{-\beta(t+\tau)}p(t+\tau,\omega)|z(t,\omega),s_t(\omega))$ $= E(e^{-\beta(t+\tau)}p(t+\tau,\omega)|p(t,\omega),s_t(\omega))$ since for given $s_t(\omega)$, $p(z,\omega)$ is invertible by theorem 2.2.

Using the fact that $1-\delta>z(t',\omega)>\delta$ for $t\leq t'\leq t+\tau$, (2.7) and (2.8), and the fact that $A(z)$, $B(z)$ and $\dot{z}(z,i)$ are C^1 on z for fixed i, we have that for each t', τ', $t'+\tau'\leq t+\tau, t\geq t'$,

$$E(e^{-\beta(t'+\tau')}p(t'+\tau',\omega)|z(t',\omega),s_{t'}(\omega)) = o_{t'}(\tau',\omega)+e^{-\beta t'}p(t',\omega)$$

where

$$\lim_{\tau'\to 0} \frac{|o_{t'}(\tau',\omega)|}{\tau'} = 0$$

uniformly on ω and t'. In particular, for any $\epsilon>0$, $|o_{t'}(\tau',\omega)|<\tau'\epsilon$, if τ' is chosen small enough. It follows from the law of iterated expectations that

$$|E(e^{-\beta(t+\tau)}p(t+\tau)|F_t)-e^{-\beta t}p(t,\omega)|\leq\epsilon \quad \text{for each} \quad \epsilon>0 \quad \text{i.e., (ii).}$$

B. **Characteristics of Equilibrium**

By solving the system (2.7)-(2.10) above we obtain a complete description of an equilibrium of the economic model. From $B(z)$ one obtains $q(z,s)$, $s=1,2$ and from $h(z,2) = -c^1(z,2)/q(z,2)$ we can solve for $c^1(z,2)$. It is also obvious that $c^1(z,1)=1$. Thus "output" in this economy is fully characterized.

It is also a consequence of theorem 1 that $d/dz\ c^1(z,2)\geq 0$ and $d/dz\ q(z,2)\geq 0$. Thus while say $s_t(\omega)=1$, aggregate output will decline as type 1 individuals accumulate assets. When the "state" s changes type 2 agents which become productive will be, on average, poor. Thus, by symmetry, output goes up and as type 2 individuals accumulate assets it will fall continuously.

It should be emphasized that the fluctuations being generated here are a result of the absence of the contingent claims markets that appear in the model in part 1. If agents could at time zero contract with each other for trades contingent on the state s the fluctuations would disappear. It is the presence of borrowing constraints that make agents consumption to depend both on their holdings of "money" and the state of nature. Also note that in contrast to the model of section 1 the average product of labor is constant (equals one) throughout the cycle.

The single asset in our model "money" yields no dividends but commands a positive price which again contrasts with the "complete markets" model. In fact, we have for each individual type from the definition of $p(t,\omega)$ and the Martingale Property,

$$(2.11) \qquad u'(c^i(t,\omega))q(t,\omega)=E\{e^{-\beta T}u'(c^i(t+\tau,\omega))q(t+\tau,\omega)|F_t\}$$

Now notice that the transversality condition at infinity holds here as in the complete market models since

$$(2.12) \qquad \lim_{t\to\infty} E\{e^{-\beta t}u'(c^1(t,\omega))q(t,\omega)\} \le \lim_{t\to\infty} e^{-\beta t}\beta^{-1} = 0$$

(and similarly for an agent of type 2).

But notice that the transversality condition just says that the expected value of an individual's wealth at t as of time zero must go to zero as t goes to infinity. It is exactly the possibility that $z^1(t,\omega)$ approaches zero that allows the r.h.s. of (2.11) to stay positive.

FOOTNOTES

[1]Cf. Scheinkman [1984] and Woodford [1984] for references to many examples.

[2]Formally, we would set $M = \bigcup_{i=1}^{\infty} (S^t x(1,2))$
If $\mathcal{M}$ denotes the set of all subsets of M we can define a measure of μ in a natural way by considering the probabilities ν_t. Given an assumption on f it is natural to identify consumption bundles with $h \in \mathcal{L}_\infty(M, \mathcal{M}, \mu)$, i.e., the set of all (essentially) bounded real valued functions in M. A price system is then a $p \in (\mathcal{L}_1(M, \mathcal{M}, \mu))_+$ i.e., a non-negative valued function in M such that $\int |p(m)| d\mu < \infty$. An equilibrium would then be a p^* such that when firms maximize profits and consumers maximize utility subject to their budget constraint supply in all contingent markets equals demand.

[3]See footnote above for a more precise statement.

[4]Equations as (1.9) are tested and preferences parameters estimated by postulating a constant relative risk aversion utility function, separable on consumption, and either (i) choosing an asset (really a combination of assets) and regressing its prices on measures of aggregate consumption or (ii) choosing a pair of assets and writing (1.9) for each and looking at differences in the rates of return.

A series of studies using aggregate data to test formulas like (1.9) and to estimate preference parameters has appeared (cf., Grossman and Shiller [1981], Hall [1981], or Hansen and Singleton [1982, 1983]). The results are at best mixed. The model is sometimes definitely rejected and the estimates of risk-aversion parameters are implausibly high and with large standard errors.

[5]On this see Kreps [1981]. There are in fact some "sumability" restrictions. More precisely, given $p(\theta^t)$ and $w_t(\theta^t)$, let $r(\theta^0, 1) = 1$ and define $r(\theta^t, \theta_{t+1}, 1) = p(\theta^t, \theta_{t+1}) \cdot r(\theta^t, 1)$ $t = 0, 1, \ldots, \theta_{t+1} \in S$ and $r(\theta^t, 2) = r(\theta^t, 1) \cdot w_t(\theta^t)$. Then one needs $\int |r(m)| d\mu < \infty$ (cf. footnote 1 above).

REFERENCES

Arrow, Kenneth. "Le rôle des valeurs boursière pour la répartition la meilleure des risques," *Econométrie*, C.N.R.S. Paris, 1953 pp. 41-47; discussion pp. 47-48, translated in *Review of Economic Studies* 31 (1964): 91-96.

Brock, William. "Asset Prices in a Production Economy," in *The Economics of Information and Uncertainty*, ed. J.J. McCall, Chicago: University of Chicago Press, 1982.

Brock, William and L.J. Mirman. "Optimal Economic Growth and Uncertainty: The Discounted Case," *Journal of Economic Theory* 4 (1972): 479-513.

Debreu, Gerard. *The Theory of Value*, New York: Wiley, 1959.

Grossman, S. and R. Shiller. "The Determinants of the Variability of Stock Market Prices," *American Economic Review* 71 (1981): 222-276.

Hall, R.E. "Intertemporal Substitution in Consumption," NBER Working Paper No. 720, 1981.

Hansen, Lars and Kenneth Singleton. "Generalized Instrumental Variables Estimation of Nonlinear Rational Expectations Models," *Econometrica* 50 (1982): 1269-1286.

________________________. "Stochastic Consumption, Risk Aversion, and the Temporal Behavior of Asset Returns," *Journal of Political Economy* 91 (1983): 249-265.

Kreps, David. "Arbitrage and Equilibrium in Economies with Infinitely Many Commodities," *Journal of Mathematical Economics* 8 (1981): 15-35.

Kydland, Finn and Edward Prescott. "Time to Build and Aggregate Fluctuations," *Econometrica* 50 (1982): 1345-70.

Lucas, Robert E. Jr. "Asset Prices in an Exchange Economy," *Econometrica* 46 (1978): 1429-1445.

______________. *Models of Business Cycles*, Oxford, England: Basil Blackwell Ltd., 1987.

Scheinkman, Jose. "Notes on Asset Pricing," manuscript, University of Chicago, 1977.

________________. "General Equilibrium Models of Economic Fluctuations: A Survey of Theory," manuscript, University of Chicago, 1984.

Scheinkman, Jose and Laurence Weiss. "Borrowing Constraints and Aggregate Economic Activity," Econometrica 54(1), January 1986: 23-45.

Woodford, Michael. "Indeterminancy of Equilibrium in the Overlapping Generations Model: A Survey," manuscript, Columbia University, 1984.

TOPICS IN NONCOOPERATIVE GAME THEORY

by

Shmuel Zamir

Hebrew University of Jerusalem, Israel

Table of Contents

Chapter 1

MINMAX AND EQUILIBRIA

The first and simplest game theoretical model we shall discuss is meant to describe the following interactive decision situation: Two decision makers, called player I and player II have to choose an action each. Player I chooses an element x of a set X while player II chooses an element y of a set Y. The choices are done simultaneously and the chosen x and y determine a certain money (or utility) transfer between the players. This motivates the following.

Definition 1.1 A *two-person zero-sum game* is an ordered triple (X, Y, h) where X and Y are sets and h is a real-valued function defined on the product set $X \times Y$.

Remarks: 1) The sets X and Y will be referred to as the *strategy sets* of player I and II, respectively. The function h is called the *pay-off function.* For $x \in X$ and $y \in Y$, $h(x, y)$ is interpreted as the amount of money that player II pays player I if I chooses x and II chooses y. In view of this interpretation player I will also be called the *maximizer* and player II the *minimizer.*

2) Two aspects of the interpretation should be emphasized for future reference: (i) The strategy choices are done *simultaneously* and *independently*, e.g. each player hands his choice to a referee who then announces (x, y) and executes the pay-off. (ii) The data of the game, namely (X, Y, h) are 'publicly' known to both players, what we shall later call a *common knowledge.*

Throughout this lecture, unless we specify otherwise, we shall say for convenience 'a game' instead of 'a two-person zero-sum game'.

Example 1.2 The special case in which X and Y are finite will be called a *finite game* or a *matrix game.* In this case, the function h is described as a *pay-off matrix* A whose rows names are labelled by the elements of X (usually denoted as $M = \{1,\dots,m\}$) and the columns by the elements of Y (denoted as $N = \{1,\dots,n\}$). Examples of matrix games are:

(i)

i \ j	1	2	3	4
1	-2	2	-1	4
2	1	6	1	2
3	9	-8	-3	-1

(ii)

i \ j	1	2
1	1	-1
2	-1	1

Definition 1.3 The *upper value* of the game $G = (X, Y, h)$ is $\bar{v} \in [-\infty, \infty]$ defined by: $\bar{v} = \inf_{y \in Y} \sup_{x \in X} h(x, y)$. The *lower value* is $\underline{v} = \sup_{x \in X} \inf_{y \in Y} h(x, y)$.

It readily follows that for any game G :

$$\underline{v} = \sup_{x\in X} \inf_{y\in Y} h(x, y) \leq \inf_{y\in Y} \sup_{x\in X} h(x, y) = \bar{v} \quad . \tag{1.1}$$

Strategies $x^* \in X$ and $y^* \in Y$ for which $\underline{v} = \inf_{y\in Y} h(x^*, y)$ and $\bar{v} = \sup_{x\in X} h(x, y^*)$ are called *minmax strategies* of the respective players. That is, if player I has a minmax strategy then the sup may be replaced by max (similarly for player II). In example (i): $\underline{v} = \max_i \min_j a_{ij} = 1$ (a minmax strategy $i = 2$)

$$\bar{v} = \min_j \max_i a_{ij} = 1 \quad \text{(a minmax strategy } j = 3) .$$

In example (ii): $\underline{v} = -1$ (both $i = 1$ and $i = 2$ are minmax strategies);
$\bar{v} = 1$ (both $j = 1$ and $j = 2$ are minmax strategies).

Definition 1.3 A game $G = (X, Y, h)$ is said to have a *value* (or a *minmax value*) if both players have minmax strategies and:

$$\sup_{x\in X} \inf_{y\in Y} h(x, y) = \inf_{y\in Y} \sup_{x\in X} h(x, y) = v \quad . \tag{1.2}$$

v is called the value of the game and the minmax strategies are then also called *optimal strategies*. So the game (i) has a value $v = 1$ with $i = 2$; $j = 3$ as optimal strategies while game (ii) does not have a value.

Definition 1.4 A pair of strategies $(x_0, y_0) \in X \times Y$ is called a *saddle-point* of the game $G = (X, Y, h)$ if

$$h(x, y_0) \leq h(x_0, y_0) \leq h(x_0, y) \quad \forall \quad (x, y) \in X \times Y \quad .$$

In game (i): (2,3) is a saddle-point with a corresponding pay-off $h(2, 3) = 1$ (which is the value of the game).

In game (ii): There is no saddle-point.

The relation between the notions of the minmax value and the saddle-point is formulated in the following lemma whose proof is rather simple and will be omitted.

Lemma 1.5 A game $G = (X, Y, h)$ has a value if and only if it has a saddle-point. In such a case:

(i) The value of the game is the pay-off corresponding to the saddle-point.

(ii) Any pair of optimal strategies is a saddle-point and any saddle-point consists of a pair of optimal strategies.

In view of non-existence of the value for matrix games such as game (ii), it is self-suggested that a player can sometimes do better by choosing his strategy randomly. For instance, if in (ii) plyaer I chooses his two strategies each with probability ½ his expected pay-off will be 0 independently of what player II does (compared to his security level $\underline{v} = -1$). This motivates the following definition:

Definition 1.6 The *mixed extension* of a matrix game $G_0 = (M, N, A)$ is the game $G = (X, Y, H)$ where

$$X = \{x \in R^m | x_i \geq 0, \ \forall \ i \in M \ ; \ \sum_{i \in M} x_i = 1\}$$

$$Y = \{y \in R^n | y_j \geq 0 \ , \ \forall \ j \in N \ ; \ \sum_{j \in N} y_j = 1\}$$

$H(x, y) = xA\tilde{y}$ (x and y are rows, $\tilde{y}$ is the transposition of y).

In other words, the strategy sets in G are the $(m - 1)$ and $(n - 1)$ dimensional simplices of probability distributions on M and N, respectively. The pay-off function H is just the expectation of the random pay-off a_{ij}. The extreme points of X (or Y) can be identified with the strategy set M (or N) in G_0. They are therefore termed *pure strategies* compared to *mixed strategies*, which is the name for general elements of X and Y.

Example. The mixed extension of the matrix game (ii) is $G = (X; Y \ H)$ where:

$$X = \{x = (x, 1 - x) | 0 \leq x \leq 1\} \ ; \qquad Y = \{y = (y, 1 - y) | 0 \leq y \leq 1\}$$

$$H(x, y) = xA\tilde{y} = 4xy - 2x - 2y + 1 \quad .$$

Unlike the original game this game has a value 0 and optimal strategies which are $(\frac{1}{2}, \frac{1}{2})$ for both players.

Theorem 1.7 (The Minmax Theorem, J. Von-Neumann, 1928). *The mixed extension of a (finite) matrix game has a value.*

Proof. Let $A = (a_{ij})$ be an $m \times n$ matrix game in which the (pure) strategy sets are $M = \{1,\ldots,m\}$, $N = \{1,\ldots,n\}$. In view of Lemma 1.5 it is enough to prove the existence of a saddle-point for the mixed extension, i.e. the existence of $x^* \in X$ and $y^* \in Y$ s.t. $\forall \ x \in X$ and $\forall \ y \in Y$:

$$H(i, y^*) \leq H(x^*, y^*) \leq H(x^*, j) \tag{1.3}$$

Here i and j stand for e^i - the i-th unit vector in X - and e^j the j-th unit vector in Y - respectively, i.e. $\forall \ x \in X \quad \forall \ y \in Y$:

$$H(i, y) = e^i A\tilde{y} = \sum_{j \in N} a_{ij} y_j$$

$$H(x, j) = xA\tilde{e}^j = \sum_{i \in M} a_{ij} x_i \quad .$$

Consider now the product space $S = X \times Y$ and define $f: S \to R^{m+n}$ as follows: For $s = (x, y) \in S$, $f(s) = (f_1(s),\ldots,f_m(s); \ f^1(s),\ldots,f^n(s))$ where:

$$f_i(s) = \max(H(i, y) - H(x, y), 0) \; ; \quad \forall \; i \in M$$

$$f^j(s) = \max(H(x, y) - H(x, j), 0) \; ; \quad \forall \; j \in N \tag{1.4}$$

Define a mapping $F: S \to S$ by: For $s = (x, y) \in S$,

$$F(s) = (F_1(s),\ldots,F_m(s); \; F^1(s),\ldots,F^n(s)) \quad \text{where}$$

$$F_i(s) = \frac{x_i + f_i(s)}{1 + \sum_{\ell \in M} f_\ell(s)} \quad , \; \forall \quad i \in M$$

$$F^j(s) = \frac{y_j + f^j(s)}{1 + \sum_{\ell \in N} f^\ell(s)} \quad , \; \forall \quad j \in N \tag{1.5}$$

S is a convex compact set (in R^{m+n}). H and f are continuous functions and therefore F is continuous. It follows by Brouwer's fixed point theorem that there exists $s^* = (x^*, y^*) \in S$ s.t. $F(s^*) = s^*$. By (1.5) this implies

$$f_i(s^*) = x_i^* \sum_{\ell \in M} f_\ell(s^*) \; ; \quad \forall \; i \in M$$

$$f^j(s^*) = y_j^* \sum_{\ell \in N} f^\ell(s^*) \; ; \quad \forall \; j \in M \tag{1.6}$$

Claim. There exists $i \in M$ s.t. $x_i^* > 0$ and $f_i(s^*) = 0$.

Assume this is not true. Using the definition of f we would have that

$x_i^* > 0$ implies $f_i(s^*) > 0$ i.e. $H(i, y^*) > H(x^*, y^*)$. Thus:

$$\sum_{\{i | x_i^* > 0\}} x_i^* H(i, y^*) > \sum_{\{i | x_i^* > 0\}} x_i^* H(x^*, y^*) \quad ,$$

which implies $\sum_{i \in M} x_i^* H(i, y^*) > H(x^*, y^*) \sum_{i \in M} x_i^*$, a contradiction since both sides equal $H(x^*, y^*)$. It follows from this claim that $\sum_{\ell \in M} f_\ell(s^*) = 0$ and since $f_\ell(s^*) \geq 0$ (by definition of f) it follows from (1.4) that $H(i, y^*) \leq H(x^*, y^*)$ $\forall \; i \in M$ which is one part of (1.3). The second part is proved in the same way showing that (x^*, y^*) is an equilibrium point and thus (by lemma 1.5) it is also a pair of optimal strategies and $H(x^*, y^*)$ is the value of the game.

Q.E.D.

Remark. The proof of the Minmax theorem given here is due to John Nash. Of the many other proofs of the theorem, at least two should be mentioned: the one using the duality theorem in linear programming, and the one using a separating hyperplane argument. Actually, the Minmax theorem is equivalent to the duality theorem in linear programming.

Extensions

The Minmax theorem was extended to apply for games far more general than mixed extensions of finite matrix games. Let us mention here two important results. The first result is that of Sion (1958) which proved the theorem for a game (X, Y, h) under rather weak properties imposed on X, Y, and h.

Theorem 1.8 (M. Sion) Let $G = (X, Y, h)$ be a game in which X and Y are convex topological spaces of which one is compact. h is an extended real-valued function defined on $X \times Y$ and satisfying the following condition: For every real c, the sets $\{y \mid h(x_0, y) \leq c\}$ and $\{x \mid h(x, y_0) \geq c\}$ are closed and convex for every $(x_0, y_0) \in X \times Y$. Then

$$\sup_{x \in X} \inf_{y \in Y} h(x, y) = \inf_{y \in Y} \sup_{x \in X} h(x, y) \quad .$$

If X (respectively, Y) is compact then sup (respectively, inf) may be replaced by max (respectively, min).

The second result to be mentioned is in the direction of extending the range of the pay-off function h: assuming that h is not necessarily a real-valued function but rather has values in some ordered field F. That is, a commutative field with a subset P of positive elements which is closed under addition and multiplication and for any $x \in F$ either $x \in P$ or $x = 0$ or $-x \in P$. The order in F is then defined in the natural way: $a > b$ iff $a - b \in P$, etc.

Theorem 1.9 Let $A = (a_{ij})$ be an $m \times n$ matrix with elements a_{ij} in an ordered field F. Then there exists a unique element v of F and there exist $x_1,\ldots,x_m$ and $y_1,\ldots,y_n$ in F s.t. $x_i \geq 0 \;\; \forall \; i \in M$, $y_j \geq 0 \;\; \forall \; j \in N$;

$$\sum_{i \in M} x_i = \sum_{j \in M} y_j = 1 \text{ and}$$

$$\sum_{j \in N} y_j a_{ij} \leq v \quad \forall \; i \in M \;, \qquad \sum_{i \in M} x_i a_{ij} \geq v \quad \forall \; j \in N \;.$$

The proof follows from the fact that a solution of an L.P. problem e.g. by the simplex method can be carried out in any ordered field. For real closed F the result follows from the standard minmax theorem using Tarski's principle.

Non-zero Sum Games

We end our first chapter by mentioning briefly a possible extension of our model of two-person zero-sum games to more players and to pay-offs not necessarily adding up to 0.

Definition 1.10 A *non-cooperative n-person game* in *strategic form* is an ordered

2n-tuple: $G = (X_1,\dots,X_n;\ h_1,\dots,h_n)$ where $X_1,\dots,X_n$ are sets and for each i, $1 \le i \le n$, h_i is a real-valued function defined on $X = X_1 \times \dots \times X_n$.

Interpretation. $N = \{1,\dots,n\}$ is the set of players, for each $i \in N$, X_i is the strategy set of player i and h_i is his pay-off function.

Remark. Our model of two-person zero-sum game (X, Y, h) is the special case in which $N = \{1, 2\}$; $X_1 = X$; $X_2 = Y$; $h_1 = h$; $h_2 = -h$.

Now two concepts were used in the two-person 0-sum case: the solution of *minmax* and that of *equilibrium*. Each of these concepts lends itself to a natural extension to the more general case. To do that let us introduce some notations. Given a game $(X_1,\dots,X_n,\ h_1,\dots,h_n)$ we let $X = \underset{i\in N}{\times} X_i$ and $\forall\ i \in N$, $X_{-i} = \underset{j\ne i}{\times} X_j$. Each $x_i \in X_i$ and $x_{-i} \in X_{-i}$ determines an element of X which is denoted by (x_i, x_{-i}) . For $x \in X$ and $\hat{x}_i \in X_i$ we denote by $(x|\hat{x}_i)$ the element of X obtained from x by replacing the i-th coordinate x_i by $\hat{x}_i$.

Definition 1.11 The *Minmax value* of player i in the game $G = (X_1,\dots,X_n,\ h_1,\dots,h_n)$ is denoted by v_i and defined by

$v_i = \sup_{x_i\in X_i} \inf_{x_{-i}\in X_{-i}} h_i(x_i, x_{-i})$. A strategy $\bar{x}_i$ which satisfies

$v_i = \inf_{x_{-i}\in X_{-i}} h_i(\bar{x}_i, x_{-i})$ is called a *minmax strategy* of player i . (Thus, if player i has a minmax strategy, the sup may be replaced by max.).

Definition 1.12 A strategy n-tuple $x^* \in X$ is called a Nash Equilibrium Point (N.E.P.) if for each $i \in N$:

$$h_i(x^*|x_i) \le h_i(x^*) \quad \forall\ x_i \in X_i \quad .$$

As the name suggests, the concept of Equilibrium was introduced by John Nash in 1950 who proved its existence for mixed extensions of finite (strategy sets) games. The proof is almost identical to the one we gave here for the two-person 0-sum case. Here again the result was generalized by considerably weakening of the conditions on the strategy sets and the pay-off functions (see, for instance Glicksberg, 1952).

It should be emphasized, however, that Lemma 1.5 is no longer true for the general case. Even if there are only two players, then generally the case is that a pair of *minmax strategies is not an E.P.* and vice versa: *a strategy in an E.P. is not a minmax strategy.* An easy example which demonstrates this diversion of the two concepts is the following two-person non-zero sum game:

$$\begin{pmatrix} 2,\ 2 & 4,\ 1 \\ 4,\ 1 & -2,\ 2 \end{pmatrix} \quad .$$

That is, each player has two strategies and the pay-off functions are given by the 2×2 matrix whose entries are ordered pairs (a_{ij}, b_{ij}) where a_{ij} is the pay-off for player I and b_{ij} for player II.

The following observations are easily verified.

(1) The minmax values are:

for player I, $v_1 = 2\frac{1}{2}$ with minmax strategy $(\frac{3}{4}, \frac{1}{4})$

for player II, $v_2 = \frac{3}{2}$ with minmax strategy $(\frac{1}{2}, \frac{1}{2})$.

(2) The unique N.E.P. is $(\frac{1}{2}, \frac{1}{2})$ for player I and $(\frac{3}{4}, \frac{1}{4})$ for player II corresponding to the pay-offs $(\frac{5}{2}, \frac{3}{2})$., So, although the equilibrium pay-offs are equal to the minmax payoffs, the equilibrium strategies are not minmax strategies, and vice versa. In other words, by playing $(\frac{1}{2}, \frac{1}{2})$ in equilibrium, player I *does not guarantee* $\frac{5}{2}$ which he can guarantee by playing $(\frac{3}{4}, \frac{1}{4})$. However, if both players will play minmax to guarantee the pay-offs $(\frac{5}{2}, \frac{3}{2})$, this will not be in equilibrium, each of them can improve his pay-off by a unilateral deviation.

Remark 1.13 It should be noted that there is no analogue of Theorem 1.9 for the N.E.P. in the non-zero sum case. In other words, a finite game with pay-offs in a certain ordered field may not have a N.E.P. in that field. To see that, consider a three-person game in which player I chooses one of two rows, player II chooses one of two columns and player III chooses one of two pay-off matrices:

$$A = \begin{pmatrix} 0,\ 3,\ 1 & 1,\ 0,\ 0 \\ 1,\ 0,\ 0 & 0,\ 1,\ 1 \end{pmatrix} \quad \text{or} \quad B = \begin{pmatrix} 2,\ 0,\ 5 & 0,\ 2,\ 0 \\ 0,-1,\ 0 & 1,\ 0,\ 0 \end{pmatrix} .$$

It can be shown that this game has a *unique* N.E.P. in which players I, II and II use the mixed strategies $(x, 1 - x)$; $(y, 1 - y)$ and $(z, 1 - z)$, respectively, where

$$x = \frac{9 + \sqrt{24}}{19} ; \qquad y = \frac{7 - \sqrt{24}}{25} ; \qquad z = \frac{12 - \sqrt{24}}{15} .$$

Hence, the game does not have a N.E.P. within the ordered field of rational numbers.

Glicksberg, I. (1952). A further generalization of the Kakutani fixed point theorem with application to Nash Equilibrium points. Proc. Amer. Math. Society, 38, 170-174.

Nash, J.F. (1950). Equilibrium points in n-person games. Proc. National Academy of Sciences, USA, 36, 48-49.

Von-Neumann, J. (1928). Zur theorie der gesellschaftesspiele. Mathematische Annalen, 100, 295-320.

Von-Neumann, J. and O. Morgenstern (1944, 1947). Theory of Games and Economic Behaviour. Princeton University Press: Princeton.

Weyl, H. (1950). Elementary proof of a minmax theorem due to Von-Neumann. Contributions to the theory of games I. Ann. Mathe. Studies, no. 24, 19-25, Princeton University Press: Princeton.

Chapter 2

GAMES IN EXTENSIVE FORM

So far we know only one way to describe a game, namely the *strategic form.* Let us try to describe the game of chess in this way. That is, we look for an ordered 4-tuple $(S_I, S_{II}, h_I, h_{II})$, where by convention I and II are the white and black players, respectively. S_I, S_{II} are their respective strategy sets and h_I, h_{II} are the pay-off functions. This game has only three outcomes: W (white wins), B (black wins, and D (draw). It is natural to have pay-offs 1 for I and -1 for II when the outcome is W ; -1 for I and 1 for II when the outcome is B; and 0 for both players when the outcome is D . This makes chess a zero-sum game. But, *what are the strategy sets?* A strategy in chess (for I or II) is a *complete instruction book* for the player which instructs him in choosing his move in any possible situation in the game, where by 'situation' we mean here a complete *history* of the play which led to that decision point.

One readily observes that:

1. The rules of chess allow only a *finite* number of moves (though very large) for each player, thus:
2. Both S_I and S_{II} are *finite but astronomically large.* Therefore:
3. By the minmax theorem we can conclude that the game of chess has a value and each player has an optimal *mixed* strategy which guarantees this value.

This description of chess looks quite artificial and not very appealing. Our strategic form model for chess suppressed its dynamic structure and condensed all decision-making into one stage. The strategies are extremely complex objects and non-manageable in any practical sense: even more so are the mixed strategies.

Is there a more appealing way to describe the game of chess? Yes, there is the natural way of describing the evolution of the play using the notions of graph theory:

I makes a move

II makes a move

I makes a move

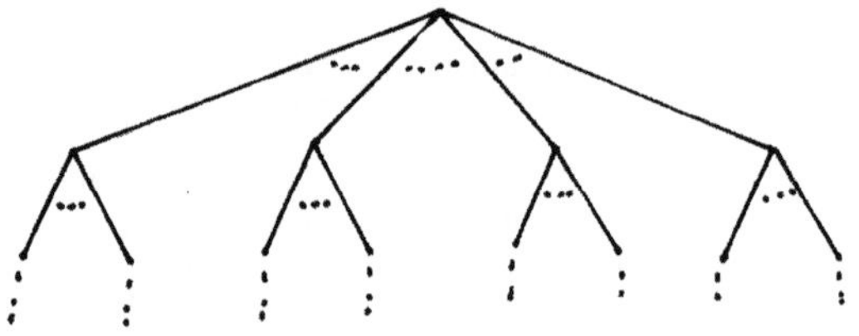

and so on until terminal points denoted by W , B or D are reached.

Such a description of a game is called an extensive form game. In its simplest version it is defined formally as follows:

<u>Definition 2.1</u> A finite two-person zero-sum game in *extensive form* is an

ordered collection $\Gamma = (X, X_I, X_{II}, X_T, x_0, f, h)$ where:

1) X is a finite set (the set of positions);

2) The sets X_I (decision positions of I), X_{II} (decision positions of II), and X_T (terminal positions) form a partition of X into disjoint sets.

3) x_0 (the initial position) is a point in $X_I \cup X_{II}$.

4) f (the immediate predecessor mapping) is a mapping from $X - \{x_0\}$ onto $X - X_T$ s.t. for any $x \in X$ there is an integer $n \geq 0$ satisfying $f^n(x) = x_0$.

5) h (pay-off function for player I) is a real-valued function defined on X_T.

An extensive form game is also called a *game tree.*

Remark. At a later stage, as we generalize our model, we shall refer to the games defined in Definition 2.1 as *extensive games with perfect information.* For the moment, since these are the only extensive games we have, we prefer to use a simple name.

A (pure) *strategy* of player I in Γ is a complete decision rule for him, i.e. a mapping s which maps each $x \in X_I$ to an alternative available for him at x, i.e. an element of the set $A(x) = \{y \in X \mid f(y) = x\}$. Denote by S_I the set of all pure strategies of I. S_{II} is derived similarly.

A *play* (or a *path*) in the game Γ is a finite sequence $p = (x_0, \ldots, x_n)$ of points in X s.t. $f(x_k) = x_{k-1}$ $\forall$ $k \geq 1$, and $x_n \in X_T$.

It is easily seen that a pair of strategies $s \in S_I$ and $t \in S_{II}$ determine uniquely a play $P(s, t) = (x_0, \ldots, x_n)$ and thus a pay-off $H(s, t) = h(x_n)$.

As long as we are interested merely in the strategies used by the players and the resulting pay-offs, any game in extensive form Γ is equivalent to the game in strategic form $\tilde{\Gamma} = (S_I, S_{II}, H)$ with the above-derived S_I, S_{II} and H. However it is important to notice the following.

1) Different extensive form games may have the same equivalent strategic form.

2) Not any finite strategic form game is obtainable from some extensive form game. For example, the matrix game $\begin{pmatrix} 1 & 0 \\ 0 & 1 \end{pmatrix}$ is not equivalent to any extensive form game as defined in Definition 2.1.

The most important feature of this structure is:

Definition 2.2 Given a game $\Gamma = (X, X_I, X_{II}, X_T, x_0, f, h)$ and any $x \in X - X_T$, the *subgame starting at* x is the game $\Gamma_x = (\tilde{X}, \tilde{X}_I, \tilde{X}_{II}, \tilde{X}_T, \tilde{f}, \tilde{h})$ where:

1) $\tilde{X} = \{y \in X \mid \text{there is } n \geq 0 \text{ s.t. } f^n(y) = x\}$.

2) $\tilde{X}_I = \tilde{X} \cap X_I$; $\tilde{X}_{II} = \tilde{X} \cap X_{II}$; $\tilde{X}_T = \tilde{X} \cap X_T$.

3) $\tilde{x}_0 = x$; $\tilde{f}$ is the restriction of f to $\tilde{X} - \{x\}$ and $\tilde{h}$ is the restriction of h to $\tilde{X}_T$.

This special structure of the game tree lends itself to a *dynamic programming* approach to determine the value of and the optimal strategies of the game by *forward or backward* induction, using the finiteness of the tree. The first result of this approach is:

Thereom 2.3 (Zermelo) Any finite zero-sum two-person game in extensive form has a value and each player has a (pure) optimal strategy.

This can be considered as the first important result in game theory, proved by Zermelo in 1912 for chess. The proof, which is a standard induction argument (on the maximal length of the game), is valid for any game given by Definition 2.1.

Note that in addition to the more appropriate description by a game tree we have here a result stronger than the one provided by the minmax theorem, namely the existence of *pure optimal* strategies. In other words, given an extensive form game, its reduction to a strategic form *itself* (rather than its mixed extension) has a minmax value.

n-person Non-zero Sum Games

Definition 2.1 has a straightforward extension to n-person non-zero sum games in extensive form. Any such game has a reduction to an equivalent strategic form game. The induction proof of Zermelo's theorem can be repeated to yield:

Theorem 2.4 Any finite n-person game in extensive form has a Nash equilibrium point (in pure strategies).

Two properties of the extensive games discussed so far were very crucial for the proof of Theorem 2.4, namely:

1. The game tree is finite.
2. The collection of positions succeeding a certain position x is a *subgame* (Definition 2.2).

In the rest of this lecture we discuss the generalizations of the model obtained by abandoning these properties.

Infinite Extensive Form Games

Infinite games in extensive form were discussed first by Gale and Stewart who considered zero-sum two person games similar to those of Definition 2.1 but with infinite length. To simplify the model, let us consider a very simple pay-off function which attains the values 1 (I wins) or -1 (II wins) only. One then obtains what is called a *win-lose* game defined as follows.

Definition 2.5 A win-lose game Γ is an ordered collection $(X, X_I, X_{II}, x_0, f, S, S_I, S_{II})$ where:

1) X is an infinite set (the set of positions);
2) X_I, X_{II} is a partition of X.

3) $x_0 \in X$.

4) f maps $X - \{x_0\}$ onto X s.t. for any $x \in X$ there is an integer $n \geq 0$ satisfying $f^n(x) = x_0$.

5) S is the set of infinite sequences $s = (s_0, s_1, \ldots)$ of elements of X satisfying $s_0 = x_0$ and $s_i = f(s_{i+1})$ for all $i \geq 0$. An element of S is called a *play*.

6) S_I (winning set for I) and S_{II} (winning set for II) form a partition of S .

Example 2.6 The two players alternate in choosing 0 or 1 . A play can then be identified with a point in $S = [0, 1]$ (i.e. the binary expansion of ..). S_I and S_{II} are two disjoint subsets s.t. $S_I \cup S_{II} = [0, 1]$.

The notion of a (pure) strategy is exactly as in the finite case, namely: A strategy of player I (respectively, II) is a function σ (respectively, τ) with domain X_I (respectively, X_{II}) satisfying $\sigma(x) \in f^{-1}(x)$ (respectively, $\tau(x) \in f^{-1}(x)$). We denote the players' strategy sets by $\Sigma_I^{(\Gamma)}$ and $\Sigma_{II}^{(\Gamma)}$. Any pair of strategies (σ, τ) , $\sigma \in \Sigma_I^{(\Gamma)}$, $\tau \in \Sigma_{II}^{(\Gamma)}$ determines in an obvious way a play $s \in S$ which we therefore write as (σ, τ) .

A strategy σ of player I is a *winning strategy* if $(\sigma, \tau) \in S_I$ for all $\tau \in \Sigma_{II}(\Gamma)$. A winning strategy for II is defined similarly. To say that the game has a minmax value is equivalent to:

Definition 2.7 A game $\Gamma = (X, X_I, X_{II}, x_0, f, S, S_I, S_{II})$ is *determined* if one of the players has a winning strategy.

An extension of Zermelo's Theorem 2.3 for infinite games would say that any such Γ is determined. However, this turned out to be false.

Theorem 2.8 (Gale and Stewart) There is an infinite game $\Gamma(X, X_I, X_{II}, x_0, f, S, S_I\ S_{II})$ which is not determined.

The proof is by constructing a counterexample of the type of Example 2.6. The construction is based on the observation that, roughly speaking, the strategy sets of the players are "very big" namely $2^{\aleph_0}$. Consequently, given any strategy of one of the players, the other can force $2^{\aleph_0}$ different plays (which is also the cardinality of the set S of all possible plays). This enables construction of two disjoint sets of plays A and B such that: given any strategy of II , player I can force an outcome in A ; and given any strategy of I player II can force an outcome in B .

In view of this negative result, the natural question is: What interesting families of games can be proved to be determined? To put that more formally, let us introduce a topology on S . Actually, there is a natural one, namely the topology in which the basic open sets are those of the form $\{s \mid \rho_n(s) = \rho_n(s_0)\}$ for some $s_0 \in S$ and for some integer $n > 0$, where ρ_n denotes the projection operator on the first n coordinate space. It is a matter of straightforward verification to prove that this is a Housdorff topology for S in which S is totally disconnected.

A game $\Gamma = (X, X_I, X_{II}, x_0, f, S_I, S_{II})$ is said to be open, closed, G_δ etc. according to whether S_I is open, closed, G_δ etc.

Theorem 2.9 (Gale and Stewart) If S_I belongs to the Boolean algebra generated by the open sets then Γ is determined.

An important consequence of this result is that any game with continuous pay-off function h has a minmax value and the players have optimal strategies.

Theorem 2.10 (Wolfe) Any win-lose game is determined if one player's winning set is G_δ .

The problem of determinacy of games in which S_I is any Borel set was a long-standing difficult problem which was finally proved by D. Martin in 1975.

Theorem 2.11 (D. Martin) Any Borel game is determined.

The consequence of this result is that any game with a measurable pay-off function h has a minmax value. However, in contrast to the continuous pay-off case, the players may not be able to guarantee the value but rather only ε-guarantee it for any $\varepsilon > 0$.

Games with Imperfect Information

Let us look now at the second property — the subgame property' used in the proof of Zermelo's theorem (and Martin's theorem). Consider the game of 'matching pennies'. Two players, I and II choose simultaneously H or T . If they both choose the same thing II pays I one dollar, otherwise I pays II one dollar. Can this game be described in extensive form? The obvious candidate for a game tree is:

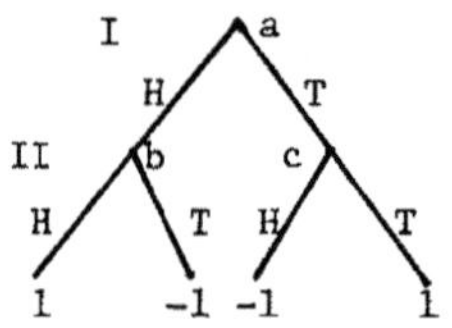

It is readily seen that this is not an appropriate description of the game unless we add more structure to it: player II cannot distinguish between positions b and c . This means in particular that he cannot choose T in b and H in c (as he would certainly like to do). We indicate this by saying that b, c is an *information set* of player II and describe it by:

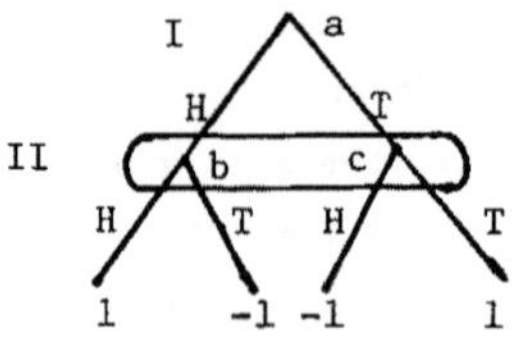

In other words, the right notion of decision point of a player is not a node in the game tree but rather a set of nodes which are indistinguishable for him. One immediately realizes that this game does not have a value. In fact, it is equivalent to the matrix game $\begin{pmatrix} 1 & -1 \\ -1 & 1 \end{pmatrix}$ which has no value (in pure strategies). This shows already that Theorem 2.3 cannot be extended to extensive form finite games with additional structure of information sets. The failure of the inductive proof is quite transparent: the part of the tree succeeding node b (or c) *is not a subgame.*

Unfortunately, the formal definition of this intuitively simple notion is quite complicated. This is so because one has to express the fact that a player cannot distinguish between two nodes in the same information set. This means, for instance, that he must be (from his point of view) in the 'same stage of the game'. Also, we allow chance moves in the game tree. This makes the pay-offs random variables whose expectations are all by convention the utilities of the corresponding players.

Definition 2.12 *Extensive form game* Γ *of* n-*players* consists of the following elements:

(1) A set $N = \{1, 2, \ldots, n\}$ of players;

(2) A finite connected graph G with no cycles called the *game tree.*

(3) A distinguished node of the tree x_0 called *the first move.* A node of degree one, different from x_0, is called a *terminal node.* The set of terminal nodes is denoted by T.

(4) The set X of non-terminal nodes is called the set of *moves* and is partitioned into $n+1$ sets $X^0, X^1, \ldots, X^n$. Elements of X^i are called *moves of player* i, while elements of X^0 are called *chance moves.*

(5) For each node in X^0 there is a probability distribution on the branches out of it with positive probability to each one of them.

(6) For each $i \in N$, there is a partition of X^i into $U_1^i, \ldots, U_{k_i}^i$, called the information sets of player i, such that for each $j \in \{1, \ldots, k_i\}$,

   (i) There is a 1 - 1 correspondence between the sets of outgoing branches of any two nodes in U_j^i.

   (ii) Any path from x_0 to a terminal node (i.e. a *play*) can cross U_j^i at most once.

(7) For each terminal node $t \in T$ attached an n-dimensional real vector $h(t) = (h^1(t), \ldots, h^n(t))$ called the pay-off vector at t.

If all information sets are singletons the game is called *a game with perfect information.* Thus the game in Definition 2.1 is a finite game with perfect information and no-chance moves, while the games of Gale and Stewart are infinite games of this kind.

A *pure strategy* of player i is a k_i-tuple $\sigma^i = (\sigma^i(U_j^i))_{j=1}^{k_i}$ where $\sigma^i(U_j^i)$ is an element of the set of alternatives available to player i in his information set U_j^i.

Denote by S^i the set of pure strategies of player i and let $S = S^1 \times \ldots \times S^n$.

Given an n-tuple of strategies $s = (s^1,\ldots,s^n) \in S$ the *expected pay-off* to player i is defined as

$$H^i(s) = \sum_{t \in T} P_s(t)\, h^i(t)$$

where $P_s(t)$ is the probability that $t \in T$ will be reached when s is played.

Any finite n-person game in normal form can be reduced to a strategic form game $(S^1,\ldots,S^n,\ H^1,\ldots,H^n)$. If the extensive form we started with was a game of perfect information, by Zermelo's proof it will have an N.E.P. in pure strategies. This result is no longer true for imperfect information games as the game of matching pennies already shows. For these games we have, by Nash's result, the existence of N.E.P. for the mixed extension.

Behaviour Strategies

In a game in extensive form, a mixed strategy means a single randomization at the beginning of the game after which a certain pure strategy is followed, i.e., a *deterministic* choice of an alternative at each information set. Another way for a player to randomize his choice is to randomize on his possible alternatives at each information set, and to do these randomizations independently in his various information sets.

Definition 2.13 A *behaviour strategy*, b^i, of player i in an extensive form game Γ is a k_i-tuple $b^i = (b^i(U^i_j))^{k_i}_{j=1}$ where $b^i(U^i_j)$ is a probability distribution over the set of alternatives at the information set U^i_j. Denote by B^i the set of behaviour strategies of player i, and denote by Σ^i his set of mixed strategies (i.e., probability distributions on S^i).

Beside its intuitive appeal for extensive form, the behaviour strategies set is usually much smaller than the mixed strategies set. For instance, consider a game in which a certain player i has three information sets with two alternatives in each. Then $|S^i| = 8$ and therefore Σ^i is seven-dimensional simplex. On the other hand, a behaviour strategy is determined by three probabilities in $[0, 1]$ and thus B^i is a three-dimensional cube.

In what circumstances can we work with B^i instead of Σ^i?

First observe that any $b^i \in B^i$ generates in a natural way a probability distribution on S^i, i.e. a mixed strategy $x^i \in \Sigma^i$. This x^i *leads to the same pay-offs as* b^i regardless of the strategies chosen by the other players. In this sense we may say that x^i is *strategically equivalent* to b^i. Denote this mapping by $\varphi\colon B^i \to \Sigma^i$. If φ is 'onto' (i.e., $\varphi(B^i) = \Sigma^i$) then any $\sigma^i \in \Sigma^i$ could be replaced by a behaviour strategy which is strategically equivalent to it, namely any $b^i \in \varphi^{-1}(\sigma^i)$. However, φ may not be 'onto' as can be seen in the following example.

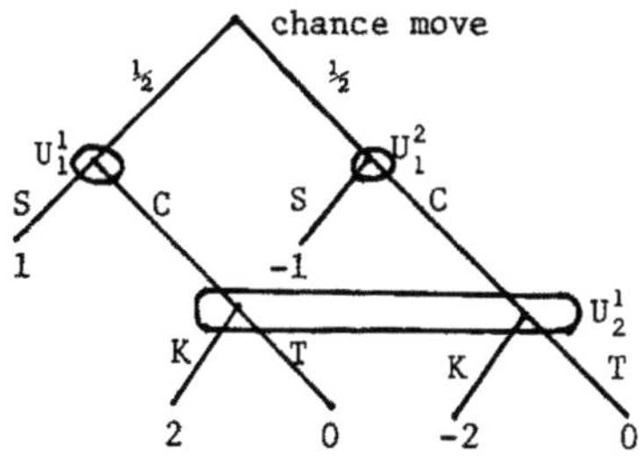

With the obvious notation player I has four pure strategies: $\{(S, K); (S, T); (C, K); (C, T)\}$. It is easily seen that if we consider the mixed strategy $\sigma^i = \frac{1}{2}(S, T) + \frac{1}{2}(C, K)$, (which happened to be the optimal strategy of player I), then there is no $b^i \in B^i$ s.t. $\varphi(b^i) = \sigma^i$. The reason for that is also quite transparent: in σ^i , the choices in the two information sets are highly correlated. This correlation cannot be produced by appropriate choices of the probability distributions comprising the behaviour strategies since player I, when in U_2^1 , *does not remember* his move in U_1^1 .

Definition 2.14 An extensive form game Γ is said to be a *game with perfect recall* if each player at each move remembers what he knew in previous moves and what choices he made at those moves.

Remark: There is no difficulty in writing this formally at the cost of introducing some more notations which we prefer to avoid here.

Theorem 2.15 (Kuhn, 1953) Let Γ be an extensive form game in which player i has perfect recall. Then, for each mixed strategy $\sigma^i \in \Sigma^i$, there is a behaviour strategy $b^i \in B^i$ which is strategically equivalent to σ^i , i.e. for each $j \in N$ and $\sigma \in \Sigma$, $H^j(\sigma) = H^j(\sigma|b^i)$, where $(\sigma|b^i)$ is the n-tuple σ in which σ^i is replaced by b^i .

Corollary 2.16 Any (finite) game Γ in extensive form has a N.E.P. in behaviour strategies.

Aumann (1964) generalized Kuhn's theorem to infinite games with perfect recall, i.e. both the length of the game and the number of alternatives at each move may be infinite.

Aumann, R.J. (1964). Mixed and behaviour strategies in infinite extensive games. Adv. Game Theory, Ann. Mathe. Studies 52, 627-650. Princeton University Press: Princeton.

Gale, D. and F.M. Stewart (1953). Infinite games with perfect information. Contributions to the Theory of Games, Vol. II. Ann. Mathe. Studies 28, 245-266. Princeton University Press: Princeton.

Kuhn, H.W. (1953). Extensive games and the problem of information. Contributions to the Theory of Games Vol. II. Ann. Mathe. Studies. 28, 193-216. Princeton University Press: Princeton.

Martin, D.A. (1975). Borel determinacy. Ann. Mathe. 102, 363-371.

Wolfe, P. (1955). The strict determinateness of certain infinite games. Pacific J. Math. 5, 891-897.

Zermelo, E. (1912). Über eine anwendung der mengenlelre auf die theorie des Schachspiels. Proc. Fifth Int. Cong. Math., Cambridge, Vol. II, 501-504.

Chapter 3

MULTISTAGE GAMES

The Notion of Super-Game

Multiperson decision situations for which we attempt to provide game theoretical models, are very seldom one-time affairs, but rather repeated over and over again. One may therefore gain additional insight about various phenomena by studying not merely the static one-shot games but also some *multi-stage* or a *repeated* game. These models seem to be the correct paradigm for studying phenomena such as communication, retaliation, flow of information, etc.

Consider the following two-person non-zero sum game known as the "Prisoner's Dilemma":

$$\begin{array}{c c} & \begin{array}{cc} G & C \end{array} \\ \begin{array}{c} G \\ C \end{array} & \begin{pmatrix} 1,\ 1 & 5,\ 0 \\ 0,\ 5 & 4,\ 4 \end{pmatrix} \end{array} .$$

The only N.E.P. in this game is (G, G) yielding a pay-off of (1, 1) which is dramatically inferior to (4, 4) from the point of view of both players. This is especially disturbing if the game is *played many times by the same players*, since one would expect some 'silent understanding' between the players and the emergence of the cooperative outcome (4, 4) at least in some of the repetitions. Can we provide a model that predicts this phenomenon?

The first attempt is to consider, say, a 1,000-times repeated prisoner's dilemma played by the same players. One easily sees that the only N.E.P. in this game is again such that each player plays G in all stages independently of what the other player does. So this is not the appropriate model we are trying to find. A moment of reflection reveals the reason. The presence of a last stage which is recognized as such by both players, aside from being unrealistic, creates unnatural end effects which propagate themselves backwards and distort the entire analysis. This suggests that a game "without an end" may be more appropriate. Without bothering much about details, let us show the following.

Proposition 3.1 In the infinitely repeated Prisoner's dilemma there is an N.E.P. with the cooperative pay-offs (4, 4) as an "average" pay-off for the players.

Proof. Consider the following strategy, σ, for a player. Play C in the first stage and keep on playing C as long as the other player continues playing C. As soon as he plays G, play G following that stage on.

Clearly, if both players play σ the pay-off sequence for both of them will be:

$$h^1(\sigma, \sigma) = h^2(\sigma, \sigma) = (4, 4, 4,\ldots) \quad .$$

If a player, say player I, uses $\hat{\sigma} \neq \sigma$, while the other player is using σ he will play G for the first time, say at stage k . His pay-off sequence will be at most (coordinate-wise): $(4,\ldots,4,5,1,1,\ldots)$ with 5 as the k-th coordinate.

By any reasonable definition of 'average pay-off' such as Cesaro limit, Abel limit, or any Banach limit, the value of $(4, 4,\ldots)$ is 4 and that of $(4,\ldots,4,5,1,1,\ldots)$ is 1 . Thus (σ, σ) is in fact a N.E.P. with 'pay-offs' (4, 4).

Q.E.D.

So, what the players could get in the one-shot game, by signing a *binding agreement* to play (C, C) can be *self-enforced* as an N.E.P. in the *super-game* (i.e., the infinitely repeated game). Many other pay-offs can be reached in the one-shot game via binding agreements. For instance, the expected pay-offs (2,2) by signing an agreement to draw a lottery (controlled by the 'authorities') to choose C or G with respective probabilit es $\frac{1}{3}$ and $\frac{2}{3}$. Whatever the outcome is both players are committed to play it. Their expected pay-off is $\frac{1}{3}(4, 4) + \frac{2}{3}(1, 1) = (2, 2)$. Can this also be sustained by an N.E.P. in the super-game? The answer is 'yes' and the N.E. strategies are the following (again, the same for both).

Play repeatedly C, G, G, C, G, G,... so long as the other player is following the same pattern. As soon as the other player deviates from this preseribed pattern, play G from there on. It is clear that when both players follow this strategy each will have the pay-off sequence $(4,1,1,4,1,1,\ldots)$ that is, worth 2 by any reasonable definition. Any unilateral deviation of one of the players will yield him a payoff sequence with at most 1 from one stage on.

The general ideas should be clear by now, and we move quickly towards the general theorem.

Consider an n-person game in strategic form $\Gamma = (S^1,\ldots,S^n,\ h^1,\ldots,h^n)$.

Definition 3.2 A *correlated strategy* of a coalition $T \subset N$ is a probability distribution on $\prod_{i \in T} S^i$.

When correlated strategies are used the set of expected vector-payoffs is the convex hull of the vector payoffs attainable by pure strategies. We denote this set by C and refer to it as the set of *correlated pay-offs*.

Definition 3.3 The individual rationality level of player i is r_i defined by:

$$r_i = \min_{\tau} \max_{\sigma} H^i(\sigma, \tau)$$

where σ ranges over the (mixed) strategies of i and τ ranges over all correlated strategies of $N \setminus \{i\}$.

A pay-off vector $(\alpha_1,\ldots,\alpha_n)$ is said to be *individually rational* if $\alpha_i \geq r_i$

for all $i \in N$.

Remark 3.4 Note that $\min_\tau \max_\sigma H^i(\sigma, \tau) = \max_\sigma \min_\tau H^i(\sigma, \tau)$ but this is so because $N \setminus \{i\}$ are allowed to use correlated strategies. It is not true if τ ranges over mixed strategies of $N \setminus \{i\}$. As an example, consider the three-person game in which I chooses a row, II chooses a column and III chooses the matrix. The pay-offs for III are

$$\begin{pmatrix} -1 & 0 \\ 0 & -3 \end{pmatrix} \begin{pmatrix} -3 & 0 \\ 0 & -1 \end{pmatrix}.$$

If we denote by $(x, 1-x)$, $(y, 1-y)$ and $(z, 1-z)$ the mixed strategies of the three players, respectively, then for player III:

$$\min_{x,y} \max_z H(x,y,z) = \min_{x,y} \max\,(-xy - 3(1-x)(1-y), -3xy - (1-x)(1-y)) = -1$$

while

$$\max_z \min_{x,y} H(x,y,z) \leq \min(-z - 3(1-z), -3z - (1-z)) \leq -2 .$$

Theorem 3.5 (the "folk theorem') The pay-off vectors to Nash equilibrium points in the super-game Γ^* are the individually rational correlated pay-offs $C_R = \{x \in C | x^i \geq r^i \;\; \forall \;\; i \in N\}$.

This theorem has been known for about 20 years but has not been published and its authorship is obscure although it is probably to be credited mainly to Aumann and Shapley. The idea of the proof is the one that can be read in our example: prescribe the right pattern of correlated moves to approach the desired point in C_R . As soon as player i deviates $N \setminus \{i\}$ switch to the *punishment* strategy, i.e., the correlated strategy that keeps his pay-off to r_i .

We shall not go through the formal definitions of the super-game Γ here. Later we shall discuss the point of the definitions of pay-offs, which is an issue of general importance to all infinite stage games.

Stochastic Games

Stochastic games are multistage games in which the game played at each stage changes randomly. The following short review of the subject will be confined to two-person zero-sum stochastic games with finitely many states and finitely many alternatives in each for both players.

The first model and result is due to Shapley (1953). There is a finite set of *states* $S = \{1,\dots,S\}$ and additional state $s = 0$ which is the 'game is over' (by abuse of notation, S denotes both the set and its cardinality as does I, J, etc.). At state $s \in S$ each player has a finite number of possible actions: $i=1,\dots,I_s$ for player 1 and $j=1,\dots,J_s$ for player 2. We may assume w.l.g. that $I_s = I$ and $J_s = J$ for all $s \in S$, and thus associate to each $s \in S$ an $I \times J$ pay-off matrix A^s (from 2 to 1). For $i \in I$, $j \in J$ and $s \in S$ there is a ***transition*** *probabilities* vector $P^s_{ij} = (P^{st}_{ij})_{t=0,1,\dots,s}$.

The stochastic game is played in stages: at each stage the game is in some state $s \in S \cup \{0\}$. If $s \neq 0$, player 1 chooses $i \in I$, player 2 chooses $j \in J$. Then (i, j) is announced, player 2 pays player 1 a^s_{ij}, the referee chooses the new state according to the probability vector P^s_{ij} and informs the players about the new state asking them to play the next stage (unless the new state is 0).

Stochastic games generalize Markov decision processes in that Markov decision processes may be viewed as stochastic games in which one of the players has only one action in each state.

The most crucial element in Shapley's first model was:

Assumption 3.6 $\quad \lambda = \min\limits_{i,j,s} P^{so}_{ij} > 0$.

Due to this assumption, expected total pay-offs are bounded and the existence of value and optimal strategies could be derived from general minmax theorems. However, we shall use an alternative approach used by Shapley and proved to be very fruitful in more general models. This is basically the dynamic programming approach.

Special Case: If $P^{so}_{ij} = \lambda$ for all i,j, and $s \in S$ we have a *λ-discounted* game: we may forget about the state o and normalize the probability vectors on S (i.e. divide by $(1 - \lambda)$). The game then has denumberably many stages and a pay-off stream $x = (x_1, x_2, \dots)$ is *evaluated* by $\sum\limits_{k=1}^{\infty} \lambda^{k-1} x_k$.

For the sake of simplicity of notations, we shall derive Shapley's results for this special case.

A *history* prior to stage n is $[(i_k, j_k, s_k)]_{k=1}^{n-1}$, where i_k, j_k are the actions chosen at stage k and s_k was the state at stage k. Denote by H_n the set of all possible such histories.

Definition 3.7

(i) A *behaviour strategy* of player 1 is a sequence $\sigma = (\sigma_n)_{n=1}^{\infty}$ where $\sigma_n : H_n \times S \to I^*$, and I^* is the simplex of probability distribucions on I.

(ii) If the mappings σ_n are to I (i.e. the extreme points of I^*), then σ is a *pure strategy*.

(iii) If the σ_n's are independent of H_n, then σ is called a *stationary strategy*.

Strategies for player 2 are defined similarly. We denote by Σ_1, Σ_2 the sets of (behaviour) strategies of the two players. Given an *initial state* $s \in S$, any pair of strategies $(\sigma, \tau) \in \Sigma_1 \times \Sigma_2$ determines a probability distribution on pay-off streams. The expected evaluation of these vector streams defines a pay-off function $H_s : \Sigma_1 \times \Sigma_2 \to R$. Denote by $\Gamma_s(\lambda)$ the two-person zero-sum game $(\Sigma_1; \Sigma_2; H_s)$ and let $\Gamma = (\Gamma_1(\lambda),\ldots,\Gamma_S(\lambda))$.

Given the pay-off matrices $A = (A^1,\ldots,A^S)$ and any $x \in R^S$ define $G(x) = (G_1(x),\ldots,G_S(x))$ where $G_s(x)$ is the $I \times J$ matrix defined by:

$$(G_s(x))_{ij} = a^s_{ij} + \sum_{t=1}^{S} p^{st}_{ij} x_t .$$

Denoting by 'val' the value operator, and $\text{val } G = (\text{val } G_1,\ldots,\text{val } G_S)$ we have:

Theorem 3.8 The stochastic games $\Gamma(\lambda) = (\Gamma_1(\lambda),\ldots,\Gamma_S(\lambda))$ have a value $V(\lambda) = (V_1(\lambda),\ldots,V_s(\lambda))$ which is the unique solution of the equation

$$x = \text{val } G((1 - \lambda)x) . \tag{3.1}$$

Proof. Observe first that with respect to the norm $|x| = \max_s |x_s|$ we have for any $x,y \in R^S$:

$$|\text{val } G(x) - \text{val } G(y)| \leq |x - y| .$$

From this it follows that the function of x, $\text{val } G((1 - \lambda)x)$ is a *contraction* and thus has a unique fixed point which is a solution for (3.1).

Next, if we denote by $\Gamma^n(\lambda) = (\Gamma^n_1(\lambda),\ldots,\Gamma^n_S(\lambda))$ the stochastic game with n-stages and its values by $V^n = (V^n_1,\ldots,V^n_S)$ we readily see that:

$$V^n = \text{val } G((1 - \lambda)V^{n-1}) ; \qquad n = 1,2,\ldots, ,$$

with $V^o = (0,\ldots,0)$. Therefore $\lim_{n\to\infty} V^n = x$, the only solution of (3.1).

Finally, for any $\varepsilon > 0$ both players can guarantee $\lim_{n\to\infty} V^n$ up to an ε by playing optimally in Γ^N for some N large enough (remember that $\lambda > 0$ and hence the contribution to the pay-off of stages $n > N$ is less than ε if N is large enough).

Q.E.D.

As for the optimal strategies, given any S-tuple of mixed strategies $x = (x^1,\ldots,x^S)$ of player 1 (or 2), in the one-stage game (i.e., elements of I^* or J^*). We identify x with the *stationary behaviour strategy* which consists of playing the mixed strategy x^s whenever the state is s.

Theorem 3.9 If for each $s \in S$, x^s is an optimal strategy in the matrix $G_s((1 - \lambda)V(\lambda))$, then $x = (x^1,\ldots,x^S)$ is a stationary optimal strategy in the λ discount game $\Gamma(\lambda)$.

Proof. For each n let $\hat{\Gamma}^n(\lambda)$ be the same game as $\Gamma^n(\lambda)$, except that when stage n is reached and the state is s, the pay-off is according to $G_s((1 - \lambda)V(\lambda))$

instead of A^s . One checks then easily that: (i) By using the stationary strategy x each player guarantees $V(\lambda)$ in $\hat{\Gamma}^n(\lambda)$. (ii) The difference in pay-offs between $\hat{\Gamma}^n(\lambda)$ and $\Gamma^n(\lambda)$ is arbitrarily small if n is large enough. Hence, for any $\varepsilon > 0$ choosing n large enough, x guarantees $V^n(\lambda) \pm \varepsilon$ in $\Gamma^n(\lambda)$ and hence $V(\lambda) \pm 2\varepsilon$ in $\Gamma(\lambda)$. Since this is true for any $\varepsilon > 0$, the result follows.

Q.E.D.

The great importance of Shapley's work is not only in formulating the first model and opening a new field of research, but also in using the *dynamic programming* approach and the *contraction mapping* which proved to be very useful tools in most of the research that followed.

However, as soon as assumption 3.6 was to be relaxed, that is, away from the λ-discount game, a lot of mathematical ingenuity and depth was needed. We are able to mention here only part of the important results.

Gillette (1957), Hoffman and Karp (1966) and Stern (1975) looked for conditions under which the undiscounted infinite stage game (to be defined later) has a min max value. Such a condition was, for instance, that for any pair of strategies used by the players, the resulting Markov chain is ergodic. An example in which this condition is not satisfied was studied by Blackwell and Ferguson (1968) under the name of "the Big Match." Their result was generalized by Kohlberg (1968) to 'games with absorbing states.' The most important breakthrough was done by Bewley and Kohlberg (1976), and finally Mertens and Neyman (1981) answered the long-standing difficult problem by proving that any stochastic game has a value.

Bewley and Kohlberg (B.K. hereafter) studied the asymptotics of stochastic games in two directions:

(i) Considering the λ-discount game $\Gamma(\lambda)$ and letting λ tend to 0 .

(ii) Considering the undiscounted $(\lambda = 0)$ n-stage game Γ^n and letting n to to ∞ .

From Shapley's result we know that for any $\lambda > 0$ the λ-discount game $\Gamma(\lambda)$ has a value $V(\lambda)$. If we think of λ as the probability of stopping the game after each stage then the expected number of stages is $1/\lambda$ and then $\lambda V(\lambda)$ can be interpreted as 'a value per stage'. B.K. proved:

Theorem 3.10 $\quad \lim_{\lambda\to 0} \lambda V(\lambda)$ exists.

Considering now the limit value of the undiscounted truncated game Γ^n , note first that there is no problem of existence for the value V^n of Γ^n . In order to compare games of different lengths one looks at the 'value per stage' V^n/n . B.K.'s next results were:

Theorem 3.11 $\quad \lim_{n\to\infty} V^n/n$ exists.

Theorem 3.12 $\quad \lim_{\lambda\to 0} \lambda V(\lambda) = \lim_{n\to\infty} V^n/n$.

Actually, B.K. managed to find the expansion of the value $V(\lambda)$ and the optimal strategies in fractional powers of λ for an interval $0 < \lambda \leq \lambda_0$. Similarly, they found an approximate expansion of V^n in powers of n. More precisely, they proved:

Theorem 3.13 There exists an integer M such that:

(i) There exists $\lambda_0 > 0$ such that the following expansion holds for $0 < \lambda \leq \lambda_0$:

$$V(\lambda) = a_M \lambda^{-1} + a_{M-1}\lambda^{-(M-1)/M} + a_{M-2}\lambda^{-(M-2)/M} + \cdots .$$

(ii) There exists a stationary strategy for player 1 described by vectors:

$$x_s(\lambda) = x_{0s} + x_{1s}\lambda^{1/M} + x_{2s}\lambda^{2/M} + \cdots ,$$

where $x_s(\lambda)$ is a probability vector in I^*, and $x_{ks} \in R^I$ for all k, and there exists $\lambda_{00} > 0$ such that for each $0 < \lambda \leq \lambda_{00}$, the stationary strategy $x(\lambda) = (x_1(\lambda),\ldots,x_S(\lambda))$ is optimal in $\Gamma(\lambda)$. The above works similarly for player 2.

(iii) There is an expansion of the form

$$w_s^n = a_s^M n + a_s^{M-1} n^{(M-1)/M} + ,\ldots, + a_s^1 n^{1/M} ,$$

such that $|v_s^n - w_s^n| < C \log (n+1)$ for some constant C.

To prove these results, B.K. adopted an algebraic approach rather than analytic. Their impressive proofs are based on the following main steps:

Step 1: Consider the ordered field F of real Puiseux series, i.e. series of the form $\sum_{k=-\infty}^{K} a_k \theta^{k/M}$, where M is a positive integer, K is any integer and a_k are real numbers. Addition and multiplications are defined in the natural way and order is defined by: $\sum_{k=-\infty}^{K} a_k \theta^{k/M} > 0$ if and only if $a_N > 0$ where N is the largest integer k s.t. $a_k \neq 0$.

Step 2: If the fundamental limit discount equation (3.1) (with θ^{-1} replacing λ),

$$x = \operatorname{val} G((1 - \theta^{-1})x) , \tag{3.2}$$

has a solution in F, then for small enough λ, substitution of λ^{-1} for θ gives $V(\lambda)$. In other words, this is then the desired expansion. Thus the problem is reduced to prove that (3.2) has a solution in F.

Step 3: As it was noted in our first lecture, the minmax theorem is true in any ordered field (Weyl, 1950), thus val G is defined for any matrix G with entries in an arbitrary ordered field, F in our case. Furthermore, an equation of the type $y = \text{val } G$ may be expressed as an *elementary formula* over F, i.e. an expression constructed in a finite number of steps from *atomic formulae* ($p > 0$ or $p = 0$, where p is a polynomial with integer coefficients, in one or more variables) by means of conjunction $(\wedge)$, disjunction $(\vee)$, negation $(\sim)$ and quantifiers of the form $\exists x$, $\forall x$.

The statement, "there exists a solution x in F to $x = \text{val } G((1 - \theta^{-1})x)$", can be expressed as an *elementary sentence in* F i.e. an elementary formula in which *all* variables are quantified by $\exists$ or $\forall$.

Step 4 (Tarski's Principle): An elementary sentence which is valid over one real closed field is valid over every real closed field. (An ordered field F is *real closed* if it has no ordered algebraic extention.)

Step 5: By Shapley's result, the elementary sentence stating, 'there is a solution in H to (3.2)', is valid over the real closed field of the real numbers.

Step 6: F is a real closed field, therefore by Steps 4 and 5 (3.2) has a solution in F.

For the n-stage values V^n the same real closed field of real Puiseux series is used with θ representing the function n.

Remark Parts (i) and (ii) of theorem 3.13 apply for non-zero sum n-person games as well. The result is then the existence of pay-off vectors $v(\lambda)$ and strategy vectors $x(\lambda)$ each of which has a convergent expansion in fractional power of λ such that in some neighborhood of $\lambda = 0$, $x(\lambda)$ is a N.E. point in the λ-discounted game with corresponding pay-offs $v(\lambda)$ (see Mertens, 1982).

The Value of the Infinite Game

In the asymptotic approach of Bewley-Kohlberg one considers the *limit of value*, either the limit of $\lambda V(\lambda)$ as $\lambda \to 0$ or the limit of V^n as $n \to \infty$. Another natural approach to study the *very long undiscounted game* is to look at *the value of the limit*, i.e. the value of the undiscounted infinite stage game Γ_∞. The strategies in Γ_∞ are defined as in definition 3.7. However, there is a technical difficulty in defining an appropriate pay-off function. This difficulty which is *common to all undiscounted infinite state games* (not necessarily stochastic) can be overcome by one of two ways:

(i) By defining the evaluation of a pay-off stream $x = (x_1, x_2 \ldots)$ as lim inf, lim sup or more generally any Banach limit of the n-stage averages $\rho_n = \frac{1}{n} \sum_{k=1}^{n} x_k$.

(ii) By avoiding the definition of pay-off function and defining directly the notion of value.

We shall adopt usually the second alterantive. More precisely, we define:

Definition 3.14 An undiscounted infinite stage game Γ_∞ is said to have a value v if $\forall\ \varepsilon > 0$ there is a strategy $\hat{\sigma}$ of player 1 and $\hat{\tau}$ of player 2 and an integer $N > 0$ s.t.

$$\rho_n(\hat{\sigma}, \tau) \geq v - \varepsilon \ ; \qquad \forall\ n > N \qquad \forall\ \tau$$

$$\rho_n(\hat{\tau}, \sigma) \leq v + \varepsilon \ ; \qquad \forall\ n > N \qquad \forall\ \sigma$$

where $\rho_n(\sigma, \tau)$ is the expected n-stage average pay-off when σ and τ are used. This implies in particular that player 1 can guarantee that lim inf ρ_n will be as close as he wishes to v and player 2 can guarantee that lim sup ρ_n will be as close as he wishes to v. We shall use the following terminology: $\hat{\sigma}$ (as well as $\hat{\tau}$) *ε-guarantee* v in Γ_∞.

Remark 3.15 Note that if Γ_∞ has a value v and if we denote by v_n the (average per stage) value of Γ_n then $\lim_n v_n$ exists and is equal to v.

The problem of existence of a value for a general undiscounted stochastic game Γ_∞ was an open problem for many years, in spite of many attempts to solve it. It was finally solved in 1981 by Mertens and Meyman who used the B.K. asymptotic theory to prove:

Theorem 3.16 The infinite game has a value which equals the asymptotic values:

$$v = \text{val}(\Gamma_\infty) = \lim_{\lambda\to 0} \lambda V(\lambda) = \lim_{n\to\infty} V^n/n \quad .$$

A rough description of the strategy of player 1 which guarantees $\liminf \rho_n \geq v - \varepsilon$ looks as follows. At stage k player 1 computes a number $\lambda_k \in (0, 1]$ and plays optimally in the λ_k-discounted game (according to the state he is in). $\lambda_k = \lambda(\xi_k)$ where $\lambda\colon [1, \infty) \to (0, 1]$ is an appropriately designed continuous decreasing function and ξ_k is a statistic updated as follows:

$$\xi_{k+1} = \text{Max}[C, \xi_k + x_k - \lambda_k V(\lambda_k) + 4\varepsilon] \quad ,$$

where $C \geq 1$ is a sufficiently large constant. So roughly speaking, ξ_k is the excess of the actual pay-offs $x_1 + x_2 + \cdots + x_k$ over the intended pay-offs $\lambda_1 V(\lambda_1) + \lambda_2 V(\lambda_2) + \cdots + \lambda_k V(\lambda_k)$. The higher ξ_k becomes the lower λ_k is, which means that he plays for lower discount rates, i.e. with more importance attached to later stages compared to the present one.

Remark 3.17 Mertens and Neyman's result holds for a class of stochastic games much wider than that treated by B.K. One does not have to make any finiteness assumptions, neither on the state space nor on the action sets, provided the following conditions hold:

(i) Pay-offs are uniformly bounded.

(ii) The value $V(\lambda)$ of the λ-discounted games exists.

(iii) $\forall \ \varepsilon < 1$ there exists a sequence λ_i decreasing to 0 such that $\lambda_{i+1} \geq \varepsilon\lambda_i \ \ \forall \ i$ and $\Sigma||V(\lambda_{i+1}) - V(\lambda_i)|| < \infty$.

It is a consequence of B.K.'s results that these conditions are always satisfied in the finite case treated there.

Aumann, R.J. (1981). Survey of repeated games. In R.J. Aumann, et al. Essays in Game Theory and Mathematical Economics in Honor of Oskar Morgenstern, Wissenschaftsverlag, Manheim, Wien, Zurich.

Bewley, T. and E. Kohlberg (1976a). The asymptotic theory of stochastic games. Math. Oper. Res. 1, 197-208.

Bewley, T. and E. Kohlberg (1976b). The asymptotic solution of a recursion equation occuring in stochastic games. Math. Oper. Res. 1, 321-336.

Blackwell, D. (1956). An analog of the minmax theorem for vector pay-offs. Pacific J. Math. 6, 1-8.

Blackwell, D. and T.S. Ferguson (1968). The big match. Ann. Math. Statist. 39, 159-163.

Gillette, D. (1957). Stochastic games with zero-stop probabilities. Contributions to the Theory of Games, Vol. III (Ann. Mathe. Studies, No.39,). Princeton University, NJ., 179-187.

Hoffman, A.J. and R.M. Karp (1966). On nonterminating stochastic games. Management Sci. 12, 359-370.

Kohlberg, E. (1974). Repeated games with absorbing states. Ann. Statist. 2, 724-738.

Mertens, J.-F. (1971-72). Repeated games: an overview of the zero-sum case. Advance Economic Theory, W. Hildenbrand (ed.). Cambridge University Press: Cambridge, 175-182.

Mertens, J.-F. and A. Neyman (1982). Stochastic games. Internat. J. Game Theory 10, 53-66.

Shapley, L. (1953). Stochastic games. Proc. Nat. Acad Sci U.S.A. 39, 1095-1100.

Stern, Martin A. (1975). On stochastic games with limiting average pay-off. Doctoral dissertation in mathematics, University of Illinois.

Chapter 4

MODELING INCOMPLETE INFORMATION

In all models we discussed so far there was an implicit but very crucial underlying assumption: the description of the game and all the data involved in this description is *known to all players*. In particular each player knows the strategy sets and the pay-off functions. On the other hand we know that this is not a very realistic assumption: players are often uncertain even about their own pay-off function and their available actions, and even more so about those of the other players. Can we model such situations in which *players are uncertain as to what game they are playing?*

Example 4.1 The state of nature is chosen by a chance move to be B (black) or W (white) with probability ½ for each possibility. Players I and II are engaged in the following situation. Player I has to choose B or W. Hearing that, player II also chooses B or W, if they both choose the same thing they receive 2 each. If one chooses B and the other W, the one choosing the real state of nature receives 5 and the other player receives 0.

Case (i). Both players do not know the real state of nature. This is the game:

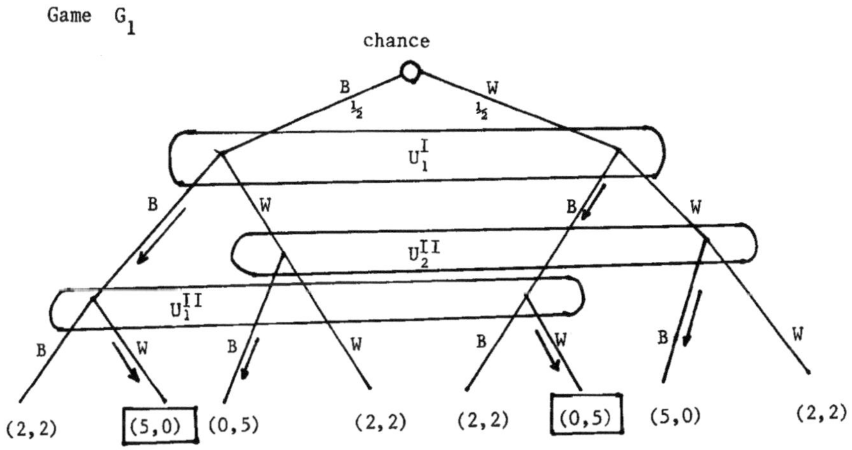

and with a unique N.E. pay-off $\frac{1}{2}(5, 0) + \frac{1}{2}(0, 5) = (2\frac{1}{2}, 2\frac{1}{2})$.

Case (ii). Player I knows the state of nature while player II does not, even though he is aware of the fact that I knows. The game is then:

Game G_2

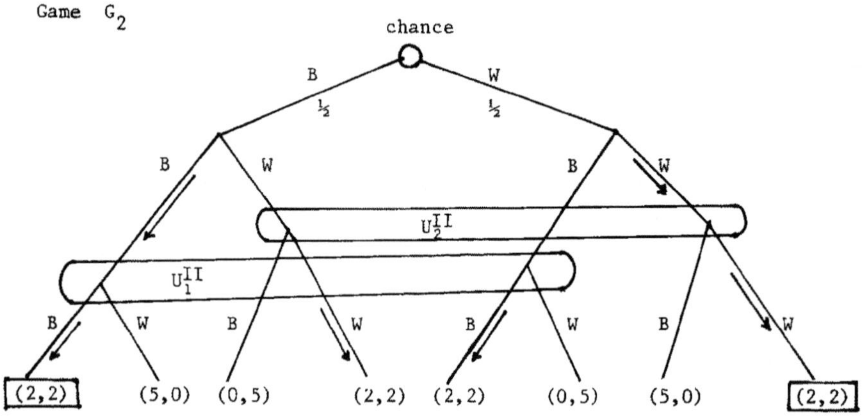

with a unique N.E. pay-off (2, 2) .

Here we already see a tricky thing about information; *additional information may be disadvantageous*. A moment of reflection shows that the problem of Player I is that *player II knows that he knows*. In fact if I could get his information without player II suspecting as much, we would get:

Case (iii). Player I (and only he) knows the state of nature and player II "thinks" that he does not know. The pattern of behaviour will be:

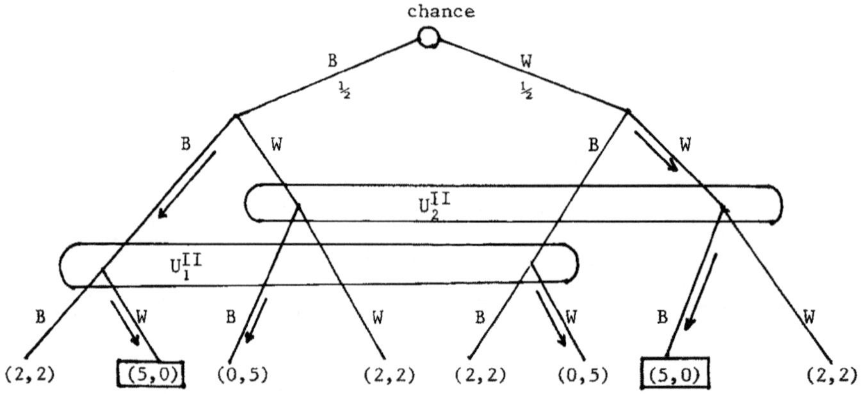

with the resulting pay-off (5, 0) -- the best possible for player I. Notice that we were careful not to call the last case a 'game'. In fact this is not a game. This is a situation in which player I knows that he is playing G_2 while II thinks that he is playing G_1 . More typically player II may not be sure whether player I knows the state of nature. In such a situation he is not sure whether he is playing G_1 or G_2 . And what about player I? What does he think about player II's beliefs concerning the real game he is playing? And what does player II think about this? The problem is getting more and more complicated and the question is how to treat it.

To fix ideas we consider a situation of incomplete information involving a set of players $N = \{1,\dots,n\}$, the members of which are uncertain about the parameters of the game they are playing which may be any element of some set S (we may think of a point of S as a full listing of the strategy sets and the pay-off functions). We shall refer to S as the set of *States of Nature.*

As we saw already in our example, a full description of the situation should include the beliefs (i.e. subjective probability distribution) of each player on S . These may be called the first level beliefs. Then we have to include what each player believes about the other player's beliefs on S . These are the second level beliefs. Then we have what a player believes are the second level beliefs of the others (i.e. what he thinks that they think that he thinks...) and so on. We are led to an infinite hierarchy of beliefs which seems inavoidable and hardly manageable.

In an attempt to overcome this difficulty, Harsanyi (1967-68) introduced the concept of *type*. A type of a player is an entity that summarizes all parameters and beliefs (of all levels) of that player. The game starts by a chance move that selects the type of each player. Of course each player knows his own type and has some beliefs (as part of his type) on the types of the other players.

The concept of type proved to be very useful but its formal derivation from the more basic notions of beliefs, beliefs on beliefs, etc. was done only some 12 years later (Böge and Eisele, 1979; Mertens and Zamir, 1985). Let us look briefly at this result.

We start with the set S of states of nature which we assume to be compact. For any compact space X we denote by $\Pi(X)$ the compact space of probability measures on X endowed with the weak* typology.

First level beliefs are just the elements of $\Pi(S)$.

Second level beliefs are elements of $\Pi(S \times [\Pi(S)]^n)$, etc. We define a sequence of spaces $\{Y_k\}_{k=0}^{\infty}$ as follows:

$Y_0 = S$ and for $k=1,2,\dots$

$Y_k = \{y_k \in Y_{k-1} \times [\Pi(Y_{k-1})]^n$ s.t. if t^i denotes the projection on the i-th copy of $[\,]^n$, then:

(a) $\forall\ i$, the marginal distribution of $t^i(y_k)$ on Y_{k-2} is $t^i(y_{k-1})$

(b) $\forall\ i$, the marginal distribution of $t^i(y_k)$ on the i-th copy of $\Pi(Y_{k-2})$ is a unit mass at $t^i(y_{k-1})\}$

Conditions (a) and (b) are coherency conditions saying that each player knows his own beliefs and any event whose probability can be computed according to beliefs of two different levels, will have the same probability in both levels.

Now let $\mathcal{Y}$ be the projective limit of $\{Y_k\}_{k=0}^{\infty}$. $\mathcal{Y}$ is a well-defined compact space if S is compact. Let $\mathcal{T}^i$ be the projection of $\mathcal{Y}$ on player i's coordinates.

$$\mathcal{Y} = S \times \mathcal{T}^1 \times \ldots \times \mathcal{T}^n \quad . \tag{4.1}$$

The set $\mathcal{T}^i$ can be called the set of *types* of player i . Clearly all $\mathcal{T}^i$'s are copies of the same set $\mathcal{T}$. An element $t^i \in \mathcal{T}^i$ defines uniquely a probability distribution on $\mathcal{Y}$ i.e. on $S \times \mathcal{T}^1 \times \ldots \times \mathcal{T}^N$. By properties (a) and (b), the marginal distribution of t^i on $\mathcal{T}^i$ is a unit mass on $\{t^i\}$. This is a formal expression of the fact that *each player knows his own type*. Therefore:

$$\mathcal{T}^i = \Pi(S \times \underset{j \neq i}{X} \mathcal{T}^j) \quad . \tag{4.2}$$

Equations (4.1) and (4.2) give the structure of what we call *the universal beliefs* (BL) *space* $\mathcal{Y}$ generated by S and n . A point $y = (s, t^1, t^2, \ldots, t^n)$ of $\mathcal{Y}$ may also be called a *state of the world* (compared to *state of nature* which is an element of S). A state of the world thus consists of a state of nature and an n-tuple of types, one for each player. A type of a player which can also be called *the state of mind* of the player is just a joint probability distribution on the states of nature and the types of the other players.

Beliefs Subspaces

As the name indicates, the universal beliefs space is a very big space. It contains all possible configurations of hierarchy of beliefs. Often the uncertainty of players is confined to a small subset of $\mathcal{Y}$

Definition 4.2 A *Beliefs subspace* (BL subspace) is a closed subset C of $\mathcal{Y}$ s.t. if $y = (s, t^1, \ldots, t^n) \in C$ then $t^i(C) = 1 \ \forall \ i$.

This is the notion of *common knowledge*, first defined formally by Aumann (1976): Every player knows that the state of the world is in C , he knows that everybody knows that the state is in C , he knows that everybody knows that everybody knows that the state is in C , etc.

Example 4.3 Players $N = \{I, II\}$; $C = \{y_1, y_2, y_3, y_4\}$ where:

$$y_1 = \{s_{11}; (\tfrac{2}{5}, \tfrac{3}{5}, 0, 0); (\tfrac{1}{3}, 0, \tfrac{2}{3}, 0)\}$$

$$y_2 = \{s_{12}; (\tfrac{2}{5}, \tfrac{3}{5}, 0, 0); (0, \tfrac{3}{4}, 0, \tfrac{1}{4})\}$$

$$y_3 = \{s_{21}; (0, 0, \tfrac{4}{5}, \tfrac{1}{5}); (\tfrac{1}{3}, 0, \tfrac{2}{3}, 0)\}$$

$$y_4 = \{s_{22}; (0, 0, \tfrac{4}{5}, \tfrac{1}{5}); (0, \tfrac{3}{4}, 0, \tfrac{1}{4})\}$$

In this BL subspace there are two types of player I:

$$I_1 = (\tfrac{2}{5}, \tfrac{3}{5}, 0, 0); \qquad I_2 = (0, 0, \tfrac{4}{5}, \tfrac{1}{5}) ,$$

and two types of player II:

$$II_1 = (\tfrac{1}{3}, 0, \tfrac{2}{3}, 0); \quad II_2 = (0, \tfrac{3}{4}, 0, \tfrac{1}{4}) .$$

The mutual beliefs of each player on the other player's types are:

I on II:

	II_1	II_2
I_1	$\frac{2}{5}$	$\frac{3}{5}$
I_2	$\frac{4}{5}$	$\frac{1}{5}$

II on I:

	II_1	II_2
I_1	$\frac{1}{3}$	$\frac{3}{4}$
I_2	$\frac{2}{3}$	$\frac{1}{4}$

This is equivalent to the situation in which the pair of types is chosen according to the following probability distribution on the product of the type sets:

	II_1	II_2
I_1	$\frac{2}{10}$	$\frac{3}{10}$
I_2	$\frac{4}{10}$	$\frac{1}{10}$

.

Then each player is told his type from which he derives his subjective probability as "the conditional probability on the types of the other player given my own type."

When such a prior on the BL subspace exists it is called a *consistent* BL subspace.

Example 4.4 $N = \{I, II\}$; $C = \{y_1, y_2, y_3, y_4\}$

$$y_1 = \{s_{11}; (\tfrac{1}{2}, \tfrac{1}{2}, 0, 0); (\tfrac{1}{3}, 0, \tfrac{2}{3}, 0)\}$$

$$y_2 = \{s_{12}; (\tfrac{1}{2}, \tfrac{1}{2}, 0, 0); (0, \tfrac{1}{5}, 0, \tfrac{4}{5})\}$$

$$y_3 = \{s_{21}; (0, 0, \tfrac{1}{4}, \tfrac{3}{4}); (\tfrac{1}{3}, 0, \tfrac{2}{3}, 0)\}$$

$$y_4 = \{s_{22}; (0, 0, \tfrac{1}{4}, \tfrac{3}{4}); (0, \tfrac{1}{5}, 0, \tfrac{4}{5})\} .$$

I on II:

	II_1	II_2
I_1	$\frac{1}{2}$	$\frac{1}{2}$
I_2	$\frac{1}{4}$	$\frac{3}{4}$

II on I:

	II_1	II_2
I_1	$\frac{1}{3}$	$\frac{1}{5}$
I_2	$\frac{2}{3}$	$\frac{4}{5}$

No prior on $\{I_1, I_2\} \times \{II_1 \times II_2\}$ can give these as conditionals which means that this is an *inconsistent case*.

To define formally the notion of consistency we need some notation. If C is a BL subspace and $y = (s, t^1,\dots,t^n) \in C$ we denote player I's type, t^i, in y (which is a probability measure on C) by t^i_y .

Definition 4.5 A BL subspace C is *consistent* if there exists a probability measure P on C s.t. $\forall\ i \in N$:

$$P = \int_C t^i_y \, dP \quad . \tag{4.3}$$

We will also say that this $P \in \Pi(C)$ is consistent. Any $y \in C$ is a consistent state of the world with respect to P .

With the appropriate measurability structure on C and on $\Pi(C)$, let $F(t^i)$ be the sub σ-field of measurable sets of $\Pi(C)$ generated by the projection t^i . Then:

Theorem 4.7 If y is a consistent state of the world w.s.t. a consistent P with finite support, then P (and in particular its support - the BL subspace containing y) is uniquely determined and is common knowledge.

In other words, each player,. with his information only, can answer the question: Is the state of the world consistent? If the state is in fact consistent all players will know that and compute correctly the same BL subspace and the prior on it.

The way for player i to find the BL subspace, which he believes contains the state of the world y , is rather straightforward. In $y = (s, t^1,\dots,t^n)$ player i knows t^i . He finds $C^i_{y,1} = \mathrm{Supp}(t^i_y)$ (i.e. support of t^i_y) and then inductively:

$$C^i_{y,k+1} = C^i_{y,k} \cup [\bigcup_{\tilde{y}\in C^i_{y,K}} \bigcup_j \mathrm{Supp}(t^j_{\tilde{y}})] \qquad k=1,2,\dots \quad .$$

We have $C^i_{y,1} \subset C^i_{y,2} \subset \dots$ and if C (the support of P) is finite we get a limit set C^i_y . Theorem 4.6 asserts that if y is consistent then C^i_y is the same for all i . Denoting this by C , it is the minimal BL subspaces containing the real state of the world *according to the beliefs of every player*.

The fact that the prior P on C can be computed correctly by each player follows from the consistency of P which implies:

If $P(z) > 0$ and $y \in \mathrm{Supp}(t^i_z)$ then $\frac{P(y)}{P(z)} = \frac{t^i_z(y)}{t^i_z(z)} > 0$. From this it follows by proceeding inductively on sets converging to C^i_y , that for any y and i either $P(C^i_y) = 0$ or $P(\cdot\,|C^i_y)$ is uniquely determined by C .

So in a consistent state of the world, players cannot draw wrong conclusions concerning the consistency. Can this happen in an inconsistent state of the world? It turns out that if y is inconsistent then player i may think wrongly that y is consistent only if $y \notin \mathrm{Supp}(t^i_y)$. Otherwise he concludes correctly that y is not consistent. For instance, in Example 4.4 in any state $y \in C$ both players will recognize correctly that the state is not consistent. On the other hand, look at the following example.

Example 4.8 Consider the following BL subspace consisting of 16 states and 4 types for each of the two players. We arrange the 16 states in a matrix as a product of the two type sets (ij means player I is of type i and II of type j). Being interested only by the beliefs structure we omit from y the state of nature s and write next to each row the corresponding type of player I which is a probability distribution on the columns (types of player II). We do similarly for player II.

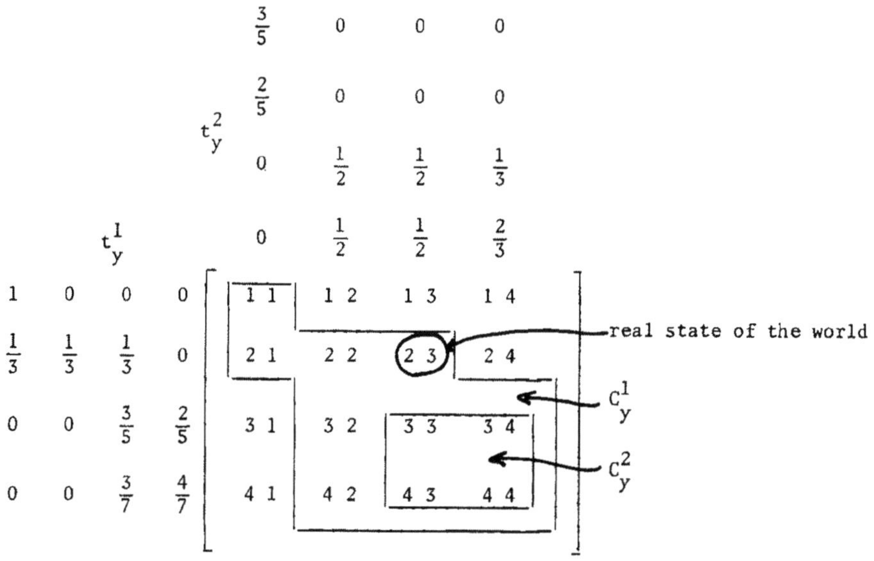

If the state of the world is $y = 23$ it is inconsistent. Also, for this state $y \in t^1_y$ but $y \notin t^2_y$ so we expect player I to get to the correct conclusion which may not be the case for player II. In fact, player I will compute $C^1_y = \{11, 21, 22, 23, 32, 33, 34, 42, 43, 44\}$ but no consistent probability distribution on it, so he will conclude that the state is inconsistent. On the other hand, player II will compute $C^2_y = \{33, 34, 42, 44\}$ with the consistent distribution $P = (1/4, 1/6, 1/4, 1/3)$ on it. So he may wrongly conclude that the state is consistent.

Approximation of a BL subspace by a Finite BL subspace

As it can be easily seen, even if we start with a finite set S , both $\mathcal{Y}$ and 'most' of its BL subspaces are sets of high cardinality. On the other hand, most of the work on games with incomplete information assumes finitely many possible states of the world. To make this discrepancy slightly less disturbing we have the following theorem which we bring without its proof which is technically quite complicated (see Mertens and Zamir, Theorem 3.1).

Theorem 4.9 For any BL subspace C of $\mathcal{Y}$ and any finite open cover $\mathcal{O}$ of $\mathcal{Y}$, there is a finite BL subspace C^* of $\mathcal{Y}$ s.t.

(i) $C \subset \cup\{0 \in \mathcal{O} | 0 \cap C^* \neq \phi\}$

(ii) $C^* \subset \cup\{0 \in \mathcal{O} | 0 \cap C \neq \phi\}$.

In other words this theorem states that *the finite BL subspaces of* $\mathcal{Y}$ *are dense* in the set of all BL subspaces of $\mathcal{Y}$ in the *Hansdorff topology* on the closed subsets of $\mathcal{Y}$.

Nash Equilibrium

Unlike Böge and Eisele who incorporated the strategy choices of the players as part of the space on which the hierarchy of beliefs are built, we adopted here the attitude of keeping this out of the BL space. So far we developed only the beliefs structure of the problem. To define a game based on $\mathcal{Y}$ we need a few more ingredients:

- $\forall\ i \in N$, player i has an action set A^i which we assume w.l.g. to be independent of his type.
- $\forall\ i \in N$, $\forall\ y \in \mathcal{Y}$ there is a *utility function* $u^i_y : \overset{n}{\underset{j=1}{X}} A^j \to R$.

Recall the type set T^i which is a projection of $\mathcal{Y}$ on one of its coordinates.

Definition 4.10 The *vector pay-off* game defined on a BL subspace C of $\mathcal{Y}$ is the game in which:

- the set of players is $N = \{1,2,\ldots,n\}$;
- the (pure) strategy set Σ^i of player i is the set of mappings $\sigma^i: C \to A^i$ which is T^i-measurable;
- the 'pay-off' to player i resulting from an n-tuple of strategies $\sigma = (\sigma^1,\ldots,\sigma^n)$ is a vector $u_i = (u_{t^i})_{t^i \in T^i}$, where

  $u_{t^i}(\sigma) = \int u^i_y(\sigma(\tilde{y}))\, dt^i(\tilde{y})$, with the interpretation that type t^i is paid $u_{t^i}(\sigma)$.

We note that u_{t^i} is T^i-measurable as it should be. Although this is not a game in the usual sense, the concept of N.E. can be defined in the usual way, namely: $\sigma = (\sigma^1,\ldots,\sigma^n)$ is N.E. if:

$$\forall\ i \in N,\ \forall\ t^i \in T^i,\ \forall\ \tilde{\sigma}^i \in \Sigma^i, \quad u_{t^i}(\sigma) \geq u_{t^i}(\sigma|\tilde{\sigma}^i) ,$$

where as usual $(\sigma|\tilde{\sigma}^i)$ is the n-tuple σ in which the i-th component is replaced by $\tilde{\sigma}^i$. This is also called a *Bayesian Equilibrium*.

When C is a finite BL subspace this game is an n-person game in which the pay-off for player i is a vector of dimension equal to $|T^i|$, the number of types of player i. This is actually the game studied by Harsanyi. We can, in this case, make this an ordinary n-person game in which the pay-off to player i is $\bar{u}_i = \sum_{t^i \in T^i} \gamma_{t^i} u_{t^i}$ where $\forall\ t^i \in T^i$, γ_{t^i} is a strictly positive constant. Clearly, *independently of the constant* γ_{t^i} we choose, this game has the same N.E. points as the above vector pay-off game. Aumann and Maschler (1967) suggested γ_{t^i} s.t. $\sum_{t^i \in T^i} \gamma_{t^i} = 1$ to treat the inconsistent case.

Notice that both the vector pay-off game and the ordinary game we defined are well defined independently of whether the BL subspace C is consistent or not. Harsanyi preferred to discuss mainly the consistent case. This is because in that case the game in strategic form is equivalent to what Harsanyi calls a "game in standard form."

Theorem 4.11 (Harsanyi): Let C be a consistent BL subspace of Y with a consistent prior P . Then the strategic vector pay-off game defined on C has the same N.E. points as the following game:

- A chance move chooses $y \in C$, then each player i is informed of t^i_y.
- $\forall\ i \in N$, player i then chooses $a^i \in A^i$ and receives $u^i_y(a^1,\ldots,a^n)$.

Proof. The proof readily follows from the definition of the games, the definition of N.E., and the fact that Supp(P) = C .

Harsanyi made the argument that the players 'should' believe in P as the prior on C . We by no means claim that here. The introduction of P is just a matter of mathematical convenience. It serves to find the original N.E. points naturally defined by C via subjective probabilities. Furthermore, since by Theorem 4.7, P is common knowledge (in the consistent case), the above-described 'game in standard form' is also common knowledge which gives even more justification for using it in analyzing the situation of incomplete information.

Aumann, R.J. (1976). Agreeing to disagree. Ann. Statist. 4, 1236-1239.

Aumann, R.J. and M. Maschler (1967). Repeated games with incomplete information: a survey of recent results. Mathematica ST-116, Ch.III, 287-403.

Boge, W. and Th. Eisele (1979). On situations of Bayesian games. Internat. J. Game Theory 8, 193-215.

Harsanyi, J.C. (1967, 1968). Games with incomplete players played by Bayesian players. Parts I, II, III. Management Sci. 14 (3,5,7).

Mertens, J.-F. and S. Zamir (1985). Formulation of Bayesian analysis for games with incomplete information. Internat. J. Game Theory 14, 1-29.

Chapter 5
REPEATED GAMES WITH INCOMPLETE INFORMATION (I)

One of the most interesting and important aspects of incomplete information situations is the strategic use of information: When and how to reveal information? When and how much to invest in collecting new information? How does information flow between players? and so on. Clearly the right setting to deal with these issues is that obtained by combining the Bayesian games of the last chapter with repeated games. This is what we plan to do here. Most of the research done so far in this direction was in the consistent 0-sum two-person games. This is because problems of information appear already in this case.

Incomplete Information on One Side

The first and simplest model of repeated games with incomplete information was presented and studied by Aumann and Maschler in 1966. In their model the state of nature was presented by a pay-off matrix chosen at random and known to one player only:

- At stage 0 chance chooses $k \in \{1, 2\}$ with probability $(1/2, 1/2)$. The result is told to player I (the maximizer) but not to player II (who knows only the probability $(1/2, 1/2)$).

- At stage m, $m=1,2,\ldots$ player I chooses $i_m \in I$ and player II chooses $j_m \in J$ and (i_m, j_m) is told to both players.

- After stage n, player II pays player I $\frac{1}{n}\sum_{m=1}^{n} a^k_{i_m j_m}$ where $A^1 = (a^1_{ij})$ and $A^2 = (a^2_{ij})$ are two $I \times J$ matrices known to both players.

Denote this game by $\Gamma_n(\frac{1}{2})$, and its (minmax) value by $v_n(\frac{1}{2})$.

<u>Example 5.1</u> $A^1 = \begin{pmatrix} 1 & 0 \\ 0 & 0 \end{pmatrix}$; $A^2 = \begin{pmatrix} 0 & 0 \\ 0 & 1 \end{pmatrix}$.

It is easily seen that $v_1(\frac{1}{2}) = 1/2$ and I's optimal strategy is to play his dominating strategy: $i = 1$ if $k = 1$ and $i = 2$ if $k = 2$. However, this strategy is *completely revealing* (CR), i.e. after the first stage II will deduce from the move of I the k chosen and from then on he can guarantee not to pay more than 0. Thus the CR strategy yields player I a pay-off $\frac{1}{2n}$ which tends to 0 as $n \to \infty$.

The other extreme behaviour of I is to play without using his information.

This will be a *non-revealing* (NR) strategy since, being independent of k, player I's move will give no information to II (about k). In this case each stage of $\Gamma_n(\frac{1}{2})$ is equivalent to the following one-stage game:

$$\Delta(\tfrac{1}{2}) = \tfrac{1}{2}A^1 + \tfrac{1}{2}A^2 = \begin{pmatrix} \frac{1}{2} & 0 \\ 0 & \frac{1}{2} \end{pmatrix}.$$

This game has the value $\frac{1}{4}$ so in any $\Gamma_n(\frac{1}{2})$ with $n \geq 2$, player I does better by not using his information than by fully using it immediately. Later we shall show that $\lim_{n\to\infty} v_n(\frac{1}{2}) = \frac{1}{4}$, thus asymptotically player I cannot get more than what he gets by playing NR.

Example 5.2 $\quad A^1 = \begin{pmatrix} -1 & 0 \\ 0 & 0 \end{pmatrix}; \quad A^2 = \begin{pmatrix} 0 & 0 \\ 0 & -1 \end{pmatrix}.$

Repeating the same discussion as in the previous example we have: By playing CR, player I can guarantee 0. By playing NR he can guarantee the value of $\Delta(\frac{1}{2}) = \begin{pmatrix} -\frac{1}{2} & 0 \\ 0 & -\frac{1}{2} \end{pmatrix}$ which is $-\frac{1}{4}$. Since clearly $v_n(\frac{1}{2}) = 0 \ \forall \ n$ it follows that in this case the CR is the best strategy for I.

Example 5.3 $\quad A^1 = \begin{pmatrix} 4 & 0 & 2 \\ 4 & 0 & -2 \end{pmatrix}, \quad A^2 = \begin{pmatrix} 0 & 4 & -2 \\ 0 & 4 & 2 \end{pmatrix}.$

- By playing CR player I guarantees 0 since the value of each matrix is 0.
- By playing NR he guarantees the value of $\Delta(\frac{1}{2}) = \begin{pmatrix} 2 & 2 & 0 \\ 2 & 2 & 0 \end{pmatrix}$ which is again 0.
- We claim that player I can do better than 0, he can guarantee 1 in any $\Gamma_n(\frac{1}{2})$

To do that player I 'prepares' two coins C^1 and C^2. Both have the outcomes $\{1, 2\}$ with probabilities $(\frac{3}{4}, \frac{1}{4})$ in C^1 and $(\frac{1}{4}, \frac{3}{4})$ in C^2. If the game is A^k he uses C^k to choose $i \in \{1, 2\}$ and then plays that move i in all stages.

The only information player II obtains is the outcome i of the coin without knowing which coin was used. However, the probability distribution of k is updated as follows:

$$P(k = 1 | i = 1) = \tfrac{3}{4}; \qquad P(k = 1 | i = 2) = \tfrac{1}{4}.$$

So, if $i = 1$, the expected (row) pay-off is:

$$\tfrac{3}{4}(4, 0, 2) + \tfrac{1}{4}(0, 4, -2) = (3, 1, 1).$$

If $i = 2$ the expected pay-off is

$$\tfrac{1}{4}(4, 0, -2) + \tfrac{3}{4}(0, 4, 2) = (1, 3, 1).$$

In any case, the expected pay-off is at least 1. We shall see later that $\lim_{n\to\infty} v_n(\frac{1}{2}) = 1$.

Limit of Value and Value of Limit

As a first step in the development of the theory it is important to clarify the notion of value for repeated games in general. As we mentioned in previous lectures one would like basically to model a *many times repeated game*. Two approaches suggest themselves: The first one which we used in discussing the examples may be called *limit of value*, and consists of considering the value of the n-stage game Γ_n (with pay-offs divided by n), letting $n \to \infty$. In the second approach *value of limit*, one defines the infinite stage game Γ_∞ and considers its value. The problem in defining Γ_∞ is the lack of an obvious candidate for a pay-off function, since the expectation of $\lim_{n\to\infty} \frac{1}{n} \sum_{m=1}^{n} g_m$, where g_m is the pay-off at stage m, may fail to exist. As we mentioned in relation to stochastic games, to overcome this difficulty we either define some kind of limiting average or we define the value of Γ_∞ *directly* without defining the pay-offs. This is what we did in definition 3.14 and this will be our attitude whenever we treat the infinite game.

Unlike the situation in stochastic games where the two approaches yield the same value, in repeated incomplete information games, they may differ. To see how this can happen let us first observe:

Remark 5.4 If v is the value of Γ_∞ then $\lim v_n$ exists and equals to v.

To see this note first that a strategy σ (or τ) in Γ_∞ defines uniquely a strategy σ_n (or τ_n) in Γ_n for n=1,2,... . This may be called the *n-stage projection* of σ (or τ). Our remark then follows from definition 3.14 which implies that if a strategy *ε-guarantees* v in Γ_∞, its n-stage projection ε-guarantees v in Γ_n for n sufficiently large.

In view of remark 5.4 the only divergence which may occur is when limit of value exists while the value of limit does not. The first example of this kind was provided by Zamir (1973). Due to time constraints we do not analyze that example here but we shall see this phenomenon later on in our lectures.

Let us now reconsider our first model generalized in the obvious way.

- The states of nature are A^k, $k \in K = \{1,\dots,K\}$, which are I × J pay-off matrices of a zero-sum two-person game in which $I = \{1,\dots,I\}$ and $J = \{1,\dots,J\}$ are the pure strategy sets of player I and II respectively.

The state of nature is chosen according to a given probability vector $p \in P = \{p = (p^1,\dots,p^K) \mid p^k \geq 0,\ \forall\ k;\ \sum_k p^k = 1\}$.

We denote the repeated games by $\Gamma_n(p)$ and their values by $v_n(p)$.

Lemma 5.5 $v_n(p)$ is concave on P for all n=1,2,... .

Proof. Let p_1, p_2 be in P and α in [0, 1] such that $\alpha p_1 + (1-\alpha)p_2 = p$. Consider the two games $\Gamma'_n(\alpha, p_1, p_2)$ and $\Gamma''_n(\alpha, p_1, p_2)$ defined as follows:

- In Γ' chance chooses $r \in \{1, 2\}$ with probability $(\alpha, 1-\alpha)$; both players are informed about the outcome. Then $\Gamma_n(p_r)$ is played.
- Γ''_n is defined in a similar way but only player I knows the r chosen.
- The above description is common knowledge.

Note that player I has the same strategy set in both games while player II's strategy set in Γ''_n is contained in that of Γ'_n. Thus, denoting by v'_n and v''_n the values of the games, it follows that $v'_n \leq v''_n$.

Now clearly $v'_n = \alpha v_n(p_1) + (1-\alpha)v_n(p_2)$. On the other hand Γ''_n has the same value as $\Gamma_n(p)$ since for player I the knowledge of r is useless (he will know k), and for player II, k is chosen (in two steps) with probability $\alpha p_1 + (1-\alpha)p_2 = p$. Hence $v''_n = v_n(p)$, and the result follows.

Q.E.D.

In considering the value of $\Gamma_n(p)$ we make use of the minmax theorem which says actually that an optimal strategy of player I guarantees the value even if player II knows that it is being used. Now given a strategy σ of player I in Γ_n, player II can compute before each stage m a *posterior probability* p_m *on* K, that is, the conditional probability distribution on K given σ and given the history up to that stage. The random variable p_m plays a very fundamental role in the theory; the role of *state variable* in the dynamic programming approach. The use of this approach is possible due to the following theorem which we mention here without proof (see Mertens and Zamir, 1971-72).

Theorem 5.6 The game $\Gamma_n(p)$ has the same value as the game in which player I announces his strategy and at stage m a new game $\Gamma_{n-m+1}(p_m)$ is played.

The most important consequence of this theorem is the following *recursive formula* for v_n.

$$v_{n+1}(p) = \frac{1}{n+1} \max_s \{\min_j (\sum_k p^k s^k A^k)_j + n \sum_i \bar{s}_i v_n(p_i)\} \qquad (5.1)$$

Here $s = (s^k)_{k\in K}$ is the first stage strategy of player I, i.e. $s^k = (s^k_i)_{i\in I}$ – a probability vector on I. $\bar{s} = \sum_k p^k s^k$ and p_i is the probability vector on K given by $p^k_i = p_k s^k_i/\bar{s}_i$.

Lemma 5.7 For all $p \in P$ the sequence $v_n(p)$ is decreasing.

Proof. $v_{n+1}(p) \leq v_n(p)$ is proved inductively using (5.1) and the concavity of v_n (Lemma 5.5) which implies: $\sum_i \bar{s}_i\, v_n(p_i) \leq v_n(p)$ Q.E.D.

Definition 5.8 The nonrevealing (NR) game is the one-stage game, denoted by $\Delta(p)$, in which the pay-off matrix is $\sum_k p^k A^k$. The value of the NR game is denoted by $u(p)$.

This is the game in which none of the players is informed about the choice of A^k.

Lemma 5.9 For all n, $v_n(p) \geq (\text{cav } u)(p)$ on P.

Here Cav u is the smallest concave function on P which is greater or equal to u.

Proof. By using an optimal strategy of $\Delta(p)$ in each stage of $\Gamma_n(p)$, player I guarantees $u(p)$ per stage thus $v_n(p) \geq u(p)$. Since v_n is concave, the result follows.

Q.E.D.

Lemma 5.10 For each n, $v_n(p)$ is Lipschitz.

Proof. It follows from the easily proved observation that if A and B are two pay-off functions of the same dimension then:

$$|\text{val}(A) - \text{val}(B)| \leq \max_{ij} |a_{ij} - b_{ij}|$$

Q.E.D.

Corollary 5.11 As $n \to \infty$, v_n uniformly converges on P to a concave function v which satisfies $v(p) \geq (\text{Cav } u)(p)$.

Proof. The proof follows from the monotonicity, the Lipschitz property, and the concavity of v_n combined with the compactness of P.

For notational simplicity only, let us assume from now on (unless otherwise specified) two states of nature $K = \{1, 2\}$. Then P can be identified with the unit interval $[0, 1]$, where $p \in [0, 1]$ is the probability of A^1.

To get a deeper understanding of the monotone convergence of v_n, let us recall the sequence $(p_n)_{n=1}^{n}$ of posterior probabilities (thus random variables in $[0, 1]$), and observe that this is a martingale bounded in P.

Lemma 5.12 For any strategy σ of player I in $\Gamma_n(p)$ we have:

$$\frac{1}{n} \sum_{m=1}^{n} E|p_{m+1} - p_m| \leq \frac{1}{\sqrt{n}} \sqrt{p(1-p)} .$$

Here E is the expectation with respect to the probability induced by σ and p.

Proof. Since p_m is a martingale with expectation p (which is p_1) we have:

$$E\left(\sum_{m=1}^{n} (p_{m+1} - p_m)^2\right) = E\left(\sum_{m=1}^{n} (p_{m+1} - p_m)\right)^2 = E(p_{n+1} - p_1)^2 \leq p(1-p) .$$

The result now follows by using Cauchy-Schwartz inequality.

Q.E.D.

The expectation $E|p_{m+1} - p_m|$ is a measure for the amount of information revealed in stage m by player I. In particular, if, at that stage, he plays NR (i.e., independently of k) then $p_{m+1} = p_m$ and thus $E|p_{m+1} - p_m|$. The next lemma says that if player I does not play NR his extra gain is somehow proportional to the information he reveals. At any stage m let $s_m = (s_m^1, s_m^2)$ be the one-stage strategy played by player I (i.e., play the mixed strategy s_m^k if the state is A^k). Let t_m be the mixed strategy of player II and let $g_m(s_m, t_m)$ be the conditional expected pay-off (given p_m) at that stage, then:

Lemma 5.13 For all s_m and t_m :

$$|g_m(s_m, t_m) - g_m(\bar{s}_m, t_m)| \leq cE_m(|p_{m+1} - p_m|) \quad , \tag{5.2}$$

where $c = 2 \max_{i,j,k} |a^k_{ij}|$, $\bar{s}_m$ is the NR strategy $\bar{s}_m = p_m s^1_m + (1 - p_m)s^2_m$, and E_m is the conditional expectation given p_m .

We omit the proof which is a matter of straightforward verification (see lemma 2 in Zamir, 1971-72).

Lemma 5.14 For all $p \in P$, $v_n(p) \leq (\text{Cav } u)(p) + O(1/\sqrt{n})$.

Proof. For any strategy σ of player I compute p_m and let player II play at stage m a mixed strategy t_m which is optimal in $\Delta(p_m)$. Denote this (response) strategy of player II by τ and by $\rho_n(\sigma, \tau)$ the expected average pay-off for σ and τ .

Since $\bar{s}_m$ is an NR strategy, $g_m(\bar{s}_m, t_m) \leq u(p_m) \leq (\text{Cav } u)(p_m)$. Using (5.2), averaging over m and using the Jensen's inequality for Cav u we obtain:

$$\rho_n(\sigma, \tau) \leq (\text{Cav } u)(p) + \frac{c}{n} \sum_{m=1}^{n} E(|p_{m+1} - p_m|) \quad .$$

Combining this with lemma 5.12 we conclude that for each σ there exists τ such that

$$\rho_n(\sigma, \tau) \leq (\text{Cav } u)(p) + \frac{c}{\sqrt{n}} \sqrt{p(1 - p)} \quad .$$

Q.E.D.

The following theorem, due to Aumann and Maschler (1967), is a corollary of what we have so far.

Theorem 5.15 (i) $\lim_{n\to\infty} v_n(p) = (\text{Cav } u)(p) \quad \forall \; p \in P$ and the convergence is uniform.

(ii) There exists $c > 0$ such that

$$0 \leq v_n(p) - (\text{Cav } u)(p) \leq \frac{c\sqrt{p(1 - p)}}{\sqrt{n}} \quad \text{for all} \quad p \in P \text{ and all } n \; .$$

Zamir has shown (1971-72) that the bound $O(1/\sqrt{n})$ for the speed of convergence is the best uniform upper bound. This was done by the following.

Example 5.16 Consider the game in which:

$$A^1 = \begin{pmatrix} 3 & -1 \\ -3 & 1 \end{pmatrix} , \qquad A^2 = \begin{pmatrix} 2 & -2 \\ -2 & 2 \end{pmatrix} \quad .$$

Here $u(p) = \text{val}\begin{pmatrix} p + 2 & p - 2 \\ -p - 2 & -p + 2 \end{pmatrix} = 0 \quad \forall \; p \in [0, 1]$.

We state without proving that $v_n(p) \geq p(1-p)/\sqrt{n}$ for all p and all n. (Here $(\text{Cav } u)(p) = u(p) = 0 \ \forall \ p \in P$.)

Remark 5.17 The central fact to emphasize in theorem 5.15 is that $\Gamma_n(p)$ cannot be analyzed for a single $0 < p < 1$ unless we study the whole family of games $\Gamma_n(p)$; $p \in P$.

Examples Revisited

Example 5.1: $u(p) = \text{val}\begin{pmatrix} p & 0 \\ 0 & 1-p \end{pmatrix} = p(1-p)$.

Since $u(p)$ is concave $\lim v_n(p) = (\text{Cav } u)(p) = p(1-p)$. In particular $\lim v_n(\frac{1}{2}) = \frac{1}{4}$.

Example 5.2: $u(p) = \text{val}\begin{pmatrix} -p & 0 \\ 0 & -(1-p) \end{pmatrix} = -p(1-p)$, whose concavification is 0.

Therefore $\lim v_n(p) = (\text{Cav } u)(p) = 0 \ \forall \ p \in [0,1]$.

Example 5.3: Here $u(p) = \text{val}\begin{pmatrix} 4p & 4(1-p) & 2(2p-1) \\ 4p & 4(1-p) & 2(1-2p) \end{pmatrix}$ is the following function:

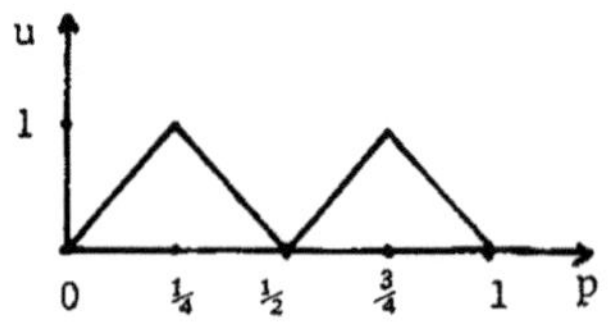

Therefore $(\text{Cav } u)(\frac{1}{2}) = \frac{1}{2}u(\frac{1}{4}) + \frac{1}{2}u(\frac{3}{4}) = 1$.

The value of $\Gamma_\infty(p)$

By remark 5.4, if $\Gamma_\infty(p)$ has a value it must be $(\text{Cav } u)(p)$. To prove this (see Definition 3.14) one has to show that:

(a) for each $\varepsilon > 0$, Player I can guarantee $(\text{Cav } u)(p) - \varepsilon$;

(b) for each $\varepsilon > 0$, Player II can guarantee $(\text{Cav } u)(p) + \varepsilon$.

The proof of (a) is the easier part. It is even true that Player 1 *can guarantee* Cav u , i.e. he has a strategy σ such that $\rho_n(\sigma, \tau) \geq (\text{Cav } u)(p)$ for all n and all τ of player II. This strategy is quite transparent in Example 5.3. There player I constructs a type-dependent lottery in such a way that given the outcome of the lottery the (posterior) probability of A^1 is either $\frac{1}{4}$ or $\frac{3}{4}$ with equal probabilities. According to the outcome of the lottery he then plays optimally in $\Delta(\frac{1}{4})$ or $\Delta(\frac{3}{4})$ in all stages of the game. In such a strategy, the revelation part is only in the first step, which we may call the *splitting* part. That is the part in which the first stage posterior is distributed in the 'right way' so that $E(p_1) = p$ and $Eu(p_1) = (\text{Cav } u)(p)$. After the splitting part, player I plays an NR strategy which is an optimal strategy in $\Delta(p_1)$.

The fact that this splitting can always be done in the desired way yields the following (see Mertens and Zamir, 1971-72, Lemma 2 or Sorin, 1980, Lemma 2.17).

Lemma 5.18 If player I can guarantee $f(p)$ in $\Gamma_\infty(p)$, he can also guarantee $(\text{Cav } f)(p)$.

Corollary 5.19 Player I can guarantee $(\text{Cav } u)(p)$ in $\Gamma_\infty(p)$.

Proof. Player I can guarantee $u(p)$ per stage by playing at every stage, and independently of his type, an optimal strategy in $\Delta(p)$. The result now follows by Lemma 5.18.

To prove (b) let τ_n be an optimal strategy of player II in $\Gamma_n(p)$. Let N_2 N_3 ... be large integers (to be specified later) and consider the following strategy τ of player 2 in $\Gamma_\infty(p)$: At the first stage play τ_1 . At the next $2N_2$ stages play N_2 times τ_2 and so on. After $1 + 2N_2 + \ldots + mN_m$ stages play N_{m+1} times τ_{m+1} . At the beginning of each 'block' player II ignores the history, as if the game newly started. With this τ player II's average pay-off for the first $(1 + 2N_2 + \ldots + mN_m)$ stages is at most:

$$(v_1 + 2N_2v_2 + \ldots + mN_mv_m)/(1 + 2N_2 + \ldots + mN_m) \quad . \tag{5.3}$$

Now given $\varepsilon > 0$ we can choose $N_2, N_3, \ldots$ so that the expression in (5.3) will be at least $v_m - \frac{\varepsilon}{2}$ for sufficiently large m . Since $\lim v_m = \text{Cav } u$ this is at least $(\text{Cav } u)(p) - \varepsilon$ for sufficiently large m .

This concludes the second result of Aumann and Maschler.

Theorem 5.20 For all $p \in P$, $(\text{Cav } u)(p)$ is the value of $\Gamma_\infty(p)$.

Admittedly, the above-described strategy of player II to ε-guarantee Cav u is far from being appealing. Even for very moderate m , τ_m may be practically nonfeasible to compute even by the largest existing computer. In contrast, we shall now describe another very elegant, appealing and easily computable ε-optimal strategy for the uninformed player, player II. This strategy relies on a fundamental paper of Blackwell (1956).

Blackwell considered a two-person game with a "pay-off matrix" B whose elements $\{b_{ij} | i \in I, \ j \in J\}$ are vectors in the K-dimensional Euclidean space R^K . The game is infinitely repeated. After stage m , both players are told the vector pay-off $g_m \in R^K$ reached at that stage so that the total information up to this stage is the $m + 1$ "history" $h_{m+1} = (g_1, \ldots, g_m)$. A strategy of a player is a sequence of mappings from histories to probability distributions on his pure strategies (I or J).

<u>Definition 5.21</u> A set $S \subset R^K$ is *approachable* for player II with τ_0 if for each $\varepsilon > 0$ there exists N_0 such that for all σ of player I, and all $n \geq N_0$ $E_{\sigma,\tau_0}(d(S,\bar{g}_n)) < \varepsilon$, where $d(\cdot, \cdot)$ is the distance in R^K, $\bar{g}_n = (1/n) \sum_{m=1}^{n} g_m$ and E_{σ,τ_0} is the expectation with respect to σ and τ_0.

S is *excludable* by player I with σ_0 if there exists $\delta > 0$ and N_0 such that for all τ and all $n \geq N_0$, $E(d(S, \bar{g}_n)) > \delta$.

Similar definitions are obtained by inversing the roles of the players. S is approachable for a player if he has a strategy with which it is approachable for him.

For each $t = (t_1, \ldots, t_J)$, a probability distribution on J, denote $R_{II}(t)$ convex hull of $\{\sum_{j \in J} t_j b_{ij} \; ; \; i \in I\}$. Hence, if player II uses t his expected pay-off will be in $R_{II}(t)$. The following theorem is the only part of Blackwell's results needed here:

<u>Theorem 5.22</u> (Blackwell 1956): Let S be a closed set in R^K. If for each $x \notin S$ there exists $t(x)$, a probability vector on J such that if y in S is the closest point to x, the hyperplane perpendicular to the line $x - y$ through y separates x from $R_{II}(t(x))$, then S is approachable for player II. An approaching strategy is given by:

- at stage 1 or if $\bar{g}_n \in S$ play anything;
- otherwise play $t_{m+1} = t(\bar{g}_m)$, $n \geq 1$.

With this theorem at hand we now construct a strategy of the uninformed player which ε-guarantees $(\mathrm{Cav}\, u)(p)$.

Step 1. Let $H = \{x \in R^K | \alpha \cdot x = \alpha \cdot p\}$ be the supporting hyperplane to Cav u at the point p, i.e. $\alpha \in R^K$ satisfies:

$$(\mathrm{Cav}\, u)(p) = \alpha \cdot p \quad \text{and} \quad u(q) \leq \alpha \cdot q \quad \text{for all } q \in P .$$

(As usual, $x \cdot y$ denotes the dot product in R^K.)

Step 2. Consider the set $S = \{y \in R^K | y^k \leq \alpha^k, \text{ for all } k \in K\}$, i.e. the 'corner set' in R^K defined by α. It is enough to show a strategy of player II with respect to which S would be approachable for him, since this would mean that the average expected pay-off up to state n will be at most $\alpha \cdot p + \varepsilon = (\mathrm{Cav}\, u)(p) + \varepsilon$ for n large enough.

Step 3. Let $x_n \in R^K$ be the average vector pay-off at the end of stage $n - 1$, and let y_n be the point in S closest to x_n. The approaching strategy for player II is as follows. At stage n:

- If $y_n = x_n$ (i.e., $x_n \in S$) play anything.

- If $x_n \notin S$ let $p' \in P$ be a vector in the direction of $x_n - y_n$. Play t_n which is optimal in $\Delta(p')$.

Note that the hyperplane H' through y_n is perpendicular to p'.
$H' = \{y \in R^K | p' \cdot y = p' \cdot y_n\}$ separates x_n from X (since S is convex). Thus in view of Theorem 5.22 it remains to show that $R_{II}(t_n)$ is on the same side of H' as S. In fact, since t_n is optimal in $\Delta(p')$ we have
$\sum_k p'^k sA^k t_n \leq u(p') \leq \alpha \cdot p'$ for all mixed strategies s of player I.

Now remark that if $p'^k > 0$ then $y_n^k = \alpha^k$ so that $\alpha \cdot p' = y_n \cdot p' < x_n \cdot p'$, i.e., when t_n is used, the resulting expected vector pay-off for that stage is on the opposite side of H' from x_n, that is to say, on the same side as S.

Remark 5.23 Comparing Definition 3.14 and the notion of approachability in Definition 5.21 we actually prove a somewhat stronger result than needed.
Not only that, for each $\varepsilon > 0$, player II has a strategy τ_ε which guarantees $\rho_n(\sigma, \tau_\varepsilon) < (\text{Cav } u)(p) + \varepsilon$ for large enough n for every σ, but he has *one strategy* τ which does this for all $\varepsilon > 0$.

Remark 5.24 When in the above-treated model the informed player is player II, the minimizer, then the Aumann-Maschler's result reads: $\lim v_n$ = value of $\Gamma_\infty = \text{Vex } u$, where $\text{Vex } u$ is the largest convex function f satisfying $f(q) \leq u(q)$ for all $q \in P$.

Chapter 6
REPEATED GAMES WITH INCOMPLETE INFORMATION (II)

Incomplete Information on Both Sides

The first model of incomplete information for both players was given by Aumann and Maschler (1967) and was the natural generalization of their first asymmetric model treated in the previous chapter.

The Model. The states of nature are $I \times J$ matrices A^{ks} where $k \in K = \{1,\ldots,K\}$, $s \in S = \{1,\ldots,S\}$. $p \in P$ and $q \in Q$ are probability distributions on K and S, respectively.

At stage 0, chance chooses the state of nature according to the product probability $p \times q$, i.e. $\Pr(A^{ks}) = p^k q^s \;\; \forall\, k, s$. Player I is told the value of k and player II is told the value of s. (That is, K and S are the type sets of players I and II respectively.)

At stage m, $m=1,2,\ldots$ player I chooses $i_m \in I$ and player II chooses $j_m \in J$ and (i_m, j_m) is announced.

In the n-repeated game, denoted by $\Gamma_n(p, q)$, the pay-off is $\frac{1}{n}\sum_{m=1}^{n} a^{ks}_{i_m j_m}$, and the value is denoted by $v_n(p, q)$. In the infinitely repeated game $\Gamma_\infty(p, q)$ we again define the value $v_\infty(p, q)$ without defining a pay-off function (Definition 3.14).

Remark 6.1 Note that in our model the types of the players are chosen independently. We shall later refer to this as *the independent case* in contrast to *the dependent case* to be introduced later.

The *nonrevealing game* (NR), denoted by $\Delta(p, q)$ is the zero-sum two-person game with the matrix pay-off $\sum_{k,s} p^k q^s A^{ks}$. Its value is denoted by $u(p, q)$.

For any real function $f(p, q)$ defined on $P \times Q$ we denote by $\operatorname{Cav}_p f(\cdot, q)$ the concavification with respect to p, the value of q being fixed. $\operatorname{Vex}_q f(p,\cdot)$ is defined similarly. With minor abuse of notation we write $\operatorname{Cav}_p f(p,q)$ and $\operatorname{Vex}_q f(p,q)$ instead of $(\operatorname{Cav}_p f(\cdot, q))(p)$ and $(\operatorname{Vex}_q f(p, \cdot))(q)$, respectively.

The Infinitely Repeated Game $\Gamma_\infty(p, q)$

We recall without repeating the notion of strategies in $\Gamma_\infty(p, q)$. Note that for player I a strategy σ can be looked at as a K-tuple $\sigma = (\sigma^k)_{k \in K}$ where σ^k is a usual infinite game strategy (used by player I if he is of type k). A similar description is valid for the strategies of player II.

Definition 6.2 $f(p, q)$ is said to be *the minmax* of $\Gamma_\infty(p, q)$ if:

(i) For each strategy τ of player II, $\forall\ \varepsilon > 0$ there is σ of player I and N such that $\rho_n(\sigma, \tau) > f(p, q) - \varepsilon$ for all $n \geq N$.

(ii) $\forall\ \varepsilon > 0$, there is $N(\varepsilon)$ and a strategy τ_ε of player II such that $\rho_n(\sigma, \tau_\varepsilon) < f(p, q) + \varepsilon$ for all σ and all $n > N(\varepsilon)$.

The notion of *maxmin* is defined similarly.

Condition (ii) says that player II can guarantee $f + \varepsilon$ in terms of lim sup. Part (i) asserts that he cannot guarantee anything lower than f even in terms of lim inf.

Theorem 6.3 The minmax of $\Gamma_\infty(p, q)$ equals $\operatorname{Vex}_q \operatorname{Cav}_p u(p, q)$.

The maxmin of $\Gamma_\infty(p, q)$ equals $\operatorname{Cav}_p \operatorname{Vex}_q u(p, q)$.

Proof. We prove only the first part, the second follows then similarly.

Step 1. If player II ignores his private information (s) and plays NR, the game $\Gamma_\infty(p, q)$ reduces then to $\bar{\Gamma}_\infty(p)$ with lack of information on one side defined by the matrices $A^k = \sum_s q^s A^{ks}$ and the probability p on K. By Theorem 5.20, in this game player II can guarantee $(\operatorname{Cav} \bar{u})(p)$ where $\bar{u}$ is the value of $\sum_k p^k A^k = \sum_{k,s} p^k q^s A^{ks}$ which is just $u(p, q)$. That is, player II can guarantee $\operatorname{Cav} u(p, q)$ in the stronger sense of Remark 5.23: he has a strategy τ which guarantees $\rho_n(\sigma, \tau) < \operatorname{Cav}_p u(p, q) + \varepsilon$ for all σ and for all $\varepsilon > 0$ for n large enough.

Step 2. By Lemma 5.18 used for the uninformed player II, he can also guarantee (in the same sense) $\operatorname{Vex}_q \operatorname{Cav}_p u(p, q)$.

This concludes the proof of (a somewhat stronger version than) (ii) in the definition of minmax. The proof of (i) is more technical, therefore we only outline the idea and main points in the proof.

- Given a strategy τ, player I can compute the posteriors q_m on S. Now $(q_m)_{m=1}^\infty$, being a martingale bounded in the simplex Q, converges with probability 1. In terms of information this means that far enough in the game, player II will reveal almost no information. Player I can therefore play NR during a large number of stages N in order "*to exhaust the maximal amount of information from* τ." Afterwards the situation is almost the same as if player II plays NR so player I can obtain $u(p, q_N)$, hence $\operatorname{Cav}_p u(p, q_n)$. His expected pay-off is (up to an ε), $E \operatorname{Cav}_p u(p, q_N)$ which is at least $\operatorname{Vex}_q \operatorname{Cav}_p u(p, q)$.

The technical steps which turn this idea into a formal proof are:

1. $E_{p,\sigma,\tau} \sum_{s} \sum_{m=1}^{\infty} (q_{m+1}^{s} - q_{m}^{s}) \leq \sum_{s} q^{s}(1 - q^{s})$ for all σ. Thus let σ^* be the strategy of player I which ε-achieves the supremum of this quantity up to stage N.

2. Since q_m depends only on q, τ, h_m and j_m, the 'average' NR strategy σ_0 which will have the same distribution on j_m will produce the same q_m as σ^* and thus will do the same job as σ^*.

3. For any strategy σ which coincides with σ_0 up to the stage N we get for all $n \geq N$, $E(\sum_{s} |q_n^s - q_N^s|) \leq M\sqrt{\varepsilon}$ for some constant M.

4. Given τ and $\varepsilon > 0$, player I plays σ_0 up to stage N, then does the 'splitting of p' to $(p_i)_{i\in I}$ with probabilities $(\lambda_i)_{i\in I}$ such that $\sum_i \lambda_i p_i = p$ and $\sum_i \lambda_i u(p_i, q_N) = \text{Cav}\, u(p, q_N)$ and then play optimally in $\Delta(p_i, q_N)$. Q.E.D.

Corollary 6.4 The infinite game has a value if and only if:

$$\underset{p}{\text{Cav}}\ \underset{q}{\text{Vex}}\ u(p, q) = \underset{q}{\text{Vex}}\ \underset{p}{\text{Cav}}\ u(p, q) \quad . \tag{6.1}$$

The following example provides a game in which (6.1) does not hold and hence $\Gamma_\infty(p, q)$ *does not have a value.*

Example 6.5 (See Mertens and Zamir 1971-72) Let $K = \{1, 2\}$, $S = \{1, 2\}$ and:

$$A^{12} = \begin{pmatrix} 0 & 0 & 0 & 0 \\ -1 & 1 & 1 & -1 \end{pmatrix} \qquad A^{12} = \begin{pmatrix} 1 & -1 & 1 & -1 \\ 0 & 0 & 0 & 0 \end{pmatrix}$$

$$A^{21} = \begin{pmatrix} -1 & 1 & -1 & 1 \\ 0 & 0 & 0 & 0 \end{pmatrix} \qquad A^{22} = \begin{pmatrix} 0 & 0 & 0 & 0 \\ 1 & -1 & 1 & -1 \end{pmatrix} .$$

$u(p, q)$, which is the value of the game

$$\begin{pmatrix} p-q & q-p & p-q & q-p \\ q'-p & p-q' & p-q' & q'-p \end{pmatrix}$$

with $p' = 1 - p$; $q' = 1 - p$, is given below together with Cav Vex u and Vex Cav u .

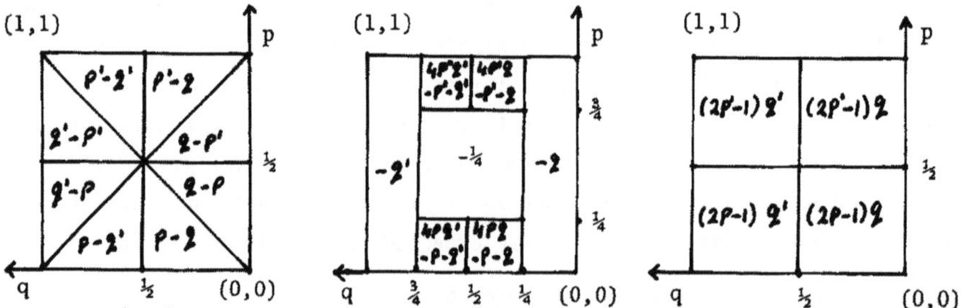

u(p,q) Cav Vex u Vex Cav u

The Finite Games $\Gamma_n(p,q)$

With the nonexistence of value for $\Gamma_\infty(p, q)$ there still remains the question of existence of the limit of $v_n(p, q)$, the value of the n-repeated games $\Gamma_n(p, q)$. This is answered by the following theorem which we bring without proof (see Mertens and Zamir, 1971-72).

Theorem 6.6 For all $(p, q) \in P \times Q$, $\lim_{n\to\infty} v_n(p, q)$ exists and is the only simultaneous solution of the following two functional equations.

$$v(p, q) = \operatorname{Vex}_q \max \{u(p, q), v(p, q)\} \tag{6.2}$$

$$v(p, q) = \operatorname{Cav}_p \min \{u(p, q), v(p, q)\} . \tag{6.3}$$

Remark 6.7 Let us show that when Cav Vex u = Vex Cav u this is also the unique solution of (6.2) and (6.3), as it should be.

- First observe that Vex Cav u *is a solution of (6.2).* In fact, notice that Cav and Vex are monotone operators, therefore, on one hand:

$$\text{Vex Cav } u = \text{Vex max } \{u, \text{Cav } u\} \geq \text{Vex max } \{u, \text{Vex Cav } u\} .$$

On the other hand, Vex Cav u $\leq$ max {u, Vex Cav u} . Taking Vex from both sides yields the other inequality and so Vex Cav u = Vex max {u, Vex Cav u }.

- Similarly, Cav Vex u is a solution of (6.3). Therefore, if

Cave Vex u = Vex Cav u , this is a common solution of (6.2) and (6.3). That it is the *only* common solution follows from:

- Any v which satisfies (6.2) and (6.3) satisfies Cav Vex u $\leq$ v $\leq$ Vex Cav u. In fact, from (6.2), v $\geq$ Vex u . Since by (6.3) v is concave we have v $\geq$ Cav Vex u . The second inequality is obtained similarly.

Extensions of the Model

Of the variants of the above-described basic model let us mention two. One is the direction of allowing a more general mechanism for revealing information than just through the moves. The other is in allowing a more general structure of prior information and *dependence* between the types of the two players.

Signaling matrices. We modify our model by introducing two matrices H_I^{ks} and H_{II}^{ks} of dimensions $I \times J$ and with elements $h_I^{ks}(ij)$ and $h_{II}^{ks}(ij)$ in some finite set H. If the state of nature drawn at stage 0 is ks and if at stage m the players choose i_m and j_m, then player I is informed of $h_I^{ks}(i_m,j_m)$ and player II of $h_{II}^{ks}(i_m,j_m)$. When $h_I^{ks}(ij) = h_{II}^{ks}(ij) = (i, j)$ for all k and s this is the usual model which we shall therefore call the *standard signaling case.*

Aumann and Maschler (1968) proved their result for the incomplete information on one side. $v = \lim v_n = \text{Cav } u$ for general signaling matrices, of course after redefining appropriately the NR game and its value u. It turns out that the signaling matrices for the informed player are immaterial for this result (they may have an effect on v_n but not on its limit).

Definition 6.8 For $p \in P$ a one-stage strategy of player I is nonrevealing (NR) if for each $j \in J$, the distribution on the letters of H in the row $h^k_{II}(ij)$ is the same for all k. (That is, this is a strategy after which the posterior on K cannot change.)

Denote by $NR(p)$ the set of nonrevealing strategies of player I at p. (Note that $NR(p)$ may be empty, but is nonempty when p is an extreme point of P.) Define the NR game $\Delta(p)$ as the game in which player I is restricted to $NR(p)$ if it is not empty. Finally:

$$u(p) = \begin{cases} \text{value of } \Delta(p) & \text{if } NR(p) \neq \phi \\ -\infty & \text{if } NR(p) = \phi \end{cases} .$$

With this definition Aumann and Maschler proved:

Theorem 6.9 $\lim_{n\to\infty} v_n(p)$ and $v(p)$ exist and both equal to $(\text{Cav } u)(p)$.

The generalization of Blackwell's approachability strategy for the uninformed player was done by Kohlberg (1975).

For incomplete information on both sides Mertens and Zamir (1980) proved the above-stated results about minmax; maxmin and $\lim v_n$ for signaling matrices which are independent of the state of nature. The model they treated was more general also in another respect, namely, they treated the dependent case which shall be explained briefly now.

The Dependent Case. As we remarked before (Remark 6.1), the Aumann Maschler model for incomplete information on both sides assumed that the types of the two players are chosen independently. In such a model the probability distribution of a player on the types of his opponent is independent on his own type.

The Model. The set K is the set of states of world and $p \in P$ is a probability distribution on K. K^I and K^{II} are two partitions of K. (The elements of K^I and K^{II} are the *types* of players I and II, respectively.) The signaling matrices H_I and H_{II} are the same for all states of nature (and this is a very crucial assumption without which the results are not valid).

As mentioned above all results to the special case were extended to this general case where $u(p)$ is the value of the one-stage game in which both players are restricted to NR strategies, i.e., strategies which produce a probability distribution on the signals of the opponent which is independent on the state of the world k (no matter what the opponent does).

The main difficulty was the extension of the operators Cav and Vex since we no longer have the natural variables p for concavification and q for convexification. The key to the right generalization is the following observation. If the distribution on K is $p \in P$, since any one-stage strategy of player I is K^I-measurable, the resulting posterior distribution on K given his move at that stage will be in the set $\Pi_1(p) \subset P$ defined by:

$$\Pi_I(p) = \{(\alpha^1 p^1, \ldots, \alpha^K p^K) \in P \mid (\alpha^k)_{k \in K} \text{ is } K^I\text{-measurable}\} .$$

Similarly,

$$\Pi_{II}(p) = \{(\beta^1 p^1, \ldots, \beta^K p^K) \in P \mid (\beta^k)_{k \in K} \text{ is } K^{II}\text{-measurable}\} .$$

Clearly for any $p \in P$ both $\Pi_I(p)$ and $\Pi_{II}(p)$ are nonempty convex and compact subsets of P. A real function f defined on P will be called I-concave if for any $p_0 \in P$, $f(p)$ restricted to $\Pi_I(p_0)$ is concave. The notion of II-convex is defined similarly. Then we define $\underset{I}{\text{Cav}}\, f$ and $\underset{II}{\text{Vex}}\, f$ in the natural way and we have:

Theorem 6.10 (a) The minmax of $\Gamma_\infty(p)$ is $\underset{II}{\text{Vex}}\, \underset{I}{\text{Cav}}\, u(p)$.

(b) The maxmin of $\Gamma_\infty(p)$ is $\underset{II}{\text{Cav}}\, \underset{I}{\text{Vex}}\, u(p)$.

(c) For each $p \in P$, $\lim v_n(p)$ exists and is the only solution v of the following two equations:

$$\text{(i)} \quad v(p) = \underset{II}{\text{Vex}} \max \{u(p), v(p)\}$$
$$\text{(ii)} \quad v(p) = \underset{I}{\text{Cav}} \min \{u(p), v(p)\} .$$

The existence of a unique solution to (i) and (ii) is an interesting duality theorem that can be proved without any mention of game theory (see Mertens and Zamir 1977b, and Sorin 1986, forthcoming).

Speed of Convergence and the Normal Distribution

We have seen that in the case of incomplete information on one side and standard signaling, the speed of convergence of $v_n(p)$ is bounded by $O(1/\sqrt{n})$ and this is the best bound. This turns out to be the case also for incomplete information on both sides with standard signaling. When signaling is by H_I and H_{II} independent of the state of nature we have a higher bound of $O(1/n^{\frac{1}{3}})$ and this is the best bound (Zamir, 1973a).

Let us recall example 5.16 with $A^1 = \begin{pmatrix} 3 & -1 \\ -3 & 1 \end{pmatrix}$, $A^2 = \begin{pmatrix} 2 & -2 \\ -2 & 2 \end{pmatrix}$. For this game $(\text{Cav}\, u)(p) = u(p) = 0 \ \forall\ p \in P$ and

$$p(1-p)/\sqrt{n} \leq v_n(p) \leq \sqrt{p(1-p)}\,/\sqrt{n} \quad . \tag{6.4}$$

The order $O(1/\sqrt{n})$ may be explained by the following argument. Since $\text{Cav}\, u(p) = u(p)$, the informed player must 'essentially' ignore his information and play the same mixed strategy $(\frac{1}{2}, \frac{1}{2})$ at each stage independently of his type. The average pay-off will be a random variable with variation (namely standard deviation) of the order of $(1/\sqrt{n})$. In the example under consideration the informed player can take advantage of this natural variation by 'pretending' to play $(\frac{1}{2}, \frac{1}{2})$, but actually deviating slightly from it. This deviation is exactly of the order that the uninformed player might expect as random but is actually used to the advantage of the informed player.

The following, quite surprising, result (Mertens and Zamir, 1976) shows a much closer connection to the Central Limit Theorem than outlined above: the normal distribution appears explicitly.

Theorem 6.11 For the game in Example 5.16: $\lim_{n\to\infty} \sqrt{n}\, v_n(p) = \phi(p)$, where $\phi(p)$ is the standard normal density evaluated at its p-quantile, i.e.

$$\phi(p) = (1/\sqrt{2\pi}) \exp(-\tfrac{1}{2}x_p^2) \quad \text{and} \quad (1/\sqrt{2\pi}) \int_{-\infty}^{x_p} \exp(-\tfrac{1}{2}x^2)dx = p \quad . \tag{6.5}$$

In a recent unpublished result, Mertens and Zamir showed that this is generally true at least for the case of two states of nature. Whenever the error term $v_n(p) - \lim v_n(p)$ is of the order of $(1/\sqrt{n})$ the coefficient is the normal density function. The proof has nothing to do with the above intuitive argument. The normal distribution comes out as a solution of a certain differential equation. At this point, this result is quite mysterious and the "something behind" is still to be discovered.

The result of Theorem 6.11 is intimately related, actually equivalent, to the following optimization problem, which makes no mention of game theory (Mertens and Zamir, 1977). Let $X(p) = p_0, p_1, \ldots p_n$ be a martingale with values in $[0, 1]$ and $p_0 \equiv p$. Let $M(p)$ be the set of all such martingales.

Theorem 6.12 $$\lim_{n\to\infty} \Big(\sup_{X(p)\in M(p)} (1/\sqrt{n}) \sum_{m=0}^{n} E|p_{m+1} - p_m| \Big) = \phi(p) ,$$

where $\phi(p)$ is given by (6.5).

The connection between the two problems should be clear by now. The $(p_m)_{m=1}^n$ are the posterior probabilities of A^1 (given that player I is using a certain strategy σ). $E|p_{m+1} - p_m|$ is a measure of the information revealed by player I at the m-th stage. This is also his pay-off at stage m (compared to $u(p_m) = 0$ that he would get if he would play NR). Therefore, the objective function to be maximized is $\sum_{m=0}^{n} E|p_{m+1} - p_m|$. But since $(p_m)_{m=1}^n$ is a martingale bounded in

[0, 1] , this expression is bounded by $O(1/\sqrt{n})$ and is in fact of that order.

Relations to Stochastic Games

By now it should be clear that repeated games of incomplete information are fundamentally different from stochastic games. In repeated games of incomplete information the state of nature is *fixed* but may be *unknown* by some players. It is the 'state of mind' of the players that changes along the play. In stochastic games, on the other hand, the state of nature *changes* randomly but it is *known* to all players. This difference is well manifested in the results: infinite undiscounted stochastic games have a value while incomplete information infinitely repeated games have no value in general (except for some special cases). Nevertheless there is a close relation between the two models which consists mainly of the fact that some incomplete information games can be transformed to equivalent stochastic games. To see that, consider the following examples.

Example 6.13 In a two-person zero-sum game Γ_{12} there are two states of nature {1, 2} chosen with equal probabilities. The pay-off matrices are:

$$A_1 = \begin{pmatrix} 0 & 0 \\ 0 & 4 \end{pmatrix} ; \quad A_2 = \begin{pmatrix} 0 & -2 \\ 2 & 0 \end{pmatrix} .$$

No player gets any prior information and both get the same signals according to the signaling matrices

$$H_1 = \begin{pmatrix} a & b \\ c & d \end{pmatrix} ; \quad H_2 = \begin{pmatrix} a & e \\ c & d \end{pmatrix} .$$

Since the values of both A_1 and A_2 are 0 it follows that:

- As soon as signal b or e is announced a pay-off -1 is made and the games moves to an absorbing state with value 0 (we denote this by $-1, \to 0^*$).
- As long as neither b nor e was announced, any signal a yields a pay-off 0 for that stage and the same game is repeated again, similarly for c and d .

We summarize this as follows:

$$\begin{pmatrix} 0, \to\text{same} & -1, \to 0^* \\ 1, \to\text{same} & 2, \to\text{same} \end{pmatrix} .$$

This means that our game is equivalent to the infinitely repeated game with one absorbing state: $\begin{pmatrix} 0 & 0^* \\ 1 & 2 \end{pmatrix}$. (We omitted the -1 since it does not affect the evaluation of the pay-off sequence which is 0 from a finite stage on.)

Now this game has clearly the value 1 , therefore this is also the value of the infinitely repeated game in our example.

Example 6.14 Consider the game Γ_{23} which is of the same type as Γ_{12} of the previous example, but with states of nature $\{2, 3\}$ and:

$$A_2 = \begin{pmatrix} 0 & -2 \\ 2 & 0 \end{pmatrix} \quad ; \quad A_3 = \begin{pmatrix} 0 & 0 \\ -4 & -2 \end{pmatrix}$$

$$H_2 = \begin{pmatrix} a & e \\ c & d \end{pmatrix} \quad ; \quad H_3 = \begin{pmatrix} f & e \\ c & d \end{pmatrix} .$$

This is equivalent to the infinitely repeated game $\begin{pmatrix} 0^* & -1 \\ -1 & -1 \end{pmatrix}$ with value -1 .

Example 6.15 (Mertens, 1982) Consider now the same type of game with three states of nature $\{1, 2, 3\}$ chosen with probabilities $(\frac{1}{3}, \frac{1}{3}, \frac{1}{3})$. The pay-off and the signaling matrices are as before:

$$A_1 = \begin{pmatrix} 0 & 0 \\ 0 & 4 \end{pmatrix} \quad ; \quad A_2 = \begin{pmatrix} 0 & -2 \\ 2 & 0 \end{pmatrix} \quad ; \quad A_3 = \begin{pmatrix} 0 & 0 \\ -4 & -2 \end{pmatrix}$$

$$H_1 = \begin{pmatrix} a & b \\ c & d \end{pmatrix} \quad ; \quad H_2 = \begin{pmatrix} a & e \\ c & d \end{pmatrix} \quad ; \quad H_3 = \begin{pmatrix} f & e \\ c & d \end{pmatrix} .$$

Using the same reasoning as before we reduce our game to:

$$\begin{pmatrix} 0 \begin{matrix} \xrightarrow{2/3} \Gamma_{12} \\ \xrightarrow{1/3} A_3 \end{matrix} & -\frac{2}{3} \begin{matrix} \xrightarrow{2/3} \Gamma_{23} \\ \xrightarrow{1/3} A_1 \end{matrix} \\ -\frac{2}{3}, \rightarrow \text{same} & -\frac{2}{3}, \rightarrow \text{same} \end{pmatrix}$$

By our previous examples $v(\Gamma_{12}) = 1$, $v(\Gamma_{23}) = -1$. Also $v(A_1) = v(A_3) = 0$. Therefore our game is equivalent to the repeated game $\frac{2}{3}\begin{pmatrix} 1^* & -1^* \\ -1 & 1 \end{pmatrix}$.

This is a special stochastic game called "The Big Match" (Blackwell and Ferguson 1968). The foregoing reduction of some games with incomplete information to games with absorbing states is due to Kohlberg and Zamir (1974). By induction on the number of states of nature they proved this type of reduction to the family of repeated two-person zero-sum games with incomplete information in which:

(i) The players have no prior information on the state of nature, i.e., $K^I = K^{II} = K$.

(ii) The signals are the same for both players.

(iii) The signals tell the players at least each other's pure strategy choices.

As a matter of fact, it was this work of Kohlberg and Zamir that motivated the generalization of Blackwell and Ferguson's results about the Big Match to general stochastic games with absorbing states. This generalization, which was accomplished by Kohlberg (1974), accelerated the research on stochastic games which was concluded in a very satisfactory way by the works of Bewley-Kohlberg (1976a, 1976b, 1978) and Mertens-Neyman (1981).

Aumann, R.J. and M. Maschler (1966). Game-theoretic aspects of gradual disarmament. Mathematica ST-80, Ch.V, 1-55.

Aumann, R.J. and M. Maschler (1967). Repeated games with incomplete information: a survey of recent results. Mathematica ST-116, Ch.III, 287-403.

Aumann, R.J. and M. Maschler (1967). Repeated games with incomplete information: the zero-sum extensive case. Mathematica ST-143, Ch.III, 37-116.

Bewley, T. and E. Kohlberg (1976a). The asymptotic theory of stochastic games. Math. Oper. Res. 1, 197-208.

Bewley, T. and E. Kohlberg (1976b). The asymptotic solution of a recursion equation occuring in stochastic games. Math. Oper. Res. 1, 321-336.

Bewley, T. and E. Kohlberg (1978). On stochastic games with stationary optimal strategies. Math. Oper. Res. 3, 104-125.

Blackwell, D. (1956). An analog of the minmax theorem for vector pay-offs. Pacific J. Math. 6, 1-8.

Blackwell, D. and T.S. Ferguson (1968). The big match. Ann. Math. Statist. 39, 159-163.

Kohlberg, E. (1974). Repeated games with absorbing states. Ann. Statist. 2, 724-738.

Kohlberg, E. (1975). Optimal strategies in repeated games of incomplete information. Internat. J. Game Theory 4, 7-24.

Kohlberg, E. and S. Zamir (1974). Repeated games of incomplete information: the symmetric case. Ann. Statist. 2, 1040-1041.

Mertens, J-F. (1971-72). Repeated games: an overview of the zero-sum case. Advances in Economic Theory, W. Hildenbrand (ed.). Cambridge University Press: Cambridge, 175-182.

Mertens, J-F. and A. Neyman (1982). Stochastic games. Internat. J. Game Theory 10, 53-66.

Mertens, J-F. and S. Zamir (1971-1972). The value of two-person zero-sum repeated games with lack of information on both sides. Internat. J. Game Theory 1, 39-64.

Mertens, J-F. and S. Zamir (1977a). The maximal variation of a bounded martingale. Israel J. of Mathe. 27, 252-276.

Mertens, J-F. and S. Zamir (1977b). A duality theory on a pair of simultaneous functional equations. J. Mathe. Anal. App. 60, 550-558.

Mertens, J-F. and S. Zamir (1980). Minmax and maxmin of repeated games with incomplete information. Internat. J. Game Theory 9, 201-215.

Sorin, S. (1980). An introduction to two-person zero-sum repeated games with incomplete information. IMSSS-Economics, Stanford University, TR 312.

Zamir, S. (1971-72). On the relation between finitely and infinitely repeated games with incomplete information. Internat. J. Game Theory 1, 179-198.

Zamir, S. (1973a). On repeated games with general information function. _Internat. J. Game Theory_ 2, 215-229.

Zamir, S. (1973b). On the notion of value for games with infinitely many stages. _Ann. Statist._ 1, 791-796.

FONDAZIONE C.I.M.E.
CENTRO INTERNAZIONALE MATEMATICO ESTIVO
INTERNATIONAL MATHEMATICAL SUMMER CENTER

"Relativistic Fluid Dynamics"

is the subject of the first 1987 C.I.M.E. Session.

The Session, sponsored by the Consiglio Nazionale delle Ricerche and the Ministero della Pubblica Istruzione, will take place under the scientific direction of Proff. ANGELO MARCELLO ANILE (Università di Catania), YVONNE CHOQUET-BRUHAT (Université de Paris 6) at «Centro Studi Noto», Noto (Siracusa), Italy, ***from May 25 to June 3, 1987.***

Courses

a) ***Relativistic Media in Astrophysics.*** (6 lectures in English).
Prof. B. CARTER (D.A.F. Observatoire de Paris, Paris).

Contents

i) The canonical theory of simple, thermally conducting and superconducting fluids. (3 lectures).
ii) Theory of elastic solid media, including variational principles, for relativistic stars and black hole accretion rings. (3 lectures).

Basic references

- B. CARTER, The canonical treatment of heat conduction and superfluidity in relativistic hydrodynamics. Random Walks in Relativity and Cosmology, ed. Dadhich, Krishna Rao, Narlikar, Vishveshwara, Wiley Eastern 1985.
- B. CARTER, Perfect fluids and magnetic field conservation laws in the theory of black hole accretion rings. Active Galactic Nuclei, ed. Hazard and Mitton, Cambridge University Press 1979.
- B. CARTER, Interaction of gravitational waves with an elastic solid medium. Gravitational Radiation, ed. Deruelle and Piran, North Holland 1983.

b) ***Global Geometric Techniques for Relativistic Fluiddynamics and Stability Theory.*** (6 lectures in English).
Prof. Darryl D. HOLM (Los Alamos National Laboratories, Los Alamos).

Contents

i) Action principle for special relativistic compressible fluiddynamics.
ii) Relativistic plasma physics and magnetohydrodynamics: Equation of motion and conservation laws. Hamilton formulation based on action principle. Casimir functionals for degenerate Poisson brackets associated to dual spaces of Lie groups. Equilibrium relations and Lyapunov functionals. Linear and nonlinear Lyapunov stability.
iii) General-relativistic compressible fluid dynamics on space-time slices. Lie-Poisson formulation of self-gravitating fluids.
iv) Special-relativistic Yang- Mills plasma dynamics.

Basic references

- D.D. HOLM, J.E. MARSDEN, T. RATIU, A. WEINSTEIN, Nonlinear Stability of Fluids and Plasma Equilibria. Phys. Rep. 123, pp. 1-116, 1985.
- D.D. HOLM, J.E. MARSDEN, T. RATIU, Hamilton Structure and Lyapunov for Ideal Continuum Dynamics, Un. of Montreal Press 1986.
- D.D. HOLM, B.A. KUPERSHMIDT, Lyapunov Stability of relativistic Fluids and Plasmas. Phys. Fluids 29, pp. 49-68, 1986.
- D.D. HOLM, Hamiltonian Formalism for General Relativistic Adiabatic Fluids, Physica D23, pp. 1-36, 1985.
- D.D. HOLM, B.A. KUPERSHMIDT, Relativistic Chromohydrodynamics and Yang-Mills-Vlasov Plasma, Phys. Lett. A 1051, pp. 225-228, 1984.

c) ***Introduction to Relativistic Hydrodynamics and Kinetic Theory.*** (6 lectures in English).
Prof. Werner ISRAEL (University of Alberta, Edmonton).

Contents

i) Mechanics and thermodynamics of relativistic fluids. Standard and "extended" phenomenological theories. Shock waves.
ii) The relativistic Boltzmann equation. Derivation of transport equation with relaxation terms.
iii) Statistical thermodynamics.
iv) Relativistic superfluids.
v) Some applications.

Basic references

- W. ISRAEL, Thermodynamics of Relativistic Systems. Physica 106a, 204, 1981.
- DE GROOT, VAN LEEUWEN, VAN WEERT, Relativistic Kinetic theory, North Holland 1981.
- W. ISRAEL, J.M. STEWART, Progress in Relativistic Thermodynamics and Electrodynamics of Continuous Media. General Relativity and Gravitation, ed A. Held, Plenum 1980.
- W. ISRAEL, Relativistic Thermodynamics, Thermofield Statistics and Superfluids. J. Irrev. Thermodynamics, II, 295, 1986.

d) ***Relativistic Plasmas.*** (6 lectures in English).
Prof. Harold WEITZNER (Courant Institute, New York).

Contents

i) Relativistic Plasma Models: Perfectly Conducing Relativistic Fluid Model. Relativistic Ohm's law Fluid Model of Friedrichs. Relativistic Vlasov Model. Warm Relativistic Fluid Model of Newcomb, Amendt and Weitzner. (3 hours).
ii) Application of Models to Laboratory Plasmas: Free electron Laser. Relativistic Beams. (3 hours).

Basic references

- K.O. FRIEDRICHS, Comm. Pure Appl. Math. 27, p. 749, 1974.
- W.A. NEWCOMB, Phys. Fluid 25, p. 846, 1982.
- P. AMENDT, H. WEITZNER, Phys. Fluids 28, p. 957, 1986.
- T.O. MARSHALL, Free-electron Laser, Mac Millan, New York, 1985.
- H. WEITZNER, A. FRUCHTMAN, P. AMENDT, To appear Phys. Fluids, 1987.
- R.C. DAVIDSON, Theory of Non-neutral Plasmas, W.A. Benjamin Inc., Reading, Massachusetts, 1974.
- C.S. GARDNER, Phys. Rev. 115, p. 791, 1959.

Prerequisites

Basic knowledge of relativistic thermodynamics, fluid dynamics and particle dynamics will be assumed.

FONDAZIONE C.I.M.E.
CENTRO INTERNAZIONALE MATEMATICO ESTIVO
INTERNATIONAL MATHEMATICAL SUMMER CENTER

"Topics in Calculus of Variations"

is the subject of the Second 1987 C.I.M.E. Session.

The Session, sponsored by the Consiglio Nazionale delle Ricerche and the Ministero della Pubblica Istruzione, will take place under the scientific direction of Prof. MARIANO GIAQUINTA (Università di Firenze) at Villa «La Querceta», Montecatini Terme (Pistoia), Italy, ***from July 20 to July 28, 1987.***

Courses

a) ***S^k-valued maps with Singularities.*** (4 lectures in English).
Prof. Haim BREZIS (Univ. Paris VI).

Outline

Motivated by models arising in the theory of liquid crystals, these lectures are concerned with various questions dealing with the energy of S^k-valued maps with singularities. Two different kinds of problems are considered. In the first type of problem the location and the degree of the singularities is prescribed; the main result is an explicit formula for the minimum value of the deformation energy. In the second type of problem the number, the location and the degree of the singularities are "free"; the main result asserts that if φ is a minimizer then all its singularities have degree ± 1; moreover φ looks like a rotation near every singularity, a fact which agrees with experimental and numerical evidence.

Basic references

1. H. BREZIS, J.M. CORON, E. LIEB, Estimations d'énergie pour des applications de R^3 à valeurs dans S^2, C.R. Acad. Sc. Paris, 303 (1986), 207-210.
2. H. BREZIS, J.M. CORON, E. LIEB, Harmonic maps with defects, Comm. Math. Phys. (to appear).
3. H. BREZIS, Liquid crystals and energy estimates for S^2-valued maps (to appear in 5.).
4. W.F. BRISKMAN, R.E. CLADIS, Defects in liquid crystals, Physics Today, May 1982, p. 48-54.
5. J. ERICKSEN, D. KINDERLEHRER, ed., Proceedings IMA Workshop on the ***Theory and Applications of Liquid Crystals***, Springer (1987).
6. R. Schoen, K. Uhlenbeck, A regularity theory for harmonic maps, J. Diff. Geom., 17 (1982), 307-335; and also 18 (1983), 253-268.

b) ***Free Boundary Problems.*** (6 lectures in English).
Prof. Luis A. CAFFARELLI (Univ. of Chicago).

Outline

These lectures will describe, through three typical variational free boundary problems, the basic techniques developed in the last decade for dealing with the regularity of weak solutions and their free boundaries. Special emphasis will be given to the Harnack's inequality approach.

A free boundary (or multiphase, or moving boundary) problem can be loosely described as a boundary value problem, for some evolving or stationary physical magnitude or system, for which some of the unknowns or their derivatives change behavior discontinuously through some value of the unknowns.

Basic references

1. H.W. ALT and L.A. CAFFARELLI, Existence and regularity for a minimum problem with free boundary, J. Reine Angew. Math., 105 (1981), 105-144.
2. ALT-CAFFARELLI and FRIEDMAN, Variational problems with two phases and their free boundaries, T.A.M.S. Vol. 282, Nr. 2, 1984, 431-461.
3. L.A. CAFFARELLI and D. KINDERLEHRER, Potential methods in variational inequalities, J. Anal. Math., 27 (1980), 285-295.
4. COLOMBINI-DE GIORGI-PICCININI, Frontiere orientate di misura minima e questioni collegate. Pisa (1972).
5. B. DAHLBERG, Estimates for harmonic measure. Arch. Rat. Mech. Anal., 65 (1977), 278-288.
6. J. FREHSE, On the regularity of the solution to a second order variational inequality, Boll. Unione Mat. Italiana, 6(4) (1972), 312-315.
7. H. LEWY and G. STAMPACCHIA, On the regularity of the solution of a variational inequality, Comm. Pure Appl. Math., 22 (1969), 153-188.
8. D. SCHAEFFER, Some examples of singularities in a free boundary, Ann. S. Norm. Pisa., 4(4) (1977), 131-144.

c) ***Minimal Foliations on a Torus.*** (4 lectures in English).
Prof. Jurgen MOSER (ETH, Zurich).

Outline

These lectures are concerned with foliations of codimension on a torus T^m whose leaves are minimals of a nonlinear variational problem. For m=2 such leaves correspond to minimal orbits of a dynamical system and a minimal foliation corresponds to an invariant torus of a Hamiltonian system. The invariant sets developed by J. Mather have as analogue a "lamination" of the torus.

Also the invariant curves theorem of twist mapping has an analogue for nonlinear elliptic partial differential equation. It is the aim to explain the connection between the mechanical problems and the higher dimensional variational problem, as well as to indicate the underlying theory.

Basic references

1. V. BANGERT, Mather Sets for Twist Maps and Geodesic Tori. Preprint, Bonn, 1985.
2. E. DI BENEDETTO, N.S. TRUDINGER, Harnack Inequality for Quasi-Minima of Variational Integrals, Annales de l'Inst. H. Poincaré, Analyse Non-Linéaire, t. 1, 1984, 295-308.
3. M. GIAQUINTA, E. GIUSTI, Quasi-minima, Ann. de l'Inst. Henri Poincaré, Analyse non lin., t. 1, 1984, 79-107.
4. M. GIAQUINTA, E. GIUSTI, Differentiability of Minima of Non-Differentiable Functionals, Inv. Math., t. 72, 1983, 285-298.
5. M. GIAQUINTA, Multiple Integrals in the Calculus of Variations and Nonlinear Elliptic Systems, Ann. Math. Studies, t. 105, Princeton, N.J., 1983.
6. G.A. HEDLUND, Geodesics on a two-dimensional Riemannian manifold with periodic coefficients, Ann. Math., t. 33, 1982, 719-739.
7. O.A. LADYZHENSKAYA, N.N. URALTSEVA, Linear and Quasilinear Elliptic Equations, Acad. Press, New York and London, 1968.
8. M.R. HERMAN, Sur les courbes invariantes par les difféomorphismes de l'anneau, Astérisque, 103-104, 1983, 1-221.
9. J.N. MATHER, Existence of quasi-periodic orbits for twist homeomorphisms of the annulus, Topology, t. 21, 1982, 457-467.
10. M. MORSE, A fundamental class of geodesics on any closed surface of genus greater than one. Trans. Am. Math. Soc., t. 26, 1924, 25-60.
11. J. MOSER, Recent Developments in the theory of Hamiltonian Systems, SIAM Review 28, Dec. 1986.
12. J. MOSER, Minimal solutions of variational problems on a torus, Ann. Inst. Henri Poincaré, Analyse non linéaire, vol. 3, No. 3, 1986, 229-272.

d) ***Variational methods in nonlinear problems.*** (4 lectures in English).
Prof. Louis NIRENBERG (Courant Institute, New York).

Outline

The course will describe the use of some min-max methods such as the mountain pass lemma, and generalization. Applications to nonlinear partial differential equations and also to ordinary differential equations such as periodic solutions for Hamiltonian systems. Some index theory will be developed and applied to obtain multiple solutions.

Basic references

1. L. NIRENBERG, Variational and topological methods in nonlinear problems, Bull. Amer. Math. Soc. 4 (1981), 267-302.
2. L. NIRENBERG, Comments on nonlinear problems. Le Matematiche 36, (1984), 109-119.
3. R. MICHALEK, G. TARANTELLO, Subharmonic solutions with prescribed minimal period for nonautonomous Hamiltonian systems, subm. to J. Diff. Eqs.

e) ***The Einstein-Hilbert energy functional on the space of Riemannian metrics.*** (6 lectures in English).
Prof. Richard SCHOEN (Univ. of California, San Diego).

Outline

We will discuss variational theory for the Einstein-Hilbert energy on the space of Riemannian metrics. The Einstein-Hilbert energy in the total scalar curvature and its critical points on the space unit volume Riemannian metrics are the Einstein metrics.

The resticted problem for metric in a given conformal class in the Yamabe problem on conformal deformation to constant scalar curvature.

We will discuss this problem in the context of recent results. Our discussion concerning the conformal problem will include conformally flat manifolds and their structure as well as existence results for complete constant scalar curvature metric of domains in S^n.

We will also discuss the unrestricted problem and summarize the present knowledge concerning this problem.

Basic references

1. N. KOISO, On the second derivative of the total scalar curvature, Osaka J. Math., 16(2) (1979), 413-421.
2. B. GIDAS, J. SPRUCK, Global and local behavior of positive solutions of nonlinear elliptic equations, Comm. pure appl. math., 34 (1981), 525-598.
3. M. GROMOV, H.B. LAWSON, Spin and scalar curvature in the presence of a fundamental group, Annals of math., 111 (1980), 209-230.
4. R. SCHOEN, Conformal deformation of a Riemannian metric to constant scalar curvature, J. Diff. Geom., 20 (1984), 479-495.
5. R. SCHOEN, S.T. YAU, On the structure of manifolds with positive scalar curvature, Manuscripta math., 28 (1979), 159-183.

The references given in paper 4. should also be studied in order to follow lectures in detail.

LIST OF C.I.M.E. SEMINARS

		Publisher
1954 -	1. Analisi funzionale	C.I.M.E.
	2. Quadratura delle superficie e questioni connesse	"
	3. Equazioni differenziali non lineari	"
1955 -	4. Teorema di Riemann-Roch e questioni connesse	"
	5. Teoria dei numeri	"
	6. Topologia	"
	7. Teorie non linearizzate in elasticità, idrodinamica, aerodinamica	"
	8. Geometria proiettivo-differenziale	"
1956 -	9. Equazioni alle derivate parziali a caratteristiche reali	"
	10. Propagazione delle onde elettromagnetiche	"
	11. Teoria della funzioni di più variabili complesse e delle funzioni automorfe	"
1957 -	12. Geometria aritmetica e algebrica (2 vol.)	"
	13. Integrali singolari e questioni connesse	"
	14. Teoria della turbolenza (2 vol.)	"
1958 -	15. Vedute e problemi attuali in relatività generale	"
	16. Problemi di geometria differenziale in grande	"
	17. Il principio di minimo e le sue applicazioni alle equazioni funzionali	"
1959 -	18. Induzione e statistica	"
	19. Teoria algebrica dei meccanismi automatici (2 vol.)	"
	20. Gruppi, anelli di Lie e teoria della coomologia	"
1960 -	21. Sistemi dinamici e teoremi ergodici	"
	22. Forme differenziali e loro integrali	"
1961 -	23. Geometria del calcolo delle variazioni (2 vol.)	"
	24. Teoria delle distribuzioni	"
	25. Onde superficiali	"
1962 -	26. Topologia differenziale	"
	27. Autovalori e autosoluzioni	"
	28. Magnetofluidodinamica	"
1963 -	29. Equazioni differenziali astratte	"
	30. Funzioni e varietà complesse	"
	31. Proprietà di media e teoremi di confronto in Fisica Matematica	"

1964 -	32. Relatività generale	C.I.M.E.
	33. Dinamica dei gas rarefatti	"
	34. Alcune questioni di analisi numerica	"
	35. Equazioni differenziali non lineari	"
1965 -	36. Non-linear continuum theories	"
	37. Some aspects of ring theory	"
	38. Mathematical optimization in economics	"
1966 -	39. Calculus of variations	Ed. Cremonese, Firenze
	40. Economia matematica	"
	41. Classi caratteristiche e questioni connesse	"
	42. Some aspects of diffusion theory	"
1967 -	43. Modern questions of celestial mechanics	"
	44. Numerical analysis of partial differential equations	"
	45. Geometry of homogeneous bounded domains	"
1968 -	46. Controllability and observability	"
	47. Pseudo-differential operators	"
	48. Aspects of mathematical logic	"
1969 -	49. Potential theory	"
	50. Non-linear continuum theories in mechanics and physics and their applications	"
	51. Questions of algebraic varieties	"
1970 -	52. Relativistic fluid dynamics	"
	53. Theory of group representations and Fourier analysis	"
	54. Functional equations and inequalities	"
	55. Problems in non-linear analysis	"
1971 -	56. Stereodynamics	"
	57. Constructive aspects of functional analysis (2 vol.)	"
	58. Categories and commutative algebra	"
1972 -	59. Non-linear mechanics	"
	60. Finite geometric structures and their applications	"
	61. Geometric measure theory and minimal surfaces	"
1973 -	62. Complex analysis	"
	63. New variational techniques in mathematical physics	"
	64. Spectral analysis	"

1974 -	65. Stability problems	Ed. Cremonese, Firenze
	66. Singularities of analytic spaces	"
	67. Eigenvalues of non linear problems	"
1975 -	68. Theoretical computer sciences	"
	69. Model theory and applications	"
	70. Differential operators and manifolds	"
1976 -	71. Statistical Mechanics	Ed. Liguori, Napoli
	72. Hyperbolicity	"
	73. Differential topology	"
1977 -	74. Materials with memory	"
	75. Pseudodifferential operators with applications	"
	76. Algebraic surfaces	"
1978 -	77. Stochastic differential equations	"
	78. Dynamical systems	Ed. Liguori, Napoli and Birkhäuser Verlag
1979 -	79. Recursion theory and computational complexity	Ed. Liguori, Napoli
	80. Mathematics of biology	"
1980 -	81. Wave propagation	"
	82. Harmonic analysis and group representations	"
	83. Matroid theory and its applications	"
1981 -	84. Kinetic Theories and the Boltzmann Equation	(LNM 1048)Springer-Verlag
	85. Algebraic Threefolds	(LNM 947) "
	86. Nonlinear Filtering and Stochastic Control	(LNM 972) "
1982 -	87. Invariant Theory	(LNM 996) "
	88. Thermodynamics and Constitutive Equations	(LN Physics 228) "
	89. Fluid Dynamics	(LNM 1047) "
1983 -	90. Complete Intersections	(LNM 1092) "
	91. Bifurcation Theory and Applications	(LNM 1057) "
	92. Numerical Methods in Fluid Dynamics	(LNM 1127) "
1984	93. Harmonic Mappings and Minimal Immersions	(LNM 1161) "
	94. Schrödinger Operators	(LNM 1159) "
	95. Buildings and the Geometry of Diagrams	(LNM 1181) "
1985 -	96. Probability and Analysis	(LNM 1206) "
	97. Some Problems in Nonlinear Diffusion	(LNM 1224) "
	98. Theory of Moduli	to appear "

<u>Note:</u> Volumes 1 to 38 are out of print. A few copies of volumes 23,28,31,32,33,34,36,38 are available on request from C.I.M.E.

1986 -	99. Inverse Problems	(LNM 1225)	Springer-Verlag
	100. Mathematical Economics	(LNM 1330)	"
	101. Combinatorial Optimization	to appear	"
1987 -	102. Relativistic Fluid Dynamics	to appear	"
	103. Topics in Calculus of Variations	to appear	"

Vol. 1173: H. Delfs, M. Knebusch, Locally Semialgebraic Spaces. XVI, 329 pages. 1985.

Vol. 1174: Categories in Continuum Physics, Buffalo 1982. Seminar. Edited by F.W. Lawvere and S.H. Schanuel. V, 126 pages. 1986.

Vol. 1175: K. Mathiak, Valuations of Skew Fields and Projective Hjelmslev Spaces. VII, 116 pages. 1986.

Vol. 1176: R.R. Bruner, J.P. May, J.E. McClure, M. Steinberger, H_∞ Ring Spectra and their Applications. VII, 388 pages. 1986.

Vol. 1177: Representation Theory I. Finite Dimensional Algebras. Proceedings, 1984. Edited by V. Dlab, P. Gabriel and G. Michler. XV, 340 pages. 1986.

Vol. 1178: Representation Theory II. Groups and Orders. Proceedings, 1984. Edited by V. Dlab, P. Gabriel and G. Michler. XV, 370 pages. 1986.

Vol. 1179: Shi J.-Y. The Kazhdan-Lusztig Cells in Certain Affine Weyl Groups. X, 307 pages. 1986.

Vol. 1180: R. Carmona, H. Kesten, J.B. Walsh, École d'Été de Probabilités de Saint-Flour XIV – 1984. Édité par P.L. Hennequin. X, 438 pages. 1986.

Vol. 1181: Buildings and the Geometry of Diagrams, Como 1984. Seminar. Edited by L. Rosati. VII, 277 pages. 1986.

Vol. 1182: S. Shelah, Around Classification Theory of Models. VII, 279 pages. 1986.

Vol. 1183: Algebra, Algebraic Topology and their Interactions. Proceedings, 1983. Edited by J.-E. Roos. XI, 396 pages. 1986.

Vol. 1184: W. Arendt, A. Grabosch, G. Greiner, U. Groh, H.P. Lotz, U. Moustakas, R. Nagel, F. Neubrander, U. Schlotterbeck, One-parameter Semigroups of Positive Operators. Edited by R. Nagel. X, 460 pages. 1986.

Vol. 1185: Group Theory, Beijing 1984. Proceedings. Edited by Tuan H.F. V, 403 pages. 1986.

Vol. 1186: Lyapunov Exponents. Proceedings, 1984. Edited by L. Arnold and V. Wihstutz. VI, 374 pages. 1986.

Vol. 1187: Y. Diers, Categories of Boolean Sheaves of Simple Algebras. VI, 168 pages. 1986.

Vol. 1188: Fonctions de Plusieurs Variables Complexes V. Séminaire, 1979–85. Edité par François Norguet. VI, 306 pages. 1986.

Vol. 1189: J. Lukeš, J. Malý, L. Zajíček, Fine Topology Methods in Real Analysis and Potential Theory. X, 472 pages. 1986.

Vol. 1190: Optimization and Related Fields. Proceedings, 1984. Edited by R. Conti, E. De Giorgi and F. Giannessi. VIII, 419 pages. 1986.

Vol. 1191: A.R. Its, V.Yu. Novokshenov, The Isomonodromic Deformation Method in the Theory of Painlevé Equations. IV, 313 pages. 1986.

Vol. 1192: Equadiff 6. Proceedings, 1985. Edited by J. Vosmansky and M. Zlámal. XXIII, 404 pages. 1986.

Vol. 1193: Geometrical and Statistical Aspects of Probability in Banach Spaces. Proceedings, 1985. Edited by X. Fernique, B. Heinkel, M.B. Marcus and P.A. Meyer. IV, 128 pages. 1986.

Vol. 1194: Complex Analysis and Algebraic Geometry. Proceedings, 1985. Edited by H. Grauert. VI, 235 pages. 1986.

Vol. 1195: J.M. Barbosa, A.G. Colares, Minimal Surfaces in $\mathbb{R}^3$. X, 124 pages. 1986.

Vol. 1196: E. Casas-Alvero, S. Xambó-Descamps, The Enumerative Theory of Conics after Halphen. IX, 130 pages. 1986.

Vol. 1197: Ring Theory. Proceedings, 1985. Edited by F.M.J. van Oystaeyen. V, 231 pages. 1986.

Vol. 1198: Séminaire d'Analyse, P. Lelong – P. Dolbeault – H. Skoda. Seminar 1983/84. X, 260 pages. 1986.

Vol. 1199: Analytic Theory of Continued Fractions II. Proceedings, 1985. Edited by W.J. Thron. VI, 299 pages. 1986.

Vol. 1200: V.D. Milman, G. Schechtman, Asymptotic Theory of Finite Dimensional Normed Spaces. With an Appendix by M. Gromov. VIII, 156 pages. 1986.

Vol. 1201: Curvature and Topology of Riemannian Manifolds. Proceedings, 1985. Edited by K. Shiohama, T. Sakai and T. Sunada. VII, 336 pages. 1986.

Vol. 1202: A. Dür, Möbius Functions, Incidence Algebras and Power Series Representations. XI, 134 pages. 1986.

Vol. 1203: Stochastic Processes and Their Applications. Proceedings, 1985. Edited by K. Itô and T. Hida. VI, 222 pages. 1986.

Vol. 1204: Séminaire de Probabilités XX, 1984/85. Proceedings. Edité par J. Azéma et M. Yor. V, 639 pages. 1986.

Vol. 1205: B.Z. Moroz, Analytic Arithmetic in Algebraic Number Fields. VII, 177 pages. 1986.

Vol. 1206: Probability and Analysis, Varenna (Como) 1985. Seminar. Edited by G. Letta and M. Pratelli. VIII, 280 pages. 1986.

Vol. 1207: P.H. Bérard, Spectral Geometry: Direct and Inverse Problems. With an Appendix by G. Besson. XIII, 272 pages. 1986.

Vol. 1208: S. Kaijser, J.W. Pelletier, Interpolation Functors and Duality. IV, 167 pages. 1986.

Vol. 1209: Differential Geometry, Peñíscola 1985. Proceedings. Edited by A.M. Naveira, A. Ferrández and F. Mascaró. VIII, 306 pages. 1986.

Vol. 1210: Probability Measures on Groups VIII. Proceedings, 1985. Edited by H. Heyer. X, 386 pages. 1986.

Vol. 1211: M.B. Sevryuk, Reversible Systems. V, 319 pages. 1986.

Vol. 1212: Stochastic Spatial Processes. Proceedings, 1984. Edited by P. Tautu. VIII, 311 pages. 1986.

Vol. 1213: L.G. Lewis, Jr., J.P. May, M. Steinberger, Equivariant Stable Homotopy Theory. IX, 538 pages. 1986.

Vol. 1214: Global Analysis – Studies and Applications II. Edited by Yu.G. Borisovich and Yu.E. Gliklikh. V, 275 pages. 1986.

Vol. 1215: Lectures in Probability and Statistics. Edited by G. del Pino and R. Rebolledo. V, 491 pages. 1986.

Vol. 1216: J. Kogan, Bifurcation of Extremals in Optimal Control. VIII, 106 pages. 1986.

Vol. 1217: Transformation Groups. Proceedings, 1985. Edited by S. Jackowski and K. Pawalowski. X, 396 pages. 1986.

Vol. 1218: Schrödinger Operators, Aarhus 1985. Seminar. Edited by E. Balslev. V, 222 pages. 1986.

Vol. 1219: R. Weissauer, Stabile Modulformen und Eisensteinreihen. III, 147 Seiten. 1986.

Vol. 1220: Séminaire d'Algèbre Paul Dubreil et Marie-Paule Malliavin. Proceedings, 1985. Edité par M.-P. Malliavin. IV, 200 pages. 1986.

Vol. 1221: Probability and Banach Spaces. Proceedings, 1985. Edited by J. Bastero and M. San Miguel. XI, 222 pages. 1986.

Vol. 1222: A. Katok, J.-M. Strelcyn, with the collaboration of F. Ledrappier and F. Przytycki, Invariant Manifolds, Entropy and Billiards; Smooth Maps with Singularities. VIII, 283 pages. 1986.

Vol. 1223: Differential Equations in Banach Spaces. Proceedings, 1985. Edited by A. Favini and E. Obrecht. VIII, 299 pages. 1986.

Vol. 1224: Nonlinear Diffusion Problems, Montecatini Terme 1985. Seminar. Edited by A. Fasano and M. Primicerio. VIII, 188 pages. 1986.

Vol. 1225: Inverse Problems, Montecatini Terme 1986. Seminar. Edited by G. Talenti. VIII, 204 pages. 1986.

Vol. 1226: A. Buium, Differential Function Fields and Moduli of Algebraic Varieties. IX, 146 pages. 1986.

Vol. 1227: H. Helson, The Spectral Theorem. VI, 104 pages. 1986.

Vol. 1228: Multigrid Methods II. Proceedings, 1985. Edited by W. Hackbusch and U. Trottenberg. VI, 336 pages. 1986.

Vol. 1229: O. Bratteli, Derivations, Dissipations and Group Actions on C*-algebras. IV, 277 pages. 1986.

Vol. 1230: Numerical Analysis. Proceedings, 1984. Edited by J.-P. Hennart. X, 234 pages. 1986.

Vol. 1231: E.-U. Gekeler, Drinfeld Modular Curves. XIV, 107 pages. 1986.

Vol. 1232: P.C. Schuur, Asymptotic Analysis of Soliton Problems. VIII, 180 pages. 1986.

Vol. 1233: Stability Problems for Stochastic Models. Proceedings, 1985. Edited by V.V. Kalashnikov, B. Penkov and V.M. Zolotarev. VI, 223 pages. 1986.

Vol. 1234: Combinatoire énumérative. Proceedings, 1985. Edité par G. Labelle et P. Leroux. XIV, 387 pages. 1986.

Vol. 1235: Séminaire de Théorie du Potentiel, Paris, No. 8. Directeurs: M. Brelot, G. Choquet et J. Deny. Rédacteurs: F. Hirsch et G. Mokobodzki. III, 209 pages. 1987.

Vol. 1236: Stochastic Partial Differential Equations and Applications. Proceedings, 1985. Edited by G. Da Prato and L. Tubaro. V, 257 pages. 1987.

Vol. 1237: Rational Approximation and its Applications in Mathematics and Physics. Proceedings, 1985. Edited by J. Gilewicz, M. Pindor and W. Siemaszko. XII, 350 pages. 1987.

Vol. 1238: M. Holz, K.-P. Podewski and K. Steffens, Injective Choice Functions. VI, 183 pages. 1987.

Vol. 1239: P. Vojta, Diophantine Approximations and Value Distribution Theory. X, 132 pages. 1987.

Vol. 1240: Number Theory, New York 1984–85. Seminar. Edited by D.V. Chudnovsky, G.V. Chudnovsky, H. Cohn and M.B. Nathanson. V, 324 pages. 1987.

Vol. 1241: L. Gårding, Singularities in Linear Wave Propagation. III, 125 pages. 1987.

Vol. 1242: Functional Analysis II, with Contributions by J. Hoffmann-Jørgensen et al. Edited by S. Kurepa, H. Kraljević and D. Butković. VII, 432 pages. 1987.

Vol. 1243: Non Commutative Harmonic Analysis and Lie Groups. Proceedings, 1985. Edited by J. Carmona, P. Delorme and M. Vergne. V, 309 pages. 1987.

Vol. 1244: W. Müller, Manifolds with Cusps of Rank One. XI, 158 pages. 1987.

Vol. 1245: S. Rallis, L-Functions and the Oscillator Representation. XVI, 239 pages. 1987.

Vol. 1246: Hodge Theory. Proceedings, 1985. Edited by E. Cattani, F. Guillén, A. Kaplan and F. Puerta. VII, 175 pages. 1987.

Vol. 1247: Séminaire de Probabilités XXI. Proceedings. Edité par J. Azéma, P.A. Meyer et M. Yor. IV, 579 pages. 1987.

Vol. 1248: Nonlinear Semigroups, Partial Differential Equations and Attractors. Proceedings, 1985. Edited by T.L. Gill and W.W. Zachary. IX, 185 pages. 1987.

Vol. 1249: I. van den Berg, Nonstandard Asymptotic Analysis. IX, 187 pages. 1987.

Vol. 1250: Stochastic Processes – Mathematics and Physics II. Proceedings 1985. Edited by S. Albeverio, Ph. Blanchard and L. Streit. VI, 359 pages. 1987.

Vol. 1251: Differential Geometric Methods in Mathematical Physics. Proceedings, 1985. Edited by P.L. García and A. Pérez-Rendón. VII, 300 pages. 1987.

Vol. 1252: T. Kaise, Représentations de Weil et GL_2 Algèbres de division et GL_n. VII, 203 pages. 1987.

Vol. 1253: J. Fischer, An Approach to the Selberg Trace Formula via the Selberg Zeta-Function. III, 184 pages. 1987.

Vol. 1254: S. Gelbart, I. Piatetski-Shapiro, S. Rallis. Explicit Constructions of Automorphic L-Functions. VI, 152 pages. 1987.

Vol. 1255: Differential Geometry and Differential Equations. Proceedings, 1985. Edited by C. Gu, M. Berger and R.L. Bryant. XII, 243 pages. 1987.

Vol. 1256: Pseudo-Differential Operators. Proceedings, 1986. Edited by H.O. Cordes, B. Gramsch and H. Widom. X, 479 pages. 1987.

Vol. 1257: X. Wang, On the C*-Algebras of Foliations in the Plane. V, 165 pages. 1987.

Vol. 1258: J. Weidmann, Spectral Theory of Ordinary Differential Operators. VI, 303 pages. 1987.

Vol. 1259: F. Cano Torres, Desingularization Strategies for Three-Dimensional Vector Fields. IX, 189 pages. 1987.

Vol. 1260: N.H. Pavel, Nonlinear Evolution Operators and Semigroups. VI, 285 pages. 1987.

Vol. 1261: H. Abels, Finite Presentability of S-Arithmetic Groups. Compact Presentability of Solvable Groups. VI, 178 pages. 1987.

Vol. 1262: E. Hlawka (Hrsg.), Zahlentheoretische Analysis II. Seminar, 1984–86. V, 158 Seiten. 1987.

Vol. 1263: V.L. Hansen (Ed.), Differential Geometry. Proceedings, 1985. XI, 288 pages. 1987.

Vol. 1264: Wu Wen-tsün, Rational Homotopy Type. VIII, 219 pages. 1987.

Vol. 1265: W. Van Assche, Asymptotics for Orthogonal Polynomials. VI, 201 pages. 1987.

Vol. 1266: F. Ghione, C. Peskine, E. Sernesi (Eds.), Space Curves. Proceedings, 1985. VI, 272 pages. 1987.

Vol. 1267: J. Lindenstrauss, V.D. Milman (Eds.), Geometrical Aspects of Functional Analysis. Seminar. VII, 212 pages. 1987.

Vol. 1268: S.G. Krantz (Ed.), Complex Analysis. Seminar, 1986. VII, 195 pages. 1987.

Vol. 1269: M. Shiota, Nash Manifolds. VI, 223 pages. 1987.

Vol. 1270: C. Carasso, P.-A. Raviart, D. Serre (Eds.), Nonlinear Hyperbolic Problems. Proceedings, 1986. XV, 341 pages. 1987.

Vol. 1271: A.M. Cohen, W.H. Hesselink, W.L.J. van der Kallen, J.R. Strooker (Eds.), Algebraic Groups Utrecht 1986. Proceedings. XII, 284 pages. 1987.

Vol. 1272: M.S. Livšic, L.L. Waksman, Commuting Nonselfadjoint Operators in Hilbert Space. III, 115 pages. 1987.

Vol. 1273: G.-M. Greuel, G. Trautmann (Eds.), Singularities, Representation of Algebras, and Vector Bundles. Proceedings, 1985. XIV, 383 pages. 1987.

Vol. 1274: N. C. Phillips, Equivariant K-Theory and Freeness of Group Actions on C*-Algebras. VIII, 371 pages. 1987.

Vol. 1275: C.A. Berenstein (Ed.), Complex Analysis I. Proceedings, 1985–86. XV, 331 pages. 1987.

Vol. 1276: C.A. Berenstein (Ed.), Complex Analysis II. Proceedings, 1985–86. IX, 320 pages. 1987.

Vol. 1277: C.A. Berenstein (Ed.), Complex Analysis III. Proceedings, 1985–86. X, 350 pages. 1987.

Vol. 1278: S.S. Koh (Ed.), Invariant Theory. Proceedings, 1985. V, 102 pages. 1987.

Vol. 1279: D. Ieşan, Saint-Venant's Problem. VIII, 162 Seiten. 1987.

Vol. 1280: E. Neher, Jordan Triple Systems by the Grid Approach. XII, 193 pages. 1987.

Vol. 1281: O.H. Kegel, F. Menegazzo, G. Zacher (Eds.), Group Theory. Proceedings, 1986. VII, 179 pages. 1987.

Vol. 1282: D.E. Handelman, Positive Polynomials, Convex Integral Polytopes, and a Random Walk Problem. XI, 136 pages. 1987.

Vol. 1283: S. Mardešić, J. Segal (Eds.), Geometric Topology and Shape Theory. Proceedings, 1986. V, 261 pages. 1987.

Vol. 1284: B.H. Matzat, Konstruktive Galoistheorie. X, 286 pages. 1987.

Vol. 1285: I.W. Knowles, Y. Saitō (Eds.), Differential Equations and Mathematical Physics. Proceedings, 1986. XVI, 499 pages. 1987.

Vol. 1286: H.R. Miller, D.C. Ravenel (Eds.), Algebraic Topology. Proceedings, 1986. VII, 341 pages. 1987.

Vol. 1287: E.B. Saff (Ed.), Approximation Theory, Tampa. Proceedings, 1985–1986. V, 228 pages. 1987.

Vol. 1288: Yu. L. Rodin, Generalized Analytic Functions on Riemann Surfaces. V, 128 pages, 1987.

Vol. 1289: Yu. I. Manin (Ed.), K-Theory, Arithmetic and Geometry. Seminar, 1984–1986. V, 399 pages. 1987.

MIX
Papier aus verantwortungsvollen Quellen
Paper from responsible sources
FSC® C105338
FSC
www.fsc.org

If you have any concerns about our products,
you can contact us on
ProductSafety@springernature.com

In case Publisher is established outside the EU,
the EU authorized representative is:
Springer Nature Customer Service Center GmbH
Europaplatz 3, 69115 Heidelberg, Germany

Printed by Libri Plureos GmbH
in Hamburg, Germany